Rugby of the Book
Herodian Books

MARK SPITZ

THE EXTRAORDINARY LIFE OF AN OLYMPIC CHAMPION

RICHARD J. FOSTER
FOREWORD BY MARK SPITZ
INTRODUCTION BY KEITH JACKSON

SANTA
MONICA
PRESS

Published by: Santa Monica Press LLC
P.O. Box 1076
Santa Monica, CA 90406-1076
1-800-784-9553
www.santamonicapress.com
books@santamonicapress.com

SANTA
MONICA
PRESS

Printed in the United States

Santa Monica Press books are available at special quantity discounts when purchased in bulk by corporations, organizations, or groups. Please call our Special Sales department at 1-800-784-9553.

ISBN-13 978-1-59580-039-8
ISBN-10 1-59580-039-5

Library of Congress Cataloging-in-Publication Data

Foster, Richard J., 1951–
Mark Spitz : the extraordinary life of an Olympic champion / by Richard J. Foster.
p. cm.
ISBN 978-1-59580-039-8
1. Spitz, Mark. 2. Swimmers—United States—Biography. I. Title.
GV838.S68F67 2008
797.2'1092—dc22
[B]
2008004278

Cover and interior design and production by cooldogdesign

Cover photograph © Rich Clarkson

Author photograph by Joe Lyman

Photographs courtesy of the International Swimming Hall of Fame: Photo insert pages 3 (upper left and upper right), 4 (upper left and upper right), 8 (lower left), 9, 11 (upper right and bottom), 12 (upper left, upper right, and lower left), 13 (bottom), 14 (bottom), 15 (lower right)

Photographs courtesy of *Swimming World Magazine* and the International Swimming Hall of Fame: Photo insert pages 2 (lower left and lower right), 5 (lower left), 6 (lower left), 7 (upper right), 8 (upper left and upper right)

Photograph courtesy of *Swimming World Magazine*: Photo insert page 3 (lower left)

CONTENTS

DEDICATION

‼‼‼

To Nancy,

You inspired me to write this book and
inspire me in so many other ways

ACKNOWLEDGMENTS

ONE MUST have the support of many to write a book like this. Thanks to all of the people who endured my interviews with them. A special thanks to the following:

Jana Hunter, who helped from start to finish. Without her research, advice, editing, and constructive criticism, this book could not have been written.

Ross Wales, who was the source of expert advice and many fantastic stories about the 1968 and 1972 Olympics. His knowledge of international swimming was extremely valuable.

Mark Wallace, who was instrumental in lining up star swimmers for interviews, but most importantly for being an outstanding source of information about Mark. Nobody knows Mark Spitz like Mark Wallace. His insights into Mark Spitz's persona were incredible.

Don Gambril, whose memory of the 1968 and 1972 Olympic Games was fabulous. He lived through those Games with Mark and his recall added much to the book.

Gary Hall, Sr., who graciously shared his stories and memories of competing with and against Mark.

Evan Morgenstein, who has an incredible insight into the minds of Olympic athletes.

Mike Sirota, whose expert advice made this work a better book than I could have written on my own.

Peter Daland, who was the source of many stories regarding the 1972 Olympic Games.

Larry Drum, who was extremely helpful in providing information on the medical issues raised in the book.

Kate Doyle, who provided insight into the horrific massacre of student protesters that occurred shortly before the Mexico City Olympic Games.

Harry Edwards, who provided valuable advice on race and sports.

Jim Montrella and Steve Genter, who provided much new information on Steve's miraculous fight to swim in the Olympics despite suffering a collapsed lung shortly before his first race.

Kurt Krumpholz, who never complained about my constant calls to get the facts right.

Stephen Smyth, whose research on numerous projects was very valuable.

Alexandra Joe, my administrative assistant, for her constant support.

My golfing buddies, Steve Pearce, Dave Olzewski, Bruce Bradley, Rocky Suares, Tom Bussa, Kevin Falskin, Nash Tejani, Vito Linuti, and John Morrison, for enduring me endlessly bouncing stories off them.

My parents, Ray and Janice, for their constant encouragement. In their minds I haven't done anything wrong since I married Nancy.

And finally, to Jeffrey Goldman at Santa Monica Press, whose commitment to telling Mark's story is much appreciated.

FOREWORD

by Mark Spitz

WHEN I FINISHED my last race at the Munich Olympics, I was relieved. Chasing the endless black lines at the bottom of the pool was no longer a concern. Nobody counted, but I easily swam over fifteen million yards and made over a half million flip turns in my career. But those kinds of numbers don't guarantee success. The magic, mystery and wonder of what makes an Olympic champion will never be figured out by an accountant, and nobody else has any sure-fire manuals on how to be a winner.

Success depends in large part on the choices we make, good and bad. I certainly didn't make all the right choices, especially in the beginning of my international career, but when I made bad choices, I learned. I don't think I could have achieved success at the 1972 Olympics in Munich if I hadn't endured the anguish of the 1968 Olympics in Mexico City.

Fortune also plays a role in success and I was fortunate to have a family who believed in me, from my parents, Arnold and Lenore, to my two sisters, Heidi and Nancy. I was also fortunate to have three of the greatest coaches in the history of swimming, Sherm Chavoor, George Haines and Doc Counsilman. Each of them taught me something different, and each significantly contributed to my success in the pool and helped me deal with life outside of the pool. This is what good coaches do. All three are gone, but I will be eternally grateful to each of them.

This book is about my journey. When Rich Foster approached me about writing my biography, I had no reservations. Rich is well known in the national and international aquatic communities and I knew that he could tell my story like few, if any, could. I knew that he would neither gloss over the bad facts nor magnify the good ones. Believe me, there are parts of this book that were difficult for me to read; but I wanted Rich to tell an accurate story and he delivered. I hope that you, as the reader, will agree.

INTRODUCTION

by Keith Jackson

IT IS FAIR THAT one should expect extraordinary achievements to come from the Olympic Games. Founded in 1896 as a celebration of sport for the youth of the world, the original intent quickly changed in 1900 when the national flags of participating countries were brought into Paris's Vélodrome de Vincennes for the first time.

"It is not the winning that matters most, but the taking part in the celebration that matters most," quickly became a thing of the past.

Winning *did* matter and it was proven immediately. And as the Games traveled on it was proven that a gold medal worn by a favorite son or daughter could in fact lift the pride and spirit of an entire nation.

I first became aware that Mark Spitz might be a special athlete during his time at Indiana University. The famed coach Doc Counsilman suggested it more than once, and West Coast club coaches George Haines and Sherm Chavoor echoed the same theme.

At the 1968 Games in Mexico City, Spitz predicted six golds but got only two. It didn't seem to disappoint him all that much—it just made his fire burn hotter, and his determination grow greater. I had never seen an athlete's eyes reflect such will; it was pure joy to watch him day after day, and the anticipation of each race was breathtaking!

It was in 1972 that the world was stunned by his remarkable performance. At the Munich Olympics, Spitz won the incredible total of *seven* gold medals, setting *seven* world records (four individual races and three relays) in the course of accomplishing this extraordinary feat.

I was the ABC announcer for every event held in the new Schwimmhalle, and by the time Spitz had won the last of his gold medals it was a miracle there was still water in the pool. The great Aussie swimmer Murray Rose was my partner on the broadcasts, and even though Rose had won several Olympic gold medals himself, he joined me and millions of others in trying to find the right words to adequately describe the remarkable performances we were so privileged to witness.

At the end of Spitz's fifth race, fifth gold medal, and fifth world record, a Russian journalist I had come to know suggested that "perhaps Olympic officials should check Spitz more closely—he may have the genes of a dolphin!"

Who is Mark Spitz? Not that many people really know, because athletes like Spitz who perform at such a high level need to be insulated in order to retain their focus. However, in this book, Rich Foster reveals the real Mark Spitz, and for that, I for one will be eternally grateful.

¡¡¡

CHAPTER 1

A FAVORITE COLOR EMERGES

Summer of 1959

A LANKY NINE-year-old boy, equipped with ocean trunks, a few weeks of simple workouts, and even fewer expectations, stepped on the starting blocks at a YMCA swim meet; it was his first experience with organized sports. He crossed the pool and touched the opposite wall first in his heat of the twenty-five-yard race.

As the youngster watched the remaining heats, his coach explained that there would be no final; the winners would be the boys who swam the six fastest times in the heats. During the awards ceremony, the young swimmer swelled with pride at the sound of his name and strode forward with great satisfaction to accept his purple ribbon, mistaken about what it signified. He hurried to show off the colorful cloth to his naturally pleased mother, who rewarded him further with a congratulatory hug and kiss on the forehead.

But the timed-heat contest had included almost forty other competitors. In the slow pace at which realization sometimes strikes youngsters, the boy became aware that the presentation had not ended. When three others stepped up on a tri-tiered podium and received white, red, and blue ribbons, he peered up at his mother with a growing sense of uneasiness.

"Why are their ribbons different colors?" he asked, his glee yielding to doubt.

"Well, those boys had the fastest times of everyone in the race," she explained. "The one on the highest step swam the fastest, so he got a blue ribbon. The boy with the red ribbon was second, and the boy with the white ribbon was third."

A scowl immediately appeared on her son's face, and he threw his ribbon on the ground in disgust. "I hate purple, I hate red, and I hate white! From now on, I'm only winning blue ribbons."

❗❗❗

Within a year, Mark Spitz had set seventeen national age-group records, and his seven gold medals in seven world records thirteen years later at the 1972 Munich Olympics was the most impressive showing ever at an Olympic Games. The initial splash of his career as the world's greatest swimmer was eclipsed in history by Alaska and Hawai'i joining the United States, Fidel Castro taking control of Cuba, and Charles Lincoln Van Doren admitting that his winnings on the popular TV quiz show *$64,000 Question* were rigged. But his maiden competitive voyage, in which he shunned the new-fangled and scanty Speedo briefs— finding them goofy-looking at best and transparent from certain angles at worst—hardly inspired the likeness of a legend.

Eventually, though, Mark—with his unprecedented success in the pool, unfailing confidence, and movie-star looks—would shine as brightly as the countless flashbulbs that accompanied his athletic performances and public appearances.

That self-assurance in his abilities, his strong-headed personality, and the inevitable attention lavished on him as his confidence and conquests continued to feed off each other, though, came with a painful price. He was ostracized, ignored, and discriminated against by jealous, psyched-out, and constantly defeated teammates and their parents. He butted heads with demanding coaches who attempted to exact their control over the sensation, wanting credit for his success. He floundered as an entertainer, fighting against unrealistic expectations for a swimmer whose audition for the part had been to swim eight to ten miles a day, win races, and sign autographs. But perhaps most hurtful and confusing were the observation, analysis, and subsequent disdain of his father's image in the press: aggressive, overbearing, and obsessed with his son's athletic prowess. But those who knew Arnold best told a different story, and it started years before his son's birth.

❗❗❗

Mark's father, Arnold Spitz, was born in 1925 to Jewish chicken ranchers in the railroad town of Turlock, California. Nestled between the Diablo Range and lower Bay Area to the west and the Sierra Nevada and famed Yosemite National Park to the east, Turlock was at the heart of agricultural development in the San Joaquin Valley in the opening decades of the twentieth century. Both of his parents were first-generation Americans whose families emigrated from Hungary in the early 1900s to escape the region's unrest surrounding World War I.

Life on a chicken ranch offered little in the way of entertainment, but Arnold recognized in himself at a young age a knack for building things. His mechanical aptitude manifested in several forms in his early years, none more important than the makeshift bridge he built in a dusty field on the farm when he was seven. He labored over the construction site, wanting nothing more than to present the masterpiece to his father and bask in the inevitable praise from his hero.

But Morris, not feeling well that afternoon, promised to see the bridge the next day. His condition worsened, though, and later that night doctors discovered a brain tumor. The Spitzes were presented with a Hobson's choice. Morris would surely die without surgery. But the alternative wasn't much better. Brain surgery was far riskier in 1932 than it is now and presented a reasonable likelihood of fatality as well. The family made the only decision that offered hope, but Morris died shortly after the operation.

"My dad was so disappointed that his father never saw that bridge," Mark said, recalling the sadness in his father's voice. "He always said that was the darkest day of his life. Whenever he was too busy to pay attention to us or couldn't be there even for a minor event in our lives, that memory and his father's early death really haunted him."

That incident and the simple fact that Arnold was robbed of the benefit of a father for the rest of his life were more crushing and ultimately defining given his mother's instability and inadequacies. An eccentric artist, Alice felt bound by the traditional role of motherhood. She openly admitted—without remorse—that she did not love her two sons equally. In possibly her singular act of conformity, Alice overtly favored the oldest, Jim, as was customary in those days, especially in families of European heritage. It was to Arnold's credit that he did not condemn his elder of four years for her behavior, and it was to Jim's credit that he did not commend himself for it. The two shared a unique closeness that sometimes represents the only silver lining of such troubling times.

Alice constantly berated Arnold, not understanding why her rough-around-the-edges, opinionated son could not emulate his brother's tact and intellect. In an attempt to avoid one of her virulent shouting episodes, Arnold once climbed to the roof of their barn. Not only was he unsuccessful in evasion, but the move further fueled his mother's fire, who augmented her verbal attack by throwing rocks and a pitchfork at him.

Even Arnold's own children could not escape his mother's propensity for partiality, enduring her unabashed favoritism of grandsons over granddaughters. On one visit, Alice spent five hours helping an artistically challenged Mark paint a mural while relegating his more talented sisters to painting alone on newsprint.

Alice remained eclectic and unable to relate personally until the end. Living in a senior care facility in 1975, she decided she'd had enough of life. Without warning or fanfare, she purposely stopped taking her medications one day and quickly passed away alone.

As many young patriotic men did in that era, Arnold transitioned into adulthood as an airman for the United States Air Force in World War II. Barely nineteen years old, he volunteered for the war effort three years after the bombing of Pearl Harbor. As a gunner on a B-29, he flew reconnaissance missions out of Guam and Tinian Island, which quickly became the prime launch site for large raids against Japan after its U.S. capture that year. Two of the B-29s based on the island were the infamous *Enola Gay*, which dropped "Little Boy"—the code name for the first atomic bomb ever used in a war—on Hiroshima on August 6, 1945, and *Bockscar*, which three days later dropped "Fat Man" on Nagasaki.

"Whenever we'd complain that we were cold, Dad would launch into stories about how he'd spent hours shivering on a bomber, trying to prove that we had it good, like the 'I walked four miles uphill in the snow' stories," Mark laughed. "But looking back, Dad hated to be cold. Every one of our family vacations was spent somewhere warm, and I don't think that was a coincidence."

Three years after returning home from the war and working as an appliance salesman for the venerable Sears, Roebuck & Company, Arnold married Lenore Smith in 1947. The couple settled in Modesto, just fourteen miles from his hometown of Turlock.

Lenore was a second-generation American whose grandparents emigrated from Russia in the early 1900s. When they entered the United States, the Ellis Island clerk didn't care for the family name—Sklotkovick. Indifferent about how his alteration of their personal history might feel, he changed the name to

Smith on the immigration papers, largely because Lenore's grandfather listed his occupation as a blacksmith.

Lenore and Arnold easily embodied the maxim "opposites attract." Arnold bluntly spoke his mind; Lenore naturally practiced diplomacy. Arnold was passionate and at times fiery, Lenore even-tempered and nurturing. Arnold polarized; Lenore was personable and well-liked. Her characteristics came through when she described her late husband with a chuckle, "He was a no-BS kind of guy who was a great husband but a better father."

Although Arnold unquestionably wore the pants in the family, Lenore quietly commanded its full respect. If she grew tired of an argument between her husband and son that showed no signs of resolution, a simple, "That's enough," would stop both in their tracks. Bewildered, they'd look at each other for a moment and then move on.

❗❗❗

By the time Mark Andrew Spitz was born on February 10, 1950, Arnold was clear about one thing: family was of the utmost importance to him, and he was committed to giving his children the presence, attention, love, protection, and opportunities that he desperately missed growing up. His experiences losing his father at a young age, being abused by his mother, and living through the atrocities of war had a significant effect on how he viewed his role as a father. While many would later view Arnold as overbearing and boorish, those that knew him best knew that his intentions were good.

But that cornerstone to his existence was in stark contrast to the public's perception that he lived vicariously through Mark's pursuits. That he pushed Mark into greatness, possibly against the boy's will. That he forced Mark to view winning as mandatory, as if he would not love a son who was anything less than a perpetual victor. The truth to their complex relationship lies somewhere in between, and both men battled that complicated blend of uninformed assessment and twisted reality for much of their lives.

Much has been made about the pair's take-no-prisoners approach to Mark's swimming career. Many reports assert that the elder infused in the younger an unsavory attitude for competition, citing Arnold's infamous and frequent mantra: "Swimming isn't everything—winning is!" Arnold uprooted the family and moved a hundred miles away when it became clear Mark needed better coaching. One of Mark's teammates admitted in adulthood to using Arnold as a model of how *not* to act as an age-group father. Mark's cousin, Sherman, remembers the pair feeding off each other's audacity at swim meets, similar to the modern-day chest bumping that pervades team athletic accomplishments.

"Dad was criticized for trying to live life through Mark," Nancy, Mark's sister, said. "But he was just trying to be as supportive as he could because of what he missed out on as a child."

Clearly Mark thrived in that atmosphere.

But outside the aquatics arena, an uncommon intensity permeated their battles. The day of Mark's bar mitzvah, Arnold insisted Mark write his thank you notes immediately. Sherman watched as Mark, in his meticulous penmanship, composed the exact same message:

Dear _____,
Thank you for my bar mitzvah present.
Mark Spitz

"Arnold was not happy when he saw the notes. He said they were unacceptable and told Mark to write them over and personalize each one," Sherman remembered. "When he left, Mark said, 'I hope I get big and strong, because one day I want to pin down that SOB and never let him up.'"

Shortly after his wedding, Arnold took a job with Learner Company, a scrap iron and steel corporation owned by his uncle Paul Learner. Learner transferred Arnold to Hawai'i in 1952 to set up a new office, and it was in the warm Pacific Ocean where Mark first learned to swim. Arnold, a lifeguard in his youth, taught his son a basic stroke, and Lenore enjoyed watching her toddler rush to the water at Waikiki Beach almost every day, knowing full well a tantrum likely would follow when they had to leave the sandy playground. "You should have seen that little boy dash into the ocean," she recounted to a *TIME* reporter in 1968. "He'd run like he was trying to commit suicide."

When Lenore became pregnant again, she asked Mark if he wanted a brother or a sister. His response was immediate: he wanted a sister. Heidi's arrival in 1952 fulfilled that wish. Unlike many two-year-olds, Mark welcomed a sibling into the family wholeheartedly, climbing into her crib daily. Worried that his mannerisms were a bit rough for a newborn, Arnold added a clasp to the top of the crib gate, presumably out of Mark's reach. It wasn't. Mark quickly figured out that he could undo the clasp if he moved a small chair next to the crib, and Heidi survived her first years of life with her constant playmate. Two years later, Lenore again asked Mark if he wanted a brother or sister, and his answer was the same. Nancy arrived in 1954. Mark didn't pester her like he had Heidi, but the directness that some thought refreshing and others thought was arrogant debuted the day he told his parents, "She looks like a monkey."

When Learner awarded employee bonuses, Arnold perceived his relatively small check as a slight from his uncle. Priding himself on a strong work ethic and dedication to the company, he believed that his performance on the job and his sacrifice in uprooting his family entitled him to a greater reward, but all he felt was yet another insult to his worthiness carried over from childhood. Not willing to remain in the "family" business, Arnold went to work for a competitor, Schnitzer Steel, back in the Bay Area, where he stayed until his first retirement.

Arnold's childhood and early professional life came during the height of anti-Semitism in America. Many universities either refused to admit or had quotas on the number of Jewish students whom they would admit. More than a few country clubs, resorts, and neighborhoods were altogether closed to Jews. Employment studies in Chicago and Los Angeles from the early 1950s revealed that twenty percent of job openings specified that non-Jews apply.

It was in that milieu that Arnold raised his family. He worked hard to shield his children from prejudice. But he also jumped to accusations of bigotry at the mere trace of a snub, keenly aware of the perceived, subtle, and overt discrimination against his people.

"Dad's protective nature, especially when he felt one of us had been slighted, was misinterpreted as being overbearing," Nancy explained. "I don't remember any discrimination, per se, but it was well-known that there were only three Jews at Santa Clara High School: Mark, Heidi, and me."

And so, given that culture and Arnold's sensitivity toward it, it seemed unusual for the Spitzes to purchase a home constructed by Joseph Eichler, a well-known German builder. His "California Modern" design—featuring floor-to-ceiling glass walls and an open floor plan—in a middle-class neighborhood appealed to the Spitzes. Arnold gave no thought to the builder's ethnicity. "The homes were gorgeous and affordable," Lenore recalled of their house on South Land Park Drive. "We had architects, engineers, and lawyers in our neighborhood, but we also had a lot of normal, middle-class families."

Arnold's brother, Jim, and Jim's wife, Helen, however, refused to consider an Eichler home, equating the German name to Nazis with an attitude that broke from Jim's customary placidity. But they misplaced their distaste for all things German with Eichler, a fellow Jew with an Austrian-Jewish immigrant father and a German-Jewish mother. He was one of the first mass home builders to establish a non-discrimination policy, selling to buyers of any race or religion. In fact, he punctuated that stance in 1958, resigning from the National Association of Home Builders when the organization refused to formally change its exclusionary ways.

Although seemingly adopting the other's personality in their home-buying decisions, the episode touched on the brothers' stark differences. Arnold's build, almost six feet tall with a strong upper body, fit his personality as a forceful individual who was direct and to the point. He was adept mechanically, very good with his hands, and successful professionally despite having never attended college. Jim was far more of an intellect, earning his master's degree and teaching high school English and drama. A tall, thin man, he made friends easily yet had no mechanical skills whatsoever. "My cousins used to joke that their dad had difficulty plugging in a toaster," Mark said.

Their bond despite their differences and Arnold's sense of family were unmistakable when Jim, a smoker, was dying of lung cancer in 1962. His hospitalization during the last month of his life took a toll on Jim's family, especially his young son. With tears streaming down his face, Jim painfully shared with Arnold his only regret: that he would not be able to watch and help his children grow up. Arnold's promise to take on that role began immediately, treating Sherman like his own son. Their trips to the barbershop and Little League baseball games were the more enjoyable duties. The toughest one was explaining the terrible disease of cancer and the finality of death with heartfelt sadness, compassion, and honesty, better preparing the eight-year-old to handle his father's passing.

"My mom wasn't able to personalize things," Sherman recalled. "She was great at PTA and women's groups, but she couldn't articulate what Dad was going through. Arnold recognized that and explained how Dad's cancer had spread and was untreatable. I felt so much better just knowing what was going on, and I was able to help my younger sister understand."

That backdrop was more than an adornment to Mark's life, more than a series of bedtime stories about a childhood, a war, a career, and a family. More than either of them were aware at the time, Arnold's upbringing provided the foundation for how he parented. It also established the example from which Mark imprinted life lessons: tact is overrated, fortitude will save you, backing down from other people is not an option, and nothing is stronger than the familial bond.

But Mark's visceral reaction to the meaning of a purple ribbon in his inaugural race demonstrated that he did not get his drive to win from his father. Nor did he learn it from his primary coaches. No doubt all these men impacted Mark's mental approach to swimming, but up until that point he was relatively free from outside psychological influences.

Craig Townsend, a clinical hypnotherapist and director of a mental training company for swimmers in Australia, has devoted his life to helping athletes develop winning attitudes. He believes early events such as Mark's encounter with the purple ribbon can become burned onto a youth's psyche.

"That incident spurred him into action to ensure he would experience the positive emotions of being a winner rather than the negative emotions attached to the feeling that he wasn't the best," Townsend explained. "It's an inner belief, a mindset, an expectation of success which continues to build over time and eventually leads to athletes attaining an absolute superhuman impression of themselves and their ability. This, in turn, propels their performances to greater heights. Once an athlete attains this level of belief, they become an *ominous adversary;* one who will never quit until they find a way to win."

Mark's intense statement, coming from a neophyte in the competitive realm, provides a glimpse into the innate mentality that propelled him to Olympic glory and to forever find the colors red and white offensive. "They still represent failure to me," Mark explained.

❡❡❡

But Mark was not yet an Olympian. He was merely a boy who was bored one summer. His foray into organized swimming began at the Sacramento YMCA in 1959, which won out over Little League simply because no local baseball teams existed. Initially, he filled his days at the Y with arts and crafts, gymnastics, basketball and playing in the pool. Then Paul Heron, who recently had swum the English Channel and was developing the organization's swim program, noticed Mark's ease in the water and invited him to join the team. With no information or knowledge about what that meant, and no visible desire to find out, Mark happily accepted and went home to announce proudly that he was now a swimmer.

Heron took a low-key approach with his team. Workouts lasted about forty-five minutes, which Mark attended two or three times a week. There was little in the way of stroke instruction; the only technique Mark learned was a flip turn and diving off the starting blocks.

Shortly after that purple-ribbon race, Mark entered a novice meet in Walnut Creek, California, held by the American Amateur Union (AAU), the governing body for all amateur sports in America at the time. Seriousness and intensity layered the event in a way the Spitzes had not experienced at the YMCA, and they found the accompanying scene at the outdoor pool quite odd.

Despite the warmth of the day, swimmers lay in sleeping bags on the deck. Arnold, embarrassed that Mark did not have one, rushed to a nearby sporting goods store. He wanted Mark to fit in, and he wanted to provide Mark whatever advantage the unusual behavior afforded the competition. Mark didn't readily conform. It was beautiful outside, he wanted to improve his tan, and he just didn't care. But Arnold insisted, conjecturing that the sun would drain the energy out of Mark, who reluctantly complied.

Still, Arnold felt like an outsider, and his lack of familiarity with the meet format and officials only increased his anxiety. Mark was relatively unfazed, taking in the scene in his still-innocent manner and almost missing his first race because they didn't know the check-in procedures. Arnold's tension lessened when Mark won. In his more relaxed state, he began to think, as so many parents of young athletes do, that his son was destined to be a champion.

From Mark's perspective, he had made good on his promise to win only blue ribbons, even at larger meets. Never mind the token competition. Mark had never stopped to consider that another level even existed. His ego, as well as his father's, began to swell.

Mark continued to swim on the AAU novice circuit, winning with much greater frequency than not, even with his minimal workouts. His passion for being the best overrode his lack of training and technical skills. In his limited world, he was becoming invincible. Likewise, with every win, Arnold became prouder.

In the fall of 1959, Mark set a regional YMCA age-group record in the 25-yard butterfly at a novice meet in Watsonville, California. The Spitz family was ecstatic, but the record didn't create much of a stir, and few other people noticed.

One person who did notice, however, was Sherm Chavoor.

‼‼
○ ○ ○

CHAPTER 2

SWIMMING FOR SHERM

SHERM CHAVOOR also began his illustrious, entrepreneurial, and innovative career at the Sacramento YMCA, coaching the summer team starting in the mid-1940s during his high school teaching days. Several years later, after coaching permeated his blood, he wanted to lead a year-round swim program. Without a local program in need of a coach, his only option was to start one. And without a facility in which to train, his only option was to build one. Thus, the Arden Hills Swim and Tennis Club was created in 1954 after Chavoor fulfilled his loan prerequisite by canvassing the neighborhood and procuring commitments from enough families to join. By the time Chavoor sold the club in 1985 and retired from coaching in 1990, his swimmers had won thirty-one Olympic medals, including twenty-one gold; set more than two hundred world and American records; captured the 1969 AAU national championship; and revered their coach who, himself, could not swim.

But that fortuitous fall in 1959, the future millionaire of French-Dutch descent still was in the process of building his dynasty. More than two hundred swimmers from the six hundred dues-paying members competed for him. But he thought the kid who surged to an age-group record in the 25-yard butterfly displayed an intense desire to win that just might help his own fortunes. Ambling over to talk to his father, he introduced himself as the owner of the private club and coach of its swim team and asked Arnold to consider becoming a member so Mark could swim for him.

Arnold smiled. After a few short months of Mark's competitive swimming career, Arnold believed his son quickly would outgrow the YMCA team, if he hadn't already. Neither the training nor the instruction matched Mark's obvious burgeoning talent, and the overtures from the coach of one of the premier swim clubs in Northern California confirmed that his analysis of his son's potential was more than the overactive imagination of a proud father. Yet Arnold, also realistic, told Chavoor that there were two problems. The first was that he couldn't afford a private swim club, and the second was that the Spitzes were Jewish.

Chavoor set about allaying Arnold's spoken fears and silent questions about whether to entrust Mark's future with him. His words conveyed the diversity of the club, which included thirty-five Jewish families, and of the team, on which Jewish and Asian swimmers competed. They also promised fees discounted to an affordable level for the Spitzes. But it was Chavoor's direct but friendly manner and obvious passion for his team, not to mention his well-formed ideas about swim training that sold Arnold after the technicalities were out of the way.

Despite Chavoor's desire to build a successful business in addition to a successful swim program, he often reduced membership dues so swimmers from poorer families could reap the benefits of being on a competitive swim team. Debbie Meyer, whose own Olympic career would thrive under Chavoor's tutelage, recalled, "Sherm always wanted kids to be able to participate on the team. If they couldn't afford it, he would make sure they could. It didn't matter what the race or religion was, Sherm liked all kids. If a family felt funny about accepting his help, he would arrange for the swimmer to do odd jobs at the club."

When the family car pulled into the property at six o'clock that first morning, the youngster's eyes widened. Arden Hills was beautiful! Even in the early morning darkness, the ten acres looked special. In addition to the swimming pool, Mark saw lighted tennis courts, beautiful buildings, and finely manicured lawns. The intimidating spread was a far cry from the Sacramento YMCA.

The very first signs of light cracked the sky as Mark and Arnold walked through the gate to the swimming pool, as temperatures hovered just over freezing on that wintry California morning. The warmth of the eighty-degree water clashed with the chill in the air to generate ten feet of dense, insulating fog over the pool surface. The only illumination came from the pool's underwater lights. Mark peered into the eerie darkness, unable to see the end of the pool. Swimmers paddled down the lanes before disappearing into the vapor about halfway down, only to reappear several seconds later. Chavoor presided over the pool with his potbelly and stopwatch.

The entire scene scared the precocious nine-year-old. Chavoor looked down, seeing a defiant look in the boy's eyes trying hard to mask apprehension and uncertainty. He told a hesitant Mark to jump in. As Mark began to look around at the other kids, he noticed Johnny Ferris and Mike Butler a few lanes over, two swimmers who had beaten him badly at a recent AAU open meet. That did nothing to lessen his anxiety. Chavoor made sure a few lanes separated the newcomer from the more advanced swimmers, knowing he was in no shape to compete with them just yet.

That first session almost overextended Mark, whose workouts at the Y represented about a warm-up at Arden Hills. Chavoor's training philosophy put a premium on yardage, lots of yardage. One of the first swim coaches to use over-distance training, his athletes usually covered ten thousand to thirteen thousand yards a day with little rest, six days a week. Mark didn't hit five digits that morning, but he swam farther than he normally did in a week.

It didn't take Mark long to learn that his new coach was a nononsense sort of guy. Chavoor ruled with stringent expectations about behavior, work ethic, and responsibility, yet managed to develop close relationships with his swimmers by applying his psychology degree to connect with each swimmer individually. After a couple of weeks, Chavoor moved Mark to the lane next to Butler and Ferris, providing him the motivation to start closing the gap. A few weeks later, Mark was keeping up with the two best swimmers in his age group. The competition between the trio got so intense they'd unintentionally sabotage the efficiency of their own strokes by looking left and right at the other two, prompting an angry Chavoor to order the three to get out of the pool and stand next to each other. "After a couple minutes of shivering, Sherm came over and said he wanted us to look closely at each other right then so that when we got back in the water, we would stop looking at each other during our swims," Mark said.

At the end of another very hard workout, Sherm told the threesome to get in one lane and swim a series of 50-yard freestyles, one boy at time. Ferris went first and morphed into the early morning fog blanketing the water. He reappeared many seconds later and posted a respectable time. Butler went second and improved on that time a little. Not to be outdone, Mark recorded the fastest time thus far. They went through three sets, each swimming faster than the preceding time. By the fourth and final set, the boys were spent. Nonetheless, Ferris managed to raise the bar yet again with the fastest time of the morning. Butler couldn't match him that time. Mark's body was really tired, but his mind quickly devised a way to outdo Ferris. He swam as hard as he could until he was sure the fog concealed him from the two swimmers and Chavoor. He then stopped and waited the estimated time it would take him to get to the far wall and back, then powered back toward Chavoor and his stopwatch. It worked. His "time" was faster than Ferris' fastest but not by enough to expose his ruse.

At the shower, Ferris and Butler were astonished that Mark could swim so fast at the end of a workout. Mark looked at the two incredulously and said, "You dummies, I didn't swim the whole way. Couldn't you figure that out?" The two immediately told Chavoor, who took the news more calmly than they expected. The disciplinarian didn't appear too upset. Chavoor knew the best swimmers psychologically manipulated their competitors, but he was amazed that Mark had started at such a young age. He also had a dilemma on his hands. If he reprimanded Mark in front of the two complainers, they would have the psychological edge. Reprimanding Mark in private would cause Ferris and Butler to question Chavoor as a coach, but letting Mark get away with it would set a bad precedent—not to mention go against every grain in his body—and allow Mark to keep the upper hand. So in front of all three, Chavoor said to Mark "I think that was brilliant. How did you think of it?" Mark shrugged. Ferris and Butler couldn't believe it. As Chavoor turned to walk away, Mark stuck his tongue out at them, but it quickly retreated when Chavoor stopped, wheeled around, pointed at Mark, and said with a stern voice, "Don't do it again."

The next time it was Arnold who witnessed firsthand Chavoor's demanding nature. Chavoor told Arnold that Mark's Hebrew lessons, which kept him out of practice Tuesday afternoons, stagnated his development, and he warned that Mark would never beat Johnny Ferris or Mike Butler if he continued to miss that workout. Arnold met with the rabbi, worked out a deal for Mark to study Hebrew on the weekends, and announced the solution to Chavoor. Curious, Chavoor asked how he'd convinced the rabbi to make an exception, and Arnold replied, "I told him that even God likes a winner."

Arnold began showing other signs of an obsession with his son's gift that would plague the duo for several decades. He reveled in his son's accomplishments and constantly drilled into Mark the importance of winning, often quizzing him during those first few years of his career:

"Mark, how many lanes in a pool?"

"Eight."

"And how many lanes win?"

"One, only one."

Mark's cousin Sherman Spitz thought a lot of what motivated Mark was the hope of making Arnold happy. "Mark was a very important obsession to Arnold. It was obvious both had a passion for winning, and it was fortunate that Arnold had a son who could win," Sherman recalled. "Their relationship was both glorious and painful. It was glorious because Arnold devoted a lot of time to his son, and they would feed on each other. At swim meets, Arnold would say, 'Mark, you liked winning that blue ribbon, but you have three more races. How many more are you going to win?' Mark would proudly and dutifully chant, 'I'm going to win three more!' The interplay between the two was something to watch, but was painful when Mark didn't do well. Arnold would complain about Mark's workout ethic. Mark would lash back by saying he would break a world record someday, and Arnold would counter with, 'You're going nowhere.' It was also painful because his devotion to Mark's career created the perception that he was Arnold's favorite."

As an adult and father, Mark can see both sides of the argument but knows they both had the goal of making him the best swimmer in the world. "It's true my dad pushed me a lot, but he loved me enough to say that his efforts were for me, not him, and I believe him. He just wanted to provide me what he had lacked in his life: a father. He always promised me the best of everything, and that's what he gave," he recalled.

Mark flourished under Chavoor, who instilled in his swimmers a drive to excel and taught them to do so with desire, determination, and dedication. At the AAU Junior Olympics in 1960, Mark beat the much bigger Butler in the 50-yard butterfly, and within a year he had broken seventeen national age-group records. Although that number is somewhat misleading, given that categories weren't uniform at the time and records could be broken in a variety of distances in yards and meters, his rate of improvement was remarkable.

A few years later, though, Arnold accepted a better job in Oakland and the family moved eighty miles southwest to Walnut Creek. Swimming regularly with Arden Hills became impossible, and Mark bounced around a couple of swim clubs in the nearby Oakland area, floundering with Laurabelle Bookstover at the Berkeley City Club before hooking up with Irvin Zador, a Chavoor recommendation. Zador had earned some international fame after leading his country's water polo team to the gold medal in the 1956 Olympics, his bloodied face from the USSR-Hungary championship game plastered on the front page of newspapers worldwide as a symbol of the Hungarian revolution. Mark liked swimming for Zador, but Arnold and Zador didn't get along, so Arnold began driving one hundred and sixty miles round-trip to Sacramento on Saturdays and Sundays so Mark could partake in intensive workouts with Chavoor.

As honored as Chavoor felt about Arnold's faith in him, he knew he couldn't come close to tapping Mark's remarkable potential with only weekend workouts. Displaying the unselfish, swimmer-focused attitude that eventually made him a lifelong mentor to Mark, Chavoor called George Haines. He asked the head coach of Santa Clara Swim Club, Arden Hill's arch rival, if he'd take on the young phenom. Not surprisingly, Haines said yes.

!?!

CHAPTER 3

THE MOVE TO SANTA CLARA

MARK'S ARRIVAL at Santa Clara Swim Club in the summer of 1964 created about as much attention as his first age-group record. That is to say, a coach noticed, but that's about it. After rising through the ranks from novice to national age-group champion at Arden Hills, Mark was back to being a little fish in a very big pond at SCSC. George Haines had started the club in 1951, the same year he coached the inaugural Santa Clara High School squad. SCSC grew from thirteen members to fifty-four by the end of that summer and later topped two hundred. Both his club and high school teams had racked up a few national and conference championships by the time Mark appeared on the roster, but that only scratched the surface of its acclaim. Individually, his swimmers had won twenty-four national titles since 1962. Nine had competed in the 1960 Olympics in Rome, where Haines served as the women's head coach. Up against that backdrop, the fourteen-year-old's accomplishments at Junior Olympics were child's play.

At first, Lenore drove her son from Walnut Creek to Santa Clara every day, a one-hundred-mile trek round-trip. According to Mark, his mom had a heavy foot on the gas pedal. "She would pick me up right when school was out and drive to Santa Clara like a bat out of hell," he laughed. While better than the one hundred and sixty miles to Arden Hills, the trips took their toll on Lenore and the family soon moved to Santa Clara. Mark benefited from swimming at morning and evening workouts for Haines, but Arnold paid the price with a ninety-four-mile daily commute.

The elite members of the club worked out at Fremont Hills Country Club in a 50-meter pool, while the younger group, with which Mark initially swam, was relegated to the 25-yard pool at Santa Clara High School. Soon, though, Mark and another younger swimmer, fifteen-year-old Mitch Ivey, graduated to the evening workouts with luminaries ranging in age from seventeen to twenty-one such as Don Schollander, who had six national titles at that point; Dick Roth, with two; Luis Nicolao, an Argentinean who held the world record in the 100-meter butterfly; as well as Gary Ilman and Mike Wall. All five would swim in the Tokyo Olympics that October, three would final, two would win medals, and Schollander would become the face of U.S. swimming with his four golds in the 100 freestyle, 400 freestyle, 4x100 freestyle relay, and 4x200 freestyle relay.

Mark responded well to Haines' workouts. Whereas Chavoor favored high yardage with little rest, Haines focused more on swimming at race pace with slightly more rest. Unwittingly, Mark's progression matched now-established training methods of developing a very strong base of fitness before concentrating on speed. At the Far Western Age Group Championships in August, he set two more national age-group records in the 200 free and 400 free in addition to winning gold medals in the 100 fly, 200 fly, and 200 individual medley.

The next summer, Mark made another leap when he qualified for the 1965 AAU national championships in Maumee, Ohio. Before his first race, the 400 free, Haines pointed to Roy Saari and asked his young contender if he knew who he was. Mark couldn't identify the winner of two medals from the 1964 Olympics and six national AAU titles. Haines gave him a brief history lesson and strategic tip: stay close to Saari and you'll make the final. Mark took second in the heat but was no match for the twenty-year-old, missing the final by three seconds.

As luck would have it, Mark drew the lane next to Saari in the last of seven preliminary heats for the 200 free. This time after a pre-race warm-up, Haines looked down at Mark and said, "You know who he is now, right?" Mark sheepishly smiled and Haines repeated his advice—stick with Saari and make your first national final. Mark touched second again, but the accomplished swimmer was too fast, outpacing him by a full four seconds. His seventeenth-place finish stung, although in reality it wasn't bad for a fifteen-year-old against stronger, more experienced swimmers. Mark did notice he beat thirty-eight other swimmers, including an older teammate from Arden Hills, Mike Burton. This eased the disappointment somewhat. Later in the meet, Mark earned his first national AAU medal when his Santa Clara "B" team of Nicolao, Kim Cummings, and Greg Buckingham placed second to the club's "A" team in the 4x200 freestyle relay, helping Santa Clara win its second straight AAU national championship.

Mark swam fast enough that summer to earn a spot in the Seventh World Maccabiah Games in Tel Aviv, Israel, his first international competition. The Games, held every four years, featured the best Jewish athletes from around the world in Open, Masters, Juniors, and Disabled divisions. The competition wasn't as robust as at AAU Nationals, but Mark made an auspicious debut on the international swim scene. His four gold medals in the 400 free, 1500 free, 400 IM, and 4x200 freestyle relay prompted *Swimming World Magazine* to opine that he might be the next Don Schollander. The comparison intrigued Mark. From that point on, Schollander became his target. Rather than quantifying his goals with times or medals or awards, he set them by what Schollander already had done or had yet to do. He wanted to fulfill that writer's prophecy.

The year ended with Mark screaming in pure satisfaction and running to show his father the December issue of *Swimming*

World Magazine. On the list of the twenty-five best long-course times for U.S. swimmers, he ranked seventh in the country in the 800 free, eighth in the 1500 free, and ninth in the 400 free.

In the spring of 1966, Mark's reputation broadened along with that of Santa Clara High School. As a sophomore, he set national prep records in the 200-yard individual medley and the 100-yard butterfly. He and Bob Jamison, Dick Eagleston, and Kim Cummings set a national record in the 400-yard freestyle relay, and he joined Mitch Ivey, Jack Faunce, and Jamison to better the standard in the 400-yard medley relay. Showing his versatility, Mark also earned high school all-American honors in the 100-yard freestyle, 200-yard freestyle, 400-yard freestyle, and 100-yard backstroke. SCHS won its first of thirteen California Interscholastic Federation Central Coast Section championships and was named the top high school swim team in the country.

After an appearance on ABC's *Wide World of Sports* in April, during which he took sixth in the 400-yard IM at the AAU national short-course championships, Mark was firmly ensconced in the first wave of Santa Clara's elite workout team. Facing off daily against Schollander, Wall, Ilman, and Nicolao made workouts extremely difficult, as each swimmer looked for any edge over his counterparts. "Every set seemed like a gold-medal race," Mark recalled.

Mark started studying Schollander's near-perfect freestyle stroke from all angles. During one early morning workout, Mark suddenly dove to the bottom of the pool to watch from below. Amazed at how smooth and effortless Schollander swam, he then rose to the surface and tried to emulate what he had just seen. "Don had a beautiful stroke," Mark said. "He was quite a bit older than me, so we weren't really friends. While I had great respect for him, he really wasn't my role model or hero, either. It may sound cold, but he was my objective. I wanted to surpass everything he had done in the pool."

Don Schollander didn't enjoy the attention Mark showed him in the pool, especially Mark's persistence in sticking close by, which Schollander described in his book, *Deep Water*: "Spitz began to work out next to me. Every day he'd be in the next lane. About the only thing Spitz lacked for competitive swimming was a sharp sense of pace and that was something that I still had, as good as ever. I figured he wanted to pick up some pointers on pace from me and it bugged me to have him there. I'd get out of the pool and move over three or four lanes; a few minutes later he would follow. I'd move again and he would follow."

Mark relished his ability to pester Schollander and remembers it much the same way. "Sometimes he would get irritated if I was swimming in the lane next to him and would move over a lane. I would quickly move over, too. If he moved to another lane, I would follow. I got a secret charge knowing that I had the capacity to exasperate him."

By that summer, though, Haines began to realize that Mark's signature event would be the 100 butterfly, despite the Schollander freestyle scrutinizing sessions. It was certainly Mark's favorite—perhaps he developed an unconscious affinity for the short fly after that first record in 1959—and he looked forward to swimming it at the 1966 AAU long-course senior nationals. His participation in 1965, the Maccabiah Games, short-course nationals, and training with the elite team in Santa Clara ushered him to Lincoln, Nebraska, with much more experience and confidence than he had the previous year.

Of his four races, the 100 fly came first. Mark's qualifying time in the preliminaries of 58.3 tied him with Nicolao, his teammate, defending champion, and world-record holder. Only Ross Wales, a freshman at Princeton who had recently won the NCAA title, swam faster in 57.7. That night in the finals, Wales slashed ahead of the pack for the first seventy-five meters before Mark made his move and surged ahead for his first AAU senior national gold medal. His 58.1 bested Wales by three-tenths of a second. Nicolao placed third.

In an extremely successful meet, Mark also placed second in the 200 fly behind Philip Houser and fifth in the 1500 free, and swam on the victorious 4x100 and 4x200 freestyle relays. Schollander still ruled the pool, garnering twenty-seven points for Santa Clara, but Mark finished third overall with twenty. The two combined for twenty-five percent of Santa Clara's national-championship total of one hundred and eighty-two points.

In that year's final issue of *Swimming World Magazine*, Mark had moved up to the world listing. Of the world's best long-course times, Mark was second in the 100 fly, fifth in the 200 fly, ninth in the 800 free, and twelfth in the 200 free.

But as good as 1966 was, 1967 turned out to be his breakout year. It started with Mark leading his high school team to such a successful season that *Swimming World Magazine* deemed the Bruins the best high school swim team in history and put Mark on its cover. The junior finished with the nation's fastest high school times in the 200-yard freestyle, 400-yard freestyle, 100-yard butterfly, and 200-yard IM; ranked fourth in the 100-yard freestyle; and swam on the fastest 400-yard freestyle and 200-yard medley relays.

Shortly after school let out, the Santa Clara Swim Club traveled up to the East Bay for a relay meet in San Leandro. The only event that wasn't a relay was the 400-yard freestyle, which had been dubbed "The Don Schollander 400 Freestyle Challenge." While warming up, Mark's friend Fred Haywood asked him what he was going to do in the 400, and Mark sarcastically replied, "I'm going to swim eight laps, and then we're done." Haywood responded, "No, I mean what are you going to do for a time?" Mark thought he would swim around a 4:30, nineteen seconds off the world record.

Not only did Mark not take the race too seriously, but he also wore two swimsuits. Ultraviolet rays pierced through the lighter portions of Santa Clara's striped suit. With the sun shining brightly that day, Mark, ever mindful of his tan, didn't want a multi-shaded rear end. "The suits were black and navy blue, with three-quarter-inch vertical stripes," he later explained. "If you stayed out in the sun for any length of time, you'd get tan marks from the sections with the lighter color, so I wore two suits to prevent that from happening. Besides, I was comfortable wearing two suits because I also played water polo for my high school. You had to wear two suits in that sport, because opposing players were always tugging on your trunks."

When Mark dove into the water, his stroke felt smooth and strong. After two laps, he was a half-body length in front of Schollander and cruising. After four laps, he was suddenly three body lengths ahead. Coming out of the sixth turn, Mark was so far ahead he couldn't see the rest of the swimmers without disrupting his stroke—something he'd avoided since shivering on Chavoor's deck that morning several years ago. Haines looked at his watch at the 300 turn and realized Mark was on world-record pace. He stood up on his chair and yelled, "Go, Mark! Go!" Spying his coach out of the corner of his eye, Mark figured he was swimming fast and thought he might break 4:20, so he turned it on the last two laps. After touching the wall, a jubilant Haines rushed over and shouted that he had just swum a 4:10.6, beating East German Frank Weigand's world record by half a second. Mark was obviously ecstatic. He had just broken his first world record, and it wasn't much of an effort. Schollander finished well back but after a few moments asked Mark what his time was. "When I told him, he was dumbfounded."

Mark still remembers the race as if it happened yesterday. "I'll never forget it. I remember the warmth of the sun, how the air and chlorinated water smelled. I remember every lap of that swim," Mark said nostalgically. "After the race, Haines could see Schollander's disappointment, so he put his arm around my shoulder and asked me to do him a favor. He told me to keep my mouth shut about beating Schollander and breaking the world record. He said that by Monday, everybody in the swimming world would know what I'd just done and finished by telling me that I had just gone from hunter to hunted."

From that point on, Mark and Schollander had a strained relationship at best. Unconscionably, despite instructing Mark to keep his mouth shut, Haines played up the rivalry by telling the press that one day Mark would be the best swimmer in the world. Mark enjoyed the attention, praise, and confidence of his coach. Others, including Schollander, didn't, and the enmity would only worsen.

Mark must have decided that because the first world record was so exciting, he might as well break some more. At the first Santa Clara Invitational about two weeks later, Mark lowered his 400 free time—perhaps swimming harder because he knew he could—to regain the record from French swimmer Alain Mosconi.

Less than a month later at the Pan American Games in Winnipeg, Canada, he set new standards in the 100 fly and 200 fly in his first international trip as a member of the USA senior team. After he bumped Nicolao from the 100 fly world-record list, Mark was concerned his teammate might feel badly and approached him after the race. "Luis patted me on the head and smiled. He told me that he had held the record long enough and was happy for me," Mark said after the meet. Nicolao's friendly treatment of Mark was quite different than he received from his roommates. As Don Havens recalled, "We had eight persons to a room and Mark was the only high school swimmer. The rest of us were mostly college juniors and seniors. Mark was immature and cocky. He would say something brash and the older swimmers would put him down. He would try to respond, but at that stage in his life he was no match for the older swimmers. It was like watching a debate between Terrell Owens and Barack Obama."

At senior nationals a week after Pan Ams, Mark improved his 200 fly time, won the 100 fly, and swam on the winning

4x200 free and 4x100 medley relays. Finally, at a meet in Berlin at which Mark lowered his 100 fly and 200 fly times, the assault ended for the year.

In all, the high school junior shattered seven world records in the span of three and a half months. For the third time in twelve months, his face graced the cover of *Swimming World Magazine*, which appropriately selected him "World Swimmer of the Year." Arden Hills teammate Debbie Meyer earned the women's honor, and both were finalists for AAU's Sullivan Award, which honors the nation's top amateur athlete. J. Randel Mattson, who broke the world's shot put record, won it that year, but Mark and Meyer's time would come.

Clearly, things were going well for Mark in the pool. Out of the pool was another matter altogether. Already extremely confident and driven, those traits morphed into arrogance and brashness with his escalating success. Jealousies brewed, especially with his older teammates, who resented that fact that this irritating, trash-talking kid was also swimming circles around them. It was one thing for Mark to make boastful claims in retaliation against Jewish taunts, slights in and out of the pool, and ostracism in the locker room. But he almost always delivered, which didn't help his social station in the club. Some viewed him as a conceited hot dog. Some simply thought he was a jerk. The rift with teammates would prove disastrous in the coming year.

Gary Conelly, a future collegiate teammate of Mark's, saw firsthand how he was treated within his club. When Conelly attended his first AAU senior national meet in 1968, he saw his hero, Greg Buckingham, standing in the lobby of the official hotel. As he watched Buckingham from a distance, Mark entered the other side of the room. Conelly couldn't believe Buckingham's "greeting," in a voice intentionally loud enough for everyone to hear, "Well, if it isn't the world's biggest asshole . . . Mark Spitz."

Unlike Chavoor, who savored his talks with Mark after practices and enjoyed visiting the Spitz household, Haines maintained only a deck relationship with his swimmers. His strict rules about calling or visiting him at home created a barrier that prevented the personal relationship that served Mark so well under Chavoor. Haines's devotion to Mark's career was unquestioned, but he didn't always relate to him in a way that could have eased the animosity. In fact, as the gulf between Mark and his teammates widened, Haines seemed to look the other way.

It didn't help that tension began to build between Arnold and Haines. Mark's father believed an undercurrent of anti-Semitism flowed through the club, affecting his family's status. After an interview, *Sports Illustrated*'s William F. Reed noted how Arnold described Mark's experiences at Santa Clara: "There were reprehensible displays. On occasion, Mark was spat upon, scratched, elbowed, kicked in the groin. Accidents perhaps? Horsing around? Possibly, but there was no doubt in Arnold Spitz's mind about the intent of the anti-Semitic jibes. 'When I was a youngster I used to fight, but that wasn't the way,' he says. 'So I tell Mark to shove it down their throats with times. Let them talk, but beat the hell out of them in the pool. This is one thing that has made him so tough.'"

As his stature grew, Lenore vigilantly attempted to read, sort, and archive each new press clipping about Mark that poured into their mailbox from around the country, but the job was becoming more and more time consuming. Suddenly, Mark's name and likeness began appearing in major magazines like *Time, Life*, and *Sports Illustrated*.

The turn of the year brought the 1968 Olympics into view, and Mark threatened to replace Schollander as the globe's premier swimmer. In February, the high school senior set an American record in the 200-yard fly and paced the club's 400-yard medley relay to a national standard in a dual meet between SCSC and Stanford University. In early March, he joined a select group of Americans who competed in the 12th Annual Bremen International Swimfest in Germany. Mark beat the best the

Europeans had to offer in the 800 free in a time faster than the world record. But because the pool was 25 meters long instead of the required 50 meters, it was not official. In the 100 fly, he edged out fellow American Doug Russell by a tenth of a second and then won the 200 fly by more two seconds over Russian Sergei Konov.

Mark capped an incredible high school career at the CIF Central Coast Section championships in May. In the outdoor pool at De Anza Junior College on a cold, rainy day, he broke Schollander's national high school mark in the 200-yard freestyle by seven-tenths of a second. He also won the 100-yard butterfly and slashed a second off the national record in the 100-yard free on the opening leg of the 4x100 freestyle relay. Mark dominated the national High School All-American awards, earning the top spot in those three events, second behind Gary Hall in the 200-yard IM, fourth in the 50-yard freestyle, and fifth in the 100-yard backstroke. He also paced Santa Clara's 200-yard medley relay and 400-yard freestyle relay to first-place rankings. SCHS was so dominant that *Swimming World Magazine* thought the team could place in the top five at the NCAA Championships.

Mark christened his long-course season with his third world record in the 400 free, eclipsing Greg Charlton's 4:08.2 with a 4:07.7. He then turned his attention to an important August, bookended by the AAU national long-course championships at the beginning and the biggest meet of Mark's career—the Olympic Trials—at the end. Mark opened nationals in Lincoln, Nebraska, by taking third in the 400 free behind Ralph Hutton and Mike Burton. The 200 free final featured Schollander, who hadn't lost the race at nationals since 1962, and a rematch with Hutton. Mark broke out of a tightly bunched pack with a furious last twenty-five meters to win. Afterward, Haines stoked the fire. "It was a good training race," he said. "It was good for Mark, because he's young and hungry. It was good for Don because I think he needs a kick in the tail to work harder."

Mark easily won his specialty, the 100 fly, but the world-record holder was upset by '64 Olympic silver-medalist and two-time national titlist Carl Robie in the 200-meter version. Robie dismissed Mark as his main competition, telling *Swimming World Magazine*, "I didn't think Spitz would win from the way he was swimming this morning. I was concerned about Ferris. I have as good a chance as any to make the [Olympic] team."

In the 100 free, Mark again faced Schollander along with UCLA great Zac Zorn. True to his three-year objective, Mark didn't care about the rest of the field. His goal was to beat Schollander for the second time in the meet. "I was focused on Schollander. I didn't think anybody could beat the two of us," recalled Mark. In an eyelash finish, Mark touched out Schollander 53.6 to 53.7, with Zorn third at 54.2.

For the second year in a row, Mark scored more points than anyone else at the meet with thirty-four and appeared in prime condition. He had world rankings in the 100 free, 200 free, and 400 free. He swam the fastest times in the past year in the 100 fly and 200 fly. He'd also had success in the individual medley and backstroke events. The big question for the Trials wasn't if he'd make the Olympic team but rather what events he'd enter.

!!!

CHAPTER 4

THE 1968 SWIM CAMP CABAL

June 1968

AT 4:30 A.M. in Arlington, Texas, the alarm clock blared. The interruption almost two hours before the sun peeked over the horizon in that interurban rail hub between Dallas and Fort Worth jolted Doug Russell from a deep sleep. With eyes half-open, his muscular arm emerged from under the covers to turn off the annoying appliance. For a brief moment, the University of Texas at Arlington junior lay in bed, his body begging him to go back to sleep. But his heart and mind prevailed. The motivation for getting out of bed that day at such a preposterous hour was the same that got him out of bed at the preposterous hour the day before, and it would get him up again the next day, and the day after that: outworking Mark Spitz to supplant him as the fastest butterfly sprinter in the world. It was important for him to know that he was up working out while Mark was still sleeping.

!!!

By the summer of 1968, Mark appeared primed to dominate his first Olympic Games. The recent high school graduate held world records in the 400-meter freestyle, 100-meter butterfly, and 200-meter butterfly, and he ranked in the top ten in the world in the 100-meter freestyle, 200-meter freestyle, and 200-meter individual medley. Individual wins at the 1967 Pan Am Games in Winnipeg proved his mettle at a major international competition, and a sweep of the butterfly events in Berlin on a European tour that fall further demonstrated his ability to cope with long travel and unfamiliar customs.

Furthermore, well-known adult figures would surround the teen, theoretically easing the strain such an event can have on rookies. The head coach of the men's Olympic team was none other than George Haines, assisted by family friend Don Gambril. Mark had verbally committed to swim for Gambril at Long Beach State after the Olympics. Sherm Chavoor, his former coach and mentor from Arden Hills, would be nearby as the women's head coach. The stars' alignment comforted not only the Spitz family but also the U.S. Olympic brass, who knew that hype for another golden boy would boost attention, funds, and the perception of the sport in the United States.

But first Mark had to make the team. Qualifying procedures were straightforward. A top-three finish in an individual event at the U.S. Olympic Swimming Trials guaranteed the athlete a trip to the Games, and high placings in certain events also qualified swimmers as relay members or alternates.

Perhaps more daunting was Haines' task of determining which race his protégé should swim at the Trials. Mark's ability and recent history indicated he could make the team in any of six events. Tempting as it was, though, entering him in all six would be greedy and foolhardy. Mark's performance could suffer by swimming in events scheduled too close together, lacking adequate time to recover between races. Likewise, entering Mark in too many events, however well-spaced, could prematurely fatigue him compared to his competitors. Maximizing the number of races he could swim at the Games without jeopardizing the quality of his performances at the Trials required Haines to carefully analyze the schedule. The key was to not double up on races on any given day.

The 100-meter and 200-meter butterfly were no-brainers. Mark specialized in that stroke, he held both world records, and the events were scheduled for the first and third days of the meet, respectively. Additionally, the fastest U.S. swimmer in the 100 fly in Mexico City earned a spot on the United States' 400-meter medley relay team. Haines also felt confident that Mark should swim the 100-meter freestyle on the fourth and final night of the Trials. Not only did it fit nicely into the overall schedule, but it, like the 100 fly, could be a three-for-one race. The top four finishers would swim on the 400 freestyle relay at the Games, and the top three would compete individually in the event. The fastest American in the 100 free at the Olympics also earned a position on the medley relay, giving Mark a second chance at the bonus race.

If Mark qualified for those three individual events and the two relays, he could bag five medals in Mexico City. Winning each race was not out of the question, and with five golds, Mark would become the most successful swimmer in Olympic history, a goal not concealed by either coach or swimmer. Any additional medals would simply brighten the star's shine.

That left a few other possible races for Mark to compete in. Mark had lowered the global standard in the 400 freestyle three times in a year's span and fared well in the 200 IM on a few occasions, but both races came with two drawbacks. Not only could their length and difficulty tire Mark, but neither offered the opportunity to collect an additional medal as a relay member.

Entering Mark in the 200-meter freestyle emerged as Haines' only real dilemma. A top-three finish at the Trials would land him in the Olympic race and on the 800-meter freestyle relay, upping his potential medal count to an unimaginable seven at a single Olympics. However, it fell on the first day of the Trials, the same day as the 100 butterfly. Mark would have to swim both events in the morning preliminaries and again that night in the finals. Haines was simply unwilling to risk Mark's fortune in his signature sprint.

But a quirk in qualifying procedures presented another avenue to a sixth event without gambling Mark's energy. The 200-meter freestyle was making its first appearance at the Olympics. Previous Trials had featured a swim-off in the 200 free to select the four swimmers for the 800-meter relay. Oddly, the U.S. Olympic Men's Swimming and Diving Committee decided that the top three in the official 200-meter freestyle would qualify for the relay, but the final position would be filled by whoever was faster: the fourth swimmer in the official 200 free or the winner of a swim-off. The swim-off would be open to any athlete who hadn't competed in the official 200 free. Since the swim-off would be the last event at the Trials, the upshot allowed Mark to enter it without affecting any of his other races.

With that, Haines positioned Mark to swim six events in Mexico City—the two butterflies, the 100-meter freestyle, the 400- and 800-meter free relays, and the 400-medley relay if he won 100 fly.

‼‼‼

A California city hosted the Men's Olympic Swim Trials for the first time since 1932, the year it became a one-meet event rather than several affairs held in various locations around the country. Long Beach, twenty miles south of Los Angeles, embraced the honor with flair, building the Belmont Plaza Olympic Pool especially for the occasion. The million-gallon, state-of-the-art pool in a Greek Modern building anchored the fashionable Belmont Shore neighborhood just south of Belmont Pier off Ocean Boulevard. Constructed at a cost of $3.7 million, the south side featured a bank of glass panel walls and sliding doors, giving spectators in the north grandstand an unabated view of the Pacific Ocean less than a sprint-distance race away. Smaller bleachers flanked the main grandstand, providing intimate settings for water polo and diving, which upped the total capacity to 2,500. Daytime temperatures hovered between the low to mid-80s during that five-day span from August 30 to September 3, heating up the arena in the preliminary events, but cool ocean breezes lowered the evening temperatures to the more comfortable mid-60s for the finals.

Gambril, also the men's head coach at the nearby Long Beach State University, remembers the natatorium as the premier indoor swim stadium in the country. "It was a beautiful, new facility that was both functional and competitive." The sellout crowds, cheering on a substantial number of regional favorites, expected fast times. They weren't disappointed.

❗❗❗
o o o

Mark's first event on the first day of the meet—the 100-meter butterfly—featured stiff competition. Mark had lowered the world record twice within the previous thirteen months, first with a hand-timed 56.3 at the Pan Am Games in Winnipeg and most recently in Berlin that October to 55.7.

But Doug Russell held the global mark for more than a month during that span. His 56.3 at the 1967 World University Games in Tokyo mirrored Mark's time. Ross Wales also posed a formidable challenge. The Ohio native had taken second in Winnipeg and won titles at the AAU championships in 1966 and the NCAA Championships in 1967. Both Russell and Wales were fast-twitch sprinters—their all-out approach almost always meant a lead at the turn—but the combination of their fade, Mark's endurance edge, and his late surge of speed kept them off the winner's stand.

All three swimmers won their heats, with Russell's 55.99 raising some eyebrows as the fastest preliminary time. Spitz turned in a 56.43, and Wales qualified third in 57.56. Of the remaining finalists—Bruce Lechler, Mike Masarie, Jerry Heidenreich, John Russell (no relation to Doug), and Carl Robie—Robie brought the most credentials, but as a 200 fly specialist he generally didn't threaten in a sprint.

Mark and Russell treated the capacity crowd to a heart-stopping battle. Russell took the first lap in blazing speed. Mark and Wales made the turn dead even. Twenty-five meters from the wall, Russell still led by a body length, but Mark was closing. The only question was whether he had enough lane left to make up the ground. In a spectacular finish, Mark forged ahead and Doug's last full stroke left him just short of the wall. The winning time of 55.6 gave Mark his third world record in the event. Russell took second in 56.1, and Wales earned the final Olympic berth with a 57.7.

Russell revealed his disappointment in an interview with *Swimming World Magazine* after the race: "I really wanted to beat Mark and show the world that I was the best flyer, but I just missed the wall. I'm not taking anything away from Mark. I probably wouldn't have beaten him anyway, but I just wish I wasn't a 97-meter butterflyer." Russell's coach, the colorful Don Easterling, knew Russell's last half-stroke probably cost him the win, but with a sly smile he added confidently, "He's got another chance—the Olympic Games."

In retrospect, Gambril believes the loss benefited Russell's preparation for the Olympics. Not only did it provide fresh incentive, but it helped Gambril convince Russell that a change in race strategy may produce a different result. "I talked to Don [Easterling] after the race, and we both felt Doug had the ability to beat Mark as long as he could swim a more controlled race and focus his training on stamina," Gambril said later.

With a day off after the 100 fly, Mark arrived at the 200-meter butterfly fully rested. Again, he entered the race as the world-record holder, having swum a 2:05.7 in Berlin. He first lowered the mark at the Pan Am Games the previous July in 2:06.4 before posting an electronic 2:06.4 in Oak Park seventeen days later at AAU Nationals. But again, another American swam the fastest time in the world at the World University Games in Tokyo when Mark's former Arden Hills teammate John Ferris touched the wall in 2:06.0.

And then there was Carl Robie, the Philadelphia Flyer and 1967 graduate of the University of Michigan. In addition to his Olympic silver medal in 1964, Robie had lowered the world record four times from 1961 to 1963 and won six AAU national 200 fly championships. He also collected the 1966 and 1967 NCAA titles. Despite his success, though, he'd already surprised many in the swimming world simply by qualifying for the Trials, having worked out at a YMCA on his own and without a coach during his first year of law school. He would drive home on weekends to work out with his high school coach, Frank Keefe. On the weekends he would get in five workouts (Friday night, two on Saturday and two on Sunday) before heading back for law school. After final exams, he worked out with Keefe full-time to train for the Olympic Trials, grinding out 15,000 to 20,000 meters a day. He had recently beaten Mark in the event at Nationals in Nebraska. His gumption made him that much more dangerous. Unbeknownst to the other competitors, Keefe thought Robie was poised to break the world record at the Trials, but a bout of dysentery caused Keefe to advise his protégé to swim for third.

Three others were given outside shots of making the team—Wales; Phil Houser, the 1966 AAU champion and 1968 NCAA champion for the University of Southern California; and Mike Burton, a middle- and long-distance freestyler who captured the bronze at Pan Ams in 1967.

This time it was Ferris at 2:07.67 and Robie at 2:07.83 who sent a ripple through the crowd by posting faster preliminary times than Mark's 2:08.32. In the finals, Wales and Ferris reached the halfway point first, with Mark and Robie at the back of the pack. The duo maintained their lead at 150 meters, turning in unison, with Houser and Robie close behind. Trailing two and a half yards behind the leaders, the world-record holder's Olympic berth seemed in jeopardy. Nervousness oozed from even his ever-confident parents.

But not from Mark. Relying on his abundant late-race energy, he began closing in the last thirty meters. Fifteen meters from the wall, he pulled even with Ferris and Robie as Wales faltered. With another signature surge, Mark shot past the leaders to win in 2:05.9, almost two-tenths ahead of Ferris and more than a second in front of Robie.

Gambril credited Haines for Mark's smart race. "In the 200 fly, most swimmers in that era simply swam as fast as they could for as long as they could," Gambril remembered. "Haines' swimmers usually had an advantage in that George was a great tactical coach. Mark definitely benefited from that wisdom."

$$\text{!!!}$$

The 100-meter freestyle, like the 100-meter dash in track and field, led the sport in popularity and excitement. Anything could happen in the all-out sprint. Racers needed a quick start off the blocks, the speed to rocket through the water, just enough endurance to ward off a late fade, and sometimes a little luck to hit the wall with a perfectly extended arm to touch out the guy in the next lane. No more than a few hundredths of a second often separated one swimmer from the next. Add to that the swimmers' intense desire to secure one of the five Olympic spots hanging in the balance—the top three competed in the event at the Olympics, the top four comprised the 4x100-meter freestyle relay, and the fifth finisher made the team as an alternate—and you have the most tension-filled races at the Trials.

It took on added importance to Mark. First and foremost, the race presented an opportunity to challenge rival Don Schollander head-to-head in one of Schollander's specialties. Mark's goal of unseating his Santa Clara Swim Club teammate as U.S. swimming's golden boy depended in part on Mark swimming the 100 free in Mexico City. The race also anointed its winner as the fastest swimmer in the nation, a distinction Mark wanted to keep after stealing it from Schollander a month earlier at AAU Nationals.

After eight heats of preliminaries, no clear-cut favorite emerged. Schollander clocked the fastest time, with a 52.93. Zac Zorn, who won the 100-yard freestyle at NCAAs that spring as a senior at UCLA, was five one-hundredths back. Mark qualified third, a mere two-tenths behind Schollander, and world-record holder Ken Walsh's time was fourth fastest. Incredibly, less than a second separated the first and eighth times. Every swimmer in the race had a shot at a Trials win or an Olympic berth.

The buzzing throng awaited a breathtaking final. Eight men approached the starting blocks as the public address announcer introduced them. Based on the roar, the reigning Olympic hero entered the race as the crowd favorite. At the last moment, though, officials delayed the start for a reason unknown to the participants or spectators. Like the other seven finalists, Schollander wondered what was going on, and the distraction completely broke his concentration. As he described the situation in his book *Deep Water*, Schollander's focus broadened to include much more than the lane into which he was about to dive. He waved to a friend in the crowd for the first time in years. Then he noticed the television lights had been turned off. Uncharacteristically, the most accomplished active swimmer in the world began worrying about his turn. Would he be able to see the wall in the darker pool? How would he judge when to begin his flip? Ten minutes passed before the starter called the swimmers to their marks, but it seemed like an eternity to Schollander.

When the gun fired, Walsh and Zorn shot off the blocks. Walsh got such a great jump that Schollander, among others, thought he false started and hesitated, expecting the race to be recalled. It wasn't. At the turn, Zorn touched in a stunning 25.2, followed by Walsh and Spitz. Schollander was dead last, a full second behind Zorn. Zorn tore through the last 50 meters to win in an apparent world record. Walsh hit the wall second, but the tight pack made it impossible to tell who snagged the third, fourth, and fifth spots.

At that time, in the era between primitive techniques and full-blown technology, race results were determined by a hierarchy of four systems. Readings from electronic touch pads always merited priority, but they didn't always function properly. In the event of a glitch, officials then reviewed the printouts from the relatively new Ritter machines that punched the order of finish on a card as swimmers touched the wall. Three officials also timed each lane, their push-buttons linked to the starter's pistol and connected to a computerized timer. Finally, a committee evaluated each piece of information.

R. Max Ritter invented his timing device in an effort to prevent this very scenario. The two-time Olympic swimmer for Germany, cofounder of FINA, and long-time American swimming official after immigrating to the U.S. in 1910 sought a better method for determining order of finish in close races after an incident at the 1960 Rome Olympics. American Lance Larson appeared to have defeated Australia's John Devitt, who actually congratulated Larson when they exited the pool. Results from the timers bore that out. But FINA rules left the decision in the hands of judges, and the third and deciding vote was cast by the chief judge watching the race from an angle rather than an elevated stand parallel to the wall as the rules stated.

Race officials labored over the results of the 100-meter freestyle final. The three timing methods were supposed to provide greater accuracy, but the lengthy interval clearly indicated the outcome was in question and likely controversial. In fact, debate swirled concerning the start of the race as much as the finish, many believing it should be swum again because of the perceived jump.

Rumors that Schollander placed third and Mark fourth began circulating, and Haines himself told Schollander that both machines verified that order. Then a new round of rumors reversed those positions. The difference between third and fourth was huge. The third-place finisher qualified for the Olympics in the 100 free, as part of the 4x100-meter freestyle relay, and with the chance to swim the 4x100 medley relay. The fourth-place finisher only swam the 400 freestyle relay. Third place represented a possible three medals; fourth only one.

After an interminable period, the announcer approached the microphone, immediately silencing the boisterous crowd. "Ladies and gentlemen, the results of the 100-meter freestyle are as follows. In first place, tying the world record in a time of 52.6, is Zac Zorn from the Phillips 66 Club in Long Beach." The crowd cheered for the hometown swimmer. "Second, with a time of 53.1, is Ken Walsh, also of Phillips 66." More cheering. "Third place goes to Mark Spitz, with a time of 53.3." The crowd drew in its collective breath and applauded half-heartedly, more out of anxiousness to hear Schollander's name called next than any disrespect to Mark. But to the shock of everyone in the pristine facility, fourth place went to Steve Rerych, the 1966 AAU champion. Schollander's fifth-place finish crushed him. The hero of the 1964 Tokyo Olympics had qualified for Mexico City in only the 200 free and the 800 free relay.

After the race, a giddy Spitz gushed, "I'm in five events now!" apparently assuming he would win the 100-meter butterfly at the Olympics to land a spot on the 400 medley relay. That remark did not go unnoticed by Russell, further fueling his resolve to outwork Mark over the next six weeks.

❢❢❢

The 200-freestyle swim-off put Brent Berk's fourth-place time of 1:57.86 on the bubble. If the winner eclipsed that time, he would bounce Berk from the Olympic relay team, although Berk also qualified in the 400 freestyle. Spitz left no doubt in the minds of the crowd, his coaches, and fellow swimmers about his ability to improve the relay, waxing the field in 1:55.92. His time bettered those from all heats and the final except Schollander's two world-record performances of 1:54.89 in the prelims and 1:54.3 in the final.

Mark's Olympic slate was almost set. He was guaranteed five races: the 100 fly, 200 fly, 100 free, 4x100 free relay, and 4x200 free relay, with a possibility of a sixth—the 4x100 medley relay—if he won the 100 fly or 100 free.

The 1968 men's Olympic swimming team also was set. The twenty-five members and seven alternates ranged in age from sixteen to twenty-three, in location from Long Beach to Philadelphia, and in number of Olympic races from one to at least five.

1. Lawrence Barbiere, 17, Vesper Boat Club (Philadelphia, PA), 100 back
2. Brent Berk, 19, Santa Clara Swim Club, 400 free
3. Gregory Buckingham; 23; Santa Clara Swim Club; 200 IM, 400 IM
4. Michael Burton; 21; Arden Hills Swim Club; 400 free, 1500 free
5. John Ferris; 19; Arden Hills Swim Club; 200 fly, 200 IM
6. Gary Hall; 17; Phillips 66 Long Beach; 200 back, 400 IM

7. Charles Hickcox; 21; Bloomington Swim Club; 100 back, 200 IM, 400 IM
8. Jackson Horsely, 16, Triton Swim Club (Lexington, KY), 200 back
9. Mitch Ivey, 19, Santa Clara Swim Club, 200 back
10. Chet Jastremski, 27, Unattached (U.S. Army), alternate-relays
11. Brian Job, 16, Santa Clara Swim Club, 200 breast
12. David Johnson, 21, Philadelphia Aquatic Club, alternate-relays
13. William Johnson, 21, Los Angeles Athletic Club, alternate-relays
14. John Kinsella, 16, Unattached (Hinsdale, IL), 1500 free
15. Phillip Long, 19, Suburban Swim Club (PA), 200 breast
16. Kenneth Merten; 23; Los Angeles Swim Club; 100 breast, 200 breast
17. Ronnie Mills, 17, Burford Swim Club (TX), 100 back
18. Donald McKenzie, 21, Bloomington Swim Club, 100 breast
19. John Nelson; 20; Unattached (Pompano Beach, FL); 200 free, 400 free, 1500 free, 4x200 FR
20. David Perkowski, 21, Bloomington Swim Club, 100 breast
21. Steven Rerych; 22; Unattached (Philadelphia, PA); 200 free, 4x200 FR
22. Ray Rivero, 18, Santa Clara Swim Club, alternate-relays
23. Carl Robie, 21, Suburban Swim Club (PA), 200 fly
24. Doug Russell, 22, Burford Swim Club (TX), 100 fly
25. Don Schollander; 22; Santa Clara Swim Club; 200 free, 4x200 FR
26. Mark Spitz; 18; Santa Clara Swim Club; 100 free, 100 fly, 200 fly, 4x100 FR, 4x200 FR
27. Andrew Strenk, 19, Los Angeles Athletic Club, alternate-relays
28. Ross Wales, 20, Princeton Aquatic Association, 100 fly

29. Mike Wall, 22, Santa Clara Swim Club, alternate-relays
30. Ken Walsh; 23; Phillips 66 Long Beach; 100 free, 4x100 FR
31. Peter Williams, 22, Spartan Swim Club (E. Lansing, MI), alternate-relays
32. Zac Zorn; 21; Phillips 66 Long Beach; 100 free, 4x100 FR

After relaxing and training a few days in Long Beach, the team flew to Colorado Springs to train at the Air Force Academy and fine-tune their bodies not only to swim the races in which they'd qualified but also to adjust to performing in the oxygen-depleted air at altitude. The Academy, higher than the Mile High City at 7,258 feet above sea level, roughly approximated Mexico City's 7,349 feet. The bulk of the swimmers would be housed at the Broadmoor hotel, but many of the distance swimmers stayed in cabins 8,500 feet above sea level.

❢❢❢

As hard as they'd worked, as much as they'd been through, as excited as they were about reaching their goals of competing in the Olympics, that group of highly skilled and motivated men had perhaps their hardest six weeks in front of them. By virtue of being at the camp, the athletes' pinpointed focus narrowed even more. This was it. This was when each would hone his technique, his fitness, his routine, his self-confidence, his mental sharpness. This was their last chance to reach down and find whatever edge they'd take to Mexico City. This was where everything came together, where every swimmer worked toward that point—mentally, physically, emotionally—from which peak performance originates.

As if that weren't pressure enough, they'd be doing it while living 'round the clock with their primary challengers. In other words, they ate, slept, carpooled, swam, and hung out with the very people they were preparing to beat. They all were team-mates now. Some also were friends. Many were rivals. A few were archenemies. But every person at camp would compete against at least two other Americans in his event at the Games. Walking the tightrope of supporting teammates while seeking or main-taining a mental edge over them requires great social skills. Too much swagger creates a negative, adversarial environment. Too much support could lead to defeat when it counted most.

For Mark, who qualified individually for three events, six of his teammates posed a direct threat. According to fellow butterflyer Ross Wales, "The seven alternates would endure the torturous training with little possibility of participating in the Olympics unless a full-fledged team member became ill or injured. Alternates could not be substituted in an individual event within thirty days of the Olympics, so two weeks into the camp their only shot at swimming in the Olympics was in a relay, but that would require three qualifiers to take sick in a stroke event, and at least two in the freestyle relay. As a result, there was a real undercurrent at work; there were two teams, those who would compete and those that were just along for the tour. Some of the latter group, envious of the qualifiers, did not add to the camaraderie of the camp." Having qualified in the most events, Mark represented the biggest roadblock for the alternates. Furthermore, a bout of tonsillitis—he would have surgery following the Olympics—kept him out of several workouts, further irritating everyone.

Santa Clara Swim Club sent seven other swimmers to camp, far and away the best-represented club, but this did not necessarily bode well for Mark. The animosity that had built up between him and his club mates over the past four years created more strife than it soothed. The camaraderie was conspicuously absent.

According to noted sports psychologist, Ken Ravizza, the conditions Mark encountered at the 1968 camp didn't forecast success at the Olympics. "In such a setting, familiar faces such as teammates become very important. The comfort of knowing others well, and of them knowing you, can ease the stress, make difficult times more tolerable, and provide support in the face of adversity or harassment," Ravizza explained. Haines, both as Mark's club coach and the Olympic coach, could have eased the tension somewhat. But instead, whether purposefully or carelessly, he compounded it. Shortly after the Trials, when a reporter asked how many of Mark's six possible events he could win, Haines responded, "Personally, I think he can win them all." The local, national, and international media pounced on such a brash statement, and a boastful and impetuous Mark echoed his coach's predictions, further increasing the attention on him. Worse, though, it intensified the maelstrom among the Olympic team itself. Forget doing the dance of decorum. Mark had just thrown down the gauntlet in no uncertain terms. Along with their coach, he had just told the world he thought he was better than any of them.

"At that time in his life, Mark was not very likable because of his immaturity," Gambril reflected. "He was one of the younger swimmers in the camp, and he would brag to the older guys that he would beat them, and then he did. That didn't sit well with such a competitive bunch. Some of them also felt the media attention on Mark was over the top, which created more ill will toward him. The resentment just continued to build."

"Mark was an unbelievably gifted swimmer," recalled Ken Walsh. "But he didn't seem to work out very hard. He missed a lot of workouts because he was supposedly sick. The rest of us were working out hard every day and Mark's lack of work ethic caused some resentment."

All in all, the assembled group was not Spitz-friendly. Gary Hall would describe the 1968 camp as the most divisive of the three camps he attended. According to Hall, "the camp was full of cliques—you had the Stanford guys, Yale guys, Long Beach guys and Indiana guys keeping to themselves. There was definitely no team attitude."

Mark was soon the butt of many jokes and pranks, and as the fog of negativity surrounding him thickened, he became painfully aware of his teammates' antipathy towards him. "I missed a lot of workouts because of my tonsillitis, and talk spread through camp that I was goldbricking—shirking my training. I'm not sure which made me feel worse, the pain in my throat or the way my teammates treated me. Most of them were older and just shunned me. If they planned to do something during our free time, they left five minutes before I found out about it. If they needed a fourth for golf and I was available, they made it a threesome."

Mark also struggled in the pool. His tonsillitis prevented him from participating in most of the first two weeks of practice. This was important because the first two weeks of training was the hardest; the coaches intended to establish a base line of conditioning from which the swimmers could begin to taper for the Olympics. By the time Mark was able to train, the team had begun the taper and he missed the hard training segment he needed to be in top shape. In addition to his inflamed tonsils, he didn't acclimate well to the altitude, having difficulty breathing at night. The combination meant he wasn't always backing up his boasts in the pool like he normally did. His confidence in his ability had always formed a shield of security around him, but the chink in his armor now threatened to expose his emotions.

Word reached Chavoor on the other side of town at the women's camp that Mark's mood was spiraling toward depression. In an effort to boost his former swimmer's spirits and distract his mental demons, Chavoor arranged for Mark, Haines, and Sue Shields, a 100-meter butterflyer on the women's team, to join him for a round of putt-putt golf. The outing backfired. While they were on the course, the foursome heard taunts launched at Mark. One person yelled out "Five gold medals? You will be lucky to win one, Jew-boy." Another one said, "Hey Jew-boy, you ain't gonna win nothing!" It would have been one thing if faceless kids were doing the heckling, but they were some of Mark's Olympic teammates. He tried to ignore the taunts, but they hurt. Mark admitted to Chavoor that he didn't have a single friend in camp.

Two swimmers—Russell and Walsh—appeared to be leaders of the unofficial anti-Spitz cabal. Both were older, more mature athletes, each with a vivid sense of humor. Both were set to compete against Mark, so each had an apparent interest in breaking his focus. "I didn't dislike Mark," said Walsh. "Mark was immature and showed some susceptibility to teasing." Mark's former Arden Hills teammate, Mike Burton, recalled that "it seemed like it was the whole camp against Mark."

Russell, the lanky, handsome, streetwise Texan, put all of his Olympic dreams in one basket. Rather than swim three events at the Trials—the 100 butterfly; the 100 backstroke, for which he briefly held the world record; and the 200 individual medley—Russell chose to focus on the 100 fly. "By the time the Olympics rolled around, Mark and I were significantly ahead of any other butterflyers in the world," Russell recalled. "I wanted to be the best in the world, and there was a clear path to that goal: beat Mark Spitz in the 100 butterfly. That's a tall order, but that was my mindset."

Walsh, a roommate of Russell's at camp, held the world record in the 100 free for more than a year before Zorn tied it at the Trials. He wanted sole possession of the record. While some thought Walsh's antics were attempts to psyche Mark out, according to Walsh, psyching out Mark was not the objective. "Mark was a good freestyler, but he wasn't my main concern. I was more worried about Zac. The team's treatment of Mark had nothing to do with competition. He was easy to kid."

As part of the immunization process prior to international travel, the USOC mandated that all U.S. Olympians receive gamma globulin shots as a precaution against Hepatitis A. Chet Jastremski, a 27-year-old alternate at the camp and medical school graduate, administered the injections to the men's swimming team one day. Playing off Mark's well-known reputation as a hypochondriac and needle-phobic, Russell and Walsh opportunistically hatched a plan.

Russell and Walsh could see that Mark was reluctant for anyone to stick a needle in his rear end, so they would actively discuss the upcoming shots when Mark was around. "One time, we talked about the needle being square and six inches long," recalled Walsh. As the team lined up outside a makeshift medical room, Russell and Walsh took their places near the front of the line. When Russell saw Mark enter the area, he told Walsh to lie on the ground as if he had passed out. When Mark walked by, he spied the prone Walsh and excitedly asked Russell "What happened to Ken?" Holding back a smile, Russell deadpanned to Mark "Oh nothing, he just had his shot." White-faced, Mark took his spot at the end of the line. Other swimmers, aware of the situation, screamed once inside the room, scaring Mark into thinking the shots were very painful. Some emerged wincing and rubbing their buttocks at the faux torture they'd just endured.

Mark's face paled as he waited his turn and in attempted nonchalance allowed others to go ahead of him. Gambril chuckled as he watched the drama unfold but suddenly Mark was nowhere to be seen. A group was dispatched to find the young swimmer and they found him standing on top of a toilet in the restroom so that it would appear that no one was in the stall. When Gary Hall opened the stall door, he observed Mark physically shaking in fear. "We had to carry him back to the end of the line to get his shot," recalled Hall. Gambril positioned himself behind Mark at the end of the line, just to make sure Mark didn't try to skip the shot entirely.

Finally, with no other swimmers to concede his spot in line to, Mark entered the room with trepidation. Somehow, Jastremski kept a straight face, although given Mark's mental state he might not have noticed anyway. A moment after dropping his pants for the injection, Russell and Walsh burst into the room with a camera and caught on film the startled teenager, pants down and a look of fear and shock on his face. They posted the photograph on the bulletin board, around which several teammates penciled crude and nasty comments.

Mark's roommate at the Broadmoor was Ronnie Mills, who had qualified for the 100-meter backstroke. A naïve Mills made the mistake of telling Russell and Walsh that he had been a cheerleader and the duo immediately gave him a new moniker "Ronnie Sue." Their room was labeled "the rejects' room." Gary Hall, who roomed with Russell and Walsh, got sick of the relentless psychological warfare against Mark and Ronnie and left his room to take one of the beds in the rejects' room.

!!!

It's not that Mark didn't try to be friendly. Nor was he always intentionally arrogant, although it often came out that way. In an effort to socialize with Russell one evening after practice, when the two were the last ones to leave the locker room, Mark asked, "Hey Doug, what are you going to do after the 100 butterfly in Mexico? Are you going to go to the beach, maybe see the pyramids?" Russell looked intently at him and replied, "Mark, I'm going to be hanging around my room getting a lot of rest, because I'll have the medley relay to swim." Russell's retort momentarily stunned Mark, for whom his victory and thus a spot on the medley relay was a foregone conclusion. He'd never considered he might lose the race. "Uh, well, uh, that's what I'm going to be doing, too" was the only response Mark could come up with. "That's why we're going to swim the race," Russell explained bluntly.

Russell's single-minded goal of winning the 100 fly, and his awareness that that meant beating Mark in the 100 fly, almost made him leave camp. When the coaches assigned lanes for workouts, they logically placed Russell with the sprinters and Mark with the middle-distance swimmers. Russell, already an excellent sprinter, knew that improving his endurance gave him the only chance of beating Mark. When Haines refused to move him to the middle-distance lanes, Russell packed his bags, feeling the workouts at camp wouldn't help him meet his goal. Gambril stepped in and agreed to the change as long as he could keep up. "I raced Mark every lap of every practice," Russell recalled. "If he went first, I went first. If he went third, I went third. Is that stalking? I guess, but he was the best butterflyer in the world, and that's where I wanted to get. As a competitor, he viewed me as no threat, and that inspired me to work even harder."

Based on a particular workout, the approach seemed to be working. After swimming twice a day during the week, Sundays consisted of a single workout called a quality set in which the athletes swam their event several times with ample rest in between. One Sunday well into camp, Russell clocked four consecutive 100 butterflies at or close to 56.0, about a half-second off Mark's world record and an impressive display of speed and endurance. As word of Russell's times spread, Mark felt the need to put an end to any consideration that Russell could outperform him. Fatigued from his own quality set and with unnecessary pride, Mark demanded to be timed in the 100 fly. Most of the guys had finished their workouts, but Mark's rash challenge piqued their interest, so they ambled back to poolside. Mark churned through the water under the curious eye of virtually everyone on the team. When coaches announced his time, more than a second slower than Russell's slowest, the swimmers left shaking their heads at his immaturity. Mark sat motionless in the pool, realizing the magnitude of his folly, and immediately began to blame his poor showing on his tough workout that day, but nobody listened.

Actually, not even Mark listened. That moment, doubt crept in, pecking at his previously stalwart faith that he would beat Russell in Mexico City. The Olympic Games is arguably the most pressure-filled athletic event in the world. Only the well-trained, deeply focused, and emotionally stable athletes can expect to succeed. Mark traveled to Mexico City with his wounded pride, diverted focus, and subpar health and fitness—not a good combination in any situation, much less given the onerously high bar his coach had set for him.

‼‼‼

CHAPTER 5

FOUR-MEDAL "FLOP" IN MEXICO CITY

"¡No queremos Olimpiadas! ¡Queremos revolución!"

TEN DAYS before the start of the 1968 Olympics, thousands of emotional college students chanted, "We don't want Olympic Games! We want revolution!" in the Plaza de las Tres Culturas in the Tlatelolco section of Mexico City. The protest on October 2 capped several months of a Mexican student movement voicing its opinions on several national issues: freedom of the press and of association, police brutality, the army's siege of the National Autonomous University of Mexico in an effort to curb the demonstrations, and the government's outlay of $140 million on the Games when poverty was so rampant in Mexico.

By sunset, police and military personnel surrounded the protesters and, when they were unable to disperse the crowd without force, they began using clubs, tear gas, and eventually guns. The exact number of people killed and wounded in the hours-long massacre remains a mystery. Details of the demonstration and especially of what happened afterward vary widely, not only because of the chaos but also because of the Mexican government's reprehensible and obstinate cover-up job. Kate Doyle, Senior Analyst of U.S. Policy in Latin America for the National Security Archive, reported that shortly after the massacre, clean-up crews were in the square mopping up the blood of the protesters. Doyle added, "Over the next few hours, government agents barged into radio and television outlets and confiscated all audio and video accounts of the tragedy."

U.S. butterfly specialist Carl Robie recalls visiting the square when he arrived in Mexico City. "My fiancée and her parents were staying in an apartment in Tlatelolco. When I visited her, the Plaza had been cleaned up. There were no blood stains, but what they couldn't clean up were machine gun marks on the walls of the apartment building. It was quite chilling to see those marks, knowing that dozens had been killed there a few days earlier," said Robie.

Most non-governmental accounts put the number in the hundreds, while the government itself claimed between twenty and fifty. Doyle has been able to document fifty-five deaths, but laments that the true number will never be known. Official government reports claimed then, and still maintain, that its forces responded in self-defense to armed radical attacks, but that stance is no longer unanimous.

Luis Echeverría, Interior Secretary over police and internal security at the time, was accused by many as the mastermind of the massacre. For years he denied ordering troops to fire and insisted they did so only in response to snipers in the crowd. But in a 1998 interview with CNN, he contradicted the party line. "These kids were not provocateurs. The majority were the sons and daughters of workers, farmers, and unemployed people." He claimed—perhaps in an attempt to lessen his culpability in the atrocity—that only his former boss, President Gustavo Díaz Ordaz, could order the police and military personnel to fire their weapons.

Regardless of who gave the command, one thing was certain. The Mexican government would tolerate no threats to the staging of the Olympic Games, least of all students protesting the hypocrisy of the Institutional Revolutionary Party's attempt to appear to the world as a progressive, democratic, and politically stable society. The goal was to show the world that Mexico was not simply a country of sombreros and siestas.

Anonymous sources within the International Olympic Committee (IOC) immediately questioned whether the Games should go on, citing the host's responsibility to guarantee the safety of athletes, coaches, officials, and spectators. IOC president Avery Brundage, still the only American to hold that position, had other motives. Cancellation of the Olympics would be a political and economic catastrophe for the IOC, already criticized for awarding the Games for the first time to a Latin American country, a developing country, and a site at high altitude. Spending only a few hours to investigate the seriousness of the combustible situation, Brundage announced that the Games would go on, accepting the Mexican government's face-saving assurances that it had succeeded in quelling the dissidents. Brundage was not alone in his stance—few outside of Mexico opposed his decision—but his quick and cosmetic analysis disrespected the slain students and neglected his duty to ensure safety at the Games.

The United States, with its own divisive situation in the Vietnam War, also endured political unrest. In January of 1968, North Vietnam forces launched the Tet Offensive, the most extensive military operation by either side up to that point and one that U.S. leaders had deemed impossible. The campaign largely failed in the field but succeeded mightily in embarrassing the United States, shaking U.S. imperialism and public opinion. Handcuffed because of the war, President Lyndon B. Johnson chose not to run for reelection, and in the days leading up to the Olympics, Richard M. Nixon and Hubert H. Humphrey campaigned intensely with the war at the forefront of the debate.

At the same time, Harry Edwards, a bright young black instructor at San Jose State College in Northern California established an organization called Olympic Project for Human Rights (OPHR). The natural evolution of the Revolt of the Black

Athlete movement protested the U.S. use of black athletes to conceal the country's continued prejudice. Many prominent black athletes joined the organization, including SJSC and international track stars John Carlos and Tommie Smith. "For years, we have participated in the Olympic Games carrying the United States on our backs with our victories, and race relations are worse than ever," he told the *New York Times Magazine* in 1972. Edwards hoped to convince black athletes to boycott the Olympic Games to draw attention to the OPHR and its cause, but when that initiative failed to take hold, he encouraged black athletes to protest in their own way.

It was with the political cauldron of 1968 as a backdrop that Mark and the other four hundred and one U.S. Olympians left the States for Mexico City. Yet upon arrival at the airport they found a festive atmosphere. Female athletes received colored corsages, mini-skirted greeters presented male athletes with miniature Olympic flags, and Olympic banners featuring doves as a symbol of peace proclaimed international brotherhood. In contrast, however, soldiers, tanks, and armored cars occupied the nearby streets. At great personal risk, unwavering protesters memorialized the victims in Plaza de las Tres Culturas by painting dripping red hearts on the doves in the banners.

As fate would have it, Mark's room in the Olympic Village sat one floor below that of Tommie Smith and John Carlos. One afternoon, commotion outside the dormitory woke Mark from his nap. Out the window he saw dozens of photographers with their cameras pointed up toward the building. In the dawn of paparazzi and given the explosion of media surrounding Mark, he mistakenly thought they were looking for him. The idea stroked his ego, so he stuck his head outside the window and waved to the whizzing and clicking of the cameras below.

This time, though, the subject of the photographs was not Mark. He looked up to see a large banner reading "BLACK POWER" hanging above his window, with Carlos and Smith displaying clenched fists. U.S. track officials and members of Mexico's Organizing Committee, uncomfortable with this display of political expression, gathered in irritation. Through a megaphone, they requested, then demanded, that Carlos and Smith remove the banner. Their ridiculous reaction accomplished nothing more than attracting yet more attention to the athletes and their sign. Once that strategy failed, the twenty or so officials headed inside, certain to settle the matter with a face-to-face confrontation. But, almost comically, the elevator got stuck and stranded them for two hours. The rescued officials, most due at the track and field stadium, sheepishly scurried off to their duties.

Having felt the pain of anti-Semitism, Mark sympathized with Carlos and Smith, but the subject didn't resonate with his fellow swimmers. In the 1960s, the sport was even whiter than it is today, as swim clubs tended to be private and expensive. Some had specific rules prohibiting the admission of blacks and Jews and others relied on unwritten policies, but the effect was the same—most clubs remained exclusive. It wasn't that the swimmers themselves were racist; they simply didn't live in a community where they observed or considered the discrimination of the nation's minorities.

On October 16, shortly after the banner incident, Smith set a world record in the 200-meter dash and Carlos finished third, the only surprise being that Australian Peter Norman nipped Carlos at the line. The real drama occurred on the medal podium. In one of the most iconic images of an Olympic medal ceremony and of the racial strife in America, Smith and Carlos each raised a black-gloved fist and bowed his head during the "Star-Spangled Banner." Smith later explained, "My raised right hand stood for the power in black America. Carlos' raised left hand stood for the unity of black America. Together they formed an arch of unity and power. The black scarf around my neck stood for black pride. The black socks with no shoes stood for black poverty in racist America. The totality of our effort was the beginning of black dignity." Norman, a white athlete, actually suggested they each wear only one glove when Carlos discovered he had left his pair at the Olympic Village. Norman, showing further solidarity that would impact the rest of his life, asked if he, too, could wear a distinctive OPHR button after seeing theirs pinned to their warm-up tops.

The scene outraged Brundage, who immediately deemed the protest an overt and improper political statement unfit for the supposedly apolitical Olympic Games. Hiding behind the IOC, he demanded that Smith and Carlos be stripped of their medals, dismissed from the U.S. team, and deported. When U.S. officials refused, Brundage threatened to kick out the entire American track team, and within two days the activist sprinters were gone. Brundage also quietly convinced the U.S. State Department and Mexican authorities to issue an All Points Bulletin for the arrest of Harry Edwards, certain he was in the city fomenting civil disobedience.

Brundage's quest for a politically impartial Games reeked with hypocrisy to those knowing his history. In 1933, the AAU considered boycotting the 1936 Berlin Games because of Nazi treatment of Jews in that country. The famed concentration camp at Dachau opened that March, but the reality of Nazi brutality had not yet reached the world's consciousness despite stories of discrimination flowing freely from Germany. Jeremiah Mahoney, head of the AAU, strongly believed that Germany had broken IOC rules forbidding discrimination based on race and religion. He worried about the prospects of German Jews participating in their country's qualifying events as well as the likely disparate treatment of U.S. Jewish and black athletes in Berlin.

Then the president of the American Olympic Committee, Brundage vehemently opposed the boycott but relented to investigate Germany's treatment of Jewish athletes. After traveling to that country to interview Olympic officials and Jewish athletes, he returned to the States with the officials' assurance that two dozen Jewish athletes would be invited to the German Olympic camp. He also spoke confidently that, based on his interviews with the athletes, the hosts had the proper Olympic ideals in mind. What he didn't report is that Nazi officials chaperoned all of his interviews with Jews in cafes, hardly the circumstances most conducive to learning the truth. Ultimately, no Jews participated in the German Olympic camp and only one, a fencer named Helene Mayer, participated in the Games. According to *The Complete Book of the Summer Olympics* by David Wallechinsky, "The Nazis rationalized their leniency toward her by stating that though she was Jewish, she had two 'Aryan' grandparents."

Brundage's ownership of the Montecito Country Club in Santa Barbara, California, which had a strict admission policy against blacks and Jews, provided perhaps the most vivid evidence of his bigotry. With those views in stark contrast of the Olympic ideals, one wonders how Brundage obtained and maintained his position as the most powerful man in the national and international organizations. A man of his stature and intelligence certainly knew that his club's policies contributed at least in premise to the country's social unrest. Racism in the United States had reached the boiling point, with riots darkening the mood from New York to California. In 1964, Congress passed the Civil Rights Act, the landmark legislation that outlawed segregation and discrimination in public places. Only the naïve or biased could have operated such an unjust establishment.

As Harry Edwards later opined, Brundage stayed in character when he overlooked the Nazi treatment of Jews, viewed the massacre of Mexican students as an administrative hurdle, and responded so harshly to the black power salute. "It was my experience over the course of establishing the Olympic Project for Human Rights and challenging Mr. Brundage and his policies that he was racist and anti-Semitic, attributes that apparently provoked little in the way of consequential negative social repercussions or professional liability in American or international sports circles."

Like the rest of the world, members of the swim team took sides on the black power salute but with dialog less emotional and more analytical. A few believed Smith and Carlos simply exercised their right to free speech. Most though, felt the Olympics were not the right venue for personal politics. Carl Robie thought the salute was inappropriate. "I knew Tommie Smith since the 1967 World Student Games in Tokyo. I was struggling with my bags at the airport and he introduced himself to me and helped me with the bags. We talked on the flight back home and I followed his races in the press. I had great respect for Tommie, but I thought that the black power salute at the 1968 games was wrong. The Olympics should be a pure forum and I thought his protest diminished the magnitude of the Olympic movement."

One of the younger members of the delegation and not yet politically minded, an uncomfortable Mark said little at the time but later expressed respect for Smith and Carlos. "I was pretty immature back then and wasn't into politics that much, but I remember thinking, 'Wow! These guys have the guts to protest like that on the Olympic stage.' They believed they had a duty to raise the issue to the world. I had no problem with what they did, and whether you agreed with them or not, it was pretty moving. It resonated with me because I had felt the sting of anti-Semitism, and they certainly shouldn't have been kicked out of the Olympic Village for a silent protest that hurt no one."

ψψψ

The same evening Smith and Carlos made history, Don Gambril told Mark to shave down in preparation for his first race the following morning. Swimmers commonly shave the hair off their arms and legs at major swimming events, less for the physiological benefit of reducing drag in the water than the psychological boost of feeling faster. "When you dove in the water after shaving down, it felt like there was no friction," Mark recalled. "When you got in bed that night, you were so smooth you thought you were going to slide off." But there was one problem. The only bathtub in the dormitory was in William Lippman's room. The chairman of the U.S. Olympic Men's Swimming & Diving Committee and team manager for swimming assigned himself the only room with a tub and television. Swimmers soon began congregating in his room to watch TV, so a greatly annoyed Lippman padlocked the previously unlockable door.

Unable to find Lippman that evening, Gambril broke the lock so that Mark and his teammates could use the tub, warning them to clean it when they left. Naturally they made Mark go last, so when Lippman returned to his room accompanied by a FINA official, he found an unlucky Mark shaving. Indignant, and probably embarrassed, a red-faced Lippman railed at him and, despite Mark's attempted explanation, continued to do so until he left. Shocked and unsettled at being treated like a low-level criminal by the team leader, Mark finished shaving in his room with a razor and a glass of water.

The slights at training camp, the shock of the student massacre, the intensity of the black power incidents, and the lack of any real friends on the team distracted and depressed Mark, who longed to open up about it all to Haines. But when the two met to discuss race strategies, Mark's pride prevailed and he kept his thoughts to himself. If Haines noticed Mark's disturbed mental state, he didn't let on.

The swimming competition ran October 17–26 in the ultra-modern Olympic Pool, with an undulating ceiling to match the waves of the water. Qualifying races began at 10:00 A.M. every day but one, with semifinals and finals starting at 5:00 P.M. The 4x100-meter relay kicked off the men's action as their only event on the first day. Olympic rules allow countries to change their relay members after the prelims, giving more athletes a chance to compete and saving their best swimmers for the final. In the morning session, Steve Rerych, Don Schollander, Mike Wall, and Bill Johnson easily put the U.S. in the finals, tying the USSR to the thousandth of a second (3:35.398) for the fastest qualifying time.

Three other Americans joined Rerych in the final, while the USSR replaced one swimmer. Zac Zorn, who had tied the world record of 52.6 in the 100 free at the Trials, sprinted to an early lead. Thinking he went out too hard in the first twenty-five meters, he backed off a bit to finish in 53.4. Nonetheless, he gave the Americans a two-body-length lead over East Germany. Rerych then streaked to a 52.8 to leave the rest of the pack out of striking distance. Mark followed with a blistering 52.7, the fastest time of the night, giving the U.S. a three-second lead over the second-place Russians. Walsh, with another 52.8, anchored the world-record performance of 3:31.7, well in front of the USSR's 3:34.2.

As soon as officials draped the medal around his neck on the podium, Mark picked it up off his chest and studied it intently. It was his first Olympic medal and it was a gold one at that. "It was nice getting a gold medal, and I remember thinking that a few months earlier, I was a long shot to qualify for the relay. It was a great way to start the Olympics," Mark recalled.

The next day, Mark swam his first individual races—the 100-meter freestyle prelims and semifinals. He easily won the first in 54.6 to earn a spot in the desired last of three semifinal heats. Robert McGregor of Britain and the Soviet Union's Leonid Ilichev touched simultaneously in 53.8 in the first one. Zorn set a new Olympic record of 53.4 in the second, with Walsh (53.9) third. In the third semifinal, Australian Michael Wenden's

52.9 broke Zorn's minutes-old Olympic mark, with Mark only one-tenth off in 53.0.

Although it was three-tenths slower than his relay leg two days earlier, the swim pleased Haines and Mark. Relay times usually are faster because swimmers get a rolling start. The swimmer on the blocks may begin his move toward the pool as long as his toes are still in contact with the block when his teammate touches the wall. It isn't until that moment when his time starts, at which point he can be almost fully extended over the water. Experts believe rolling starts give relay swimmers about a half-second advantage over someone starting flat on the blocks.

As usual, mere tenths of a second separated the men's times in the finals the following evening. The field was so strong that Walsh, the world-record holder, was relegated to an outside lane as the seventh qualifier. Peter Daland, commentating for *Swimming World Magazine*, predicted a Zorn victory, with Mark second, and McGregor third. A half hour before the race, officials shepherded the eight qualifiers to the staging room. They sat in near silence after the door closed, no one wanting to speak first. The tension weighed on Mark in his first individual experience in a staging room. He felt awkward, preferring to be outside on the deck interacting with his coaches and the crowd. It seemed like an eternity before a race official finally opened the door and asked the men to line up according to their lanes.

The parade to the starting blocks helped soothe Mark's pre-race jitters, and his adrenaline surged with the sellout crowd's cheers. As he took off his warm-ups and stretched before climbing on the block, Mark heard his teammates encouraging Walsh and Zorn but not him. It was yet another stab he tried to ignore as he focused on the race, but it bothered him.

In typical fashion, Zorn blasted off the blocks and quickly led by a half-body length. At the turn, Wenden and Mark were close behind. With twenty-five meters to go, Zorn faltered and Wenden blew past to finish a body length ahead of the field in a new world record of 52.2. Ken Walsh took the silver in 52.8, and Mark had to settle for the bronze with a 53.0. Zorn faded hard to finish eighth in 53.9.

"Wenden really wasn't on our radar," recalled Walsh. "Back then, communications weren't as they are now and Australia was always bringing in some threat you'd never heard of before." Wenden's exuberant teammates carried off the new Olympic champion on their shoulders and the three Americans could do nothing but watch. An exuberant Wenden told *Swimming World Magazine*, "I figured I'd have to go out hard because Zorn is a notorious fast first-fifty-meter swimmer. I thought if I could be a yard or so behind at the fifty, maybe with him at sixty or catch him at seventy-five meters, that would be just right." The key to Wenden's victory, though, was a timely comment from fellow Aussie, Bob Windle, who had swam against Zorn while attending Indiana University. "Windle told me that he knew that Zorn would certainly touch the wall first. He told me that if I could still see Zorn's feet at the turn I would be all right, because Zorn would burn out. I'm glad I knew that before the race, because Zorn's early lead would have been a difficult test on my mental toughness," recalled Wenden.

Alternately, a disconsolate Mark tried to mask his disappointment with a statement that contradicted his infamous confidence. "I'm pretty happy with the way it came out. I tried my hardest, and it's my best time. I was going to go as hard as I could tonight, and I had a feeling I would be the first or second American." His finish behind Walsh cost Mark the freestyle leg on the 400-meter medley relay. His only remaining shot to swim on the medley required a win in the 100-meter butterfly.

!!!

After four swims over the previous three days, Mark faced up to four in the next two if he advanced to the finals in the 100 fly and the 800 free relay. Considering that Mark held the global standard in the individual event and the U.S. won four golds in the relay in the past five Olympiads, the world expected just that. Mark's most serious threat came by way of Doug Russell, but Ross Wales also had the ability to stage an upset. Luis Nicolao presented the only other concern from Mark's standpoint. The Argentine lowered the world record twice in his career and trained with the Santa Clara Swim Club, so Mark knew firsthand he could be dangerous. The goal in the preliminary heats simply was to be among the fastest twenty-four swimmers and thus qualify for the semifinals.

Russell drew attention when he set an Olympic record (57.3) in the first prelim. Though it was well short of Mark's 55.6 world record, it startled Mark that Russell would swim so hard in the prelims. Mark considered making a statement in the fifth heat by beating Doug's new record, but he wisely saved his energy and glided to the finish at 58.5. Wales and Nicolao won their heats as well.

The semifinals that evening would be more serious but still wouldn't require maximum effort from Mark. His goal was to secure one of the three middle lanes for the final reserved for the fastest qualifiers. Mark lowered his time to 57.4 in the first of three semifinals, a tenth of a second off Russell's Olympic record—a very solid result. As he gathered his things after the race, he noticed that only seven swimmers took the blocks for the second semifinal and quickly figured out Nicolao was missing. He learned later a traffic jam caused by the marathon ensnared Luis within eyesight of the pool. He sat helplessly as his dreams of being an Olympic champion crawled by.

Mark stuck around to watch Russell and Wales in the third semifinal. Russell blazed to a 55.9, only three-tenths off Mark's world record and more than two seconds ahead of Wales. That type of speed still was unnecessary to win the heat or qualify for the final, but Russell wanted to finish setting the table in preparation for the final. It had the intended effect.

In the staging room prior to the final the next night, Mark eyed his antagonist nervously. In nine previous meetings, the script had never changed. Russell led at fifty meters, at seventy-five meters, sometimes even at ninety meters. But Mark always caught and passed him in the final strokes. Losing any race irritated Russell, but to do so in the same agonizing way to the same arrogant guy over and over and over tormented him.

"I don't know if you can appreciate being a competitor, especially at that level," Russell explained later, "but when you want to win and you're really close every time, it gets inside your head. It got to the point where I was expecting him to catch me, and my insides were trying to fight off that thought."

Russell intended to break the cycle. Everyone expected to see his hell-bent sprinting style, which he overtly displayed in the qualifying rounds. But Gambril had spent the past six weeks preaching a different tactic. "Don kept trying to tell me that I could swim as fast as everybody else without swimming as hard as everybody else," Russell remembered. The idea was counterintuitive to a guy who loved to swim all-out, but he had to change something if he was going to make history. As the eight finalists filed to the starting blocks, Russell kept his thoughts positive: "This race is mine. This race is mine. Control yourself early, then get to the wall first." His intensity unnerved Mark, who nevertheless expected the same outcome.

When Russell hit the water, he felt the usual urge to take the lead, but he managed to hold back. For the first time against Russell, Mark was fastest to the half-way point. Russell felt sure Mark's confidence skyrocketed when he turned first. With twenty-five meters to go, Russell, Wales, and Mark were dead even, matching stroke for stroke. "We looked like a little topless synchronized swimming team," Russell chuckled.

At that point, Russell knew he was going to win because he still hadn't let himself loose yet. "I knew the way I felt that I was going to be able to accelerate all the way to the wall, and I was already celebrating." His only problem was holding off his burst until the right moment. With each stroke he thought, "Do I need to go now? No, wait one more." Finally, he went. Whirling through his strokes to win by half of a body length, he bested Mark, 55.9 to 56.4. Gary Hall later called it the most strategic race in Olympic swimming history. Wales won the bronze with a 57.2 to give the U.S. its second sweep of the Games.

Russell exorcised his demon but in the process created a new one for Mark, who couldn't believe he lost. "I owned that race, but I lost. I have nobody to blame but myself, but now Doug owned the race and I couldn't get used to that feeling."

On the medal stand, the two competitors occupied different worlds. While the national anthem played, Russell basked in peace with himself. "It takes forever to get to that point, and there are a lot of bumps in the road," Russell said, recalling the moment. "But the feeling wasn't jubilation or 'In your face!' or 'I kicked Mark's rear end.' At that level it's more about you than about any single competitor. That's really where the battle is—it's not with the competitors."

Mark stood one step below Russell in a trance. "I couldn't believe I lost. I was going over the race in my mind, trying to figure out what I had done wrong. When the ceremony was over someone had to nudge me to get off the podium. I felt like the loneliest person on earth."

But the evening wasn't over. The 800-meter freestyle relay final, less than a half-hour later, would be Mark's eighth swim in five days. In the morning session, Bill Johnson, Andy Strenk, Dave Johnson, and Mike Wall teamed to qualify the U.S. second behind the Australians, who had swum their "A" team.

John Nelson, the U.S.'s freestyle specialist who would compete the 200 free, 400 free, and 1500 free later in the meet, led off the final with a strong swim, coming in about two-tenths behind the East German. Rerych, whose second leg gave the U.S. a comfortable lead in the 4x100 free four days earlier, matched Nelson's 1:58.6 split to put the Americans two and a half seconds ahead of Australia. Mark, obviously drained from his butterfly final, couldn't break two minutes. His 2:00.5 fell almost five seconds short of his swim-off time at the Trials and lost almost a second to Robert Windle of Australia, which anchored with 100 free world-record holder and gold medalist Michael Wenden. Schollander posted a team-best 1:54.6 to hold off a closing Wenden, but Mark's swim cost them an Olympic and world record.

In the locker room, Mark's teammates erupted in anger instead of celebrating the win. They criticized Mark for not ceding his spot on the relay for the good of the team, arguing that his medal greed had cost them a record that any one of six other swimmers could have helped set. Mark's already bruised ego took another hit. Schollander later diplomatically told the press, "The reason we didn't get the world record here was because we've all swam in other races. In Tokyo we had a fresh team with two days rest. I think this team would easily go under 7:50 at sea level."

Mark spent the three days until his final race, the 200-meter butterfly, attempting to regroup mentally and emotionally so that physically he could perform up to his capabilities. It seemed to have worked, as Mark tied former Arden Hills teammate John Ferris with the fastest time in the prelims. Their 2:10.6 led a tightly packed field. Lars Peter Feil of Sweden registered the eighth-fastest time only 1.3 seconds slower, not a large margin in the 200 fly. Robie, the silver medalist in 1964, Victor Sharygin and Valentin Kusmin from the Soviet Union, Martyn Woodroffe from Great Britain, and Volkert Meeuw from West Germany all clocked times within a second of the leaders.

Robie was dangerous because he was viewed as an exceptional high-altitude swimmer. He won the 200-yard butterfly at the

NCAA Championships at the Air Force Academy and the 200-meter butterfly at the Mexico City pre-Olympic test event in 1967. He was predicted to win three gold medals in the 1964 Tokyo Olympics, but spread himself too thin and garnered only one silver medal. For the 1968 Olympics, Robie decided to put all of his eggs in one basket—the 200-meter butterfly. This would be the last race of his career, so it was all or nothing. After qualifying fifth, he calmly told his friends and family that he was going to win. He proceeded to the starting blocks with such focus, that a college roommate, watching the event on television said that he could tell Robie was going to win by his demeanor and look on his face.

Uncharacteristically, the officials prohibited swimmers from jumping in the water to prepare for the race, so the three Americans agreed to false start together in a mini-protest. Under current Olympic rules, the three would have been disqualified, but in 1968 swimmers were allowed two false starts. The starter's scowl displayed his contempt for the three as they pulled themselves out of the pool and back onto their blocks.

At the first turn, Woodroffe, Meeuw, and Robie touched almost simultaneously, slightly ahead of the field. Mark struggled in last place, with Ferris at his side. At 100 meters, Robie inched ahead of Woodroffe, with Feil close behind. Mark still brought up the rear, two and a half seconds back. Ferris, finally realizing that tailing Mark wasn't a good idea this time, began to gain on the field. At 150 meters, Robie and Woodroffe were almost dead even, with Feil, Kuzman, and Ferris still within striking distance. Robie touched in 2:08.7, just three-tenths ahead of Woodroffe, who touched out Ferris by the same margin. Mark was never in contention, finishing a disappointing last place in 2:13.5, four and a half seconds off the lead and an embarrassing two seconds behind the seventh-place finisher.

Ferris, upset after the race, not-so-subtly blamed Mark for his third-place showing. "I had everything left after the race," he told the *Swimming World Magazine.* "I was swimming against Mark Spitz. I would have taken it out a lot harder if I could do it again. I'm disappointed with third. I expected Mark to be the one to beat, but he wasn't. If I had known before the race that Mark was going to do this, there would have been no doubt in my mind that I would win. I would have swam my usual race and gone out hard. I was trying something new here, like Doug Russell did. I figured this might work for me too. But I went out slower even considering that I wanted to be out slow because of the fact that I wanted to be with Mark." So, in a few short days, Mark was the reason Russell was an Olympic champion and the reason Ferris, in his own mind, was not.

Mark's sisters, Nancy and Heidi, watched Mark's flop at home on television. "I felt so badly for Mark," said Nancy. "The media really hyped him up to win all these gold medals and it just didn't happen."

❗❗❗

Even though Mark's tribulation in the pool at his first Olympics mercifully had ended, his misery had not. Despite winning four medals, his entire experience in Mexico City had been disastrous. The press had labeled him a failure. He had no support or friends on the team. He had nothing left to do but sit in his room, reviewing his dismal 200 fly the previous day. And then Doug Russell burst through the door in a fury.

Minutes earlier Russell caught wind of a rumor that Mark made a sulky comment to a teammate that he hoped Russell failed his drug test. The implications that Russell couldn't beat Mark unless he cheated, and that he was capable of cheating in the first place, infuriated him. Russell's pride in outworking Mark to win the gold medal overshadowed the actual piece of hardware, so he threw it on Mark's bed and shouted, "If you need this thing that bad, then here! You can have it!" slamming the door on his way out.

Mark sat frozen on his bed and had barely begun to process what just happened when Russell stormed back in seconds later after reconsidering his rash offer. "That thing had better be in my room when I get back from lunch!"

Stunned, sheepish, and despondent, Mark stared at the ornate hunk of metal, which looked almost exactly like his own two gold medals. It measured two and a quarter inches in diameter and about an eighth of an inch thick. On the front, four images stood in bold relief—XIX Olimpiada Mexico 1968, a seated woman in a flowing robe holding a wreath above her head, a Greek urn, and the decorative archways along the top of a stadium. A victor riding on the shoulders of an admiring throng dominated the scene on the reverse side, with another stadium in the background. A small, flat plate connected the medal and the red ribbon. The Olympic swimming logo embellished the front, but the similarities ended with the back of the plate. Inscribed on Mark's were the names of the two relays he swam, but Russell's read "100 butterfly," and that made all the difference.

The previous six weeks in particular but the last few years in general had exposed his last nerve. He wondered if the emotional and mental anguish—far more taxing and distressing than the physical challenges of being a world-class athlete—was worth it if it could so negatively impact his performances. Swimming had never been so hard, and the temptation strengthened to move on from childhood games to the more serious matters of life. He had hit bottom, and he sat alone in his dorm room brooding over the past, contemplating the future, and agonizing about the present.

"That damn medal . . . that damn medal," Mark thought to himself for several minutes, alternately staring at it and the wall at the end of his bed. "It should have been mine. How did that happen? What happened?"

Finally, he picked it up and walked dejectedly to Russell's room. Thankfully, no one answered the knock. He opened the unlocked door and, after one last look at the medal, placed it neatly on Russell's bed. As he returned to his room, though, a sense of tranquility replaced his angst, and he knew instantly what it meant. "This will never happen to me again," he thought. "In Munich, I'm going to show my teammates, the press, the world, but most importantly myself, that I am the best ever."

‽‽‽

CHAPTER 6

FINDING DOC

WHEN THE time came to choose a college during Mark's senior year of high school, his decision was easy: Stanford University. In addition to being in his backyard, the school had an excellent swimming program that had finished in the top ten at the NCAA Championships about every year since 1937. (They had just won their first NCAA Championship in March 1967.) Academically, it rivaled the Ivy schools on the East Coast. In fact, Stanford was the only school to which he initially applied. The University of California at Berkeley met two of his criteria—a top-notch academic institution located in the Bay Area—but its swimming program had not yet become a player on the national scene, effectively striking Cal from the list. Stanford's rejection of his application devastated Mark, not to mention left him a bit aimless, and prompted Arnold to make anti-Semitic claims—a short-lived theory without factual basis.

Two other California schools actively recruited him, so Mark turned his attention to Long Beach State, which had recently won the 1968 NCAA Division II Championship, and the University of Southern California, winner of five NCAA titles in the sixties. Both interested Mark, but ultimately he applied only to Long Beach.

The 49ers made sense for a number of reasons. First and foremost, the Spitzes were familiar with their coach, Don Gambril. One of Mark's few bright memories from training camp was the bond he and Gambril developed during their bouts of tonsillitis, although his tactical assistance to Doug Russell in the

100 fly left a bad taste in Mark's mouth. Also, Gambril and his wife had developed a close relationship with Arnold and Lenore. Gambril's wife booked the same Olympic tour as the Spitzes, and the two couples vacationed together afterward in Acapulco, where Don and Arnold went fishing for sailfish and marlins. When Gambril was recruiting Mark, he traveled to Sacramento several times and attended Santa Clara High School football games with Mark's parents.

Gambril also assured the Spitzes that his school was entering an important time in its young history. After twenty years of existence, several 49er teams were beginning to dominate their conference, and the 1967 arrival of athletic director Fred Miller portended even greater things to come. He backed up his mission of Long Beach State going big time in three sports—football, men's basketball, and swimming—by making three important hires in his first two years: Jim Stangeland, an assistant football coach for USC's 1967 national title team who also had won three national titles in five years at Long Beach City College; Jerry Tarkanian, who coached Pasadena City College to three California junior college basketball championships; and Gambril.

Miller quickly met his objectives. Stangeland led the football team to two conference championships and the only bowl game in the school's history, the 1970 Pasadena Bowl. Tarkanian immediately put the basketball team on the map, lifting a mediocre program to four conference titles and four NCAA appearances in five years before moving on to fame and infamy at UNLV and Fresno State. Gambril won NCAAs his first season and assembled an impressive international cast of Olympians who had competed in Mexico City, including finalists Hans Fassnacht, Michael Holthaus, and Reinhard Merkel from Germany; Swede Hans Ljungberg; José Silvio Fiolo of Brazil; and Australian Graham White. Mark knew that training alongside such talented swimmers would be good for his career.

Swimming daily in the beautiful Belmont Plaza Olympic Pool during the 49ers' season added to the attraction. So did the pleasant Southern California climate, with warm summers and mild winters, and the city's substantial aquatics history.

Despite the obvious perks, committing to Long Beach State didn't overjoy him. It looked good on paper, and his parents felt strongly about it, but his reservation showed subtly that May when he signed an Inter-Conference Letter of Intent instead of a National Letter of Intent. The agreement restricted Mark from receiving a scholarship from any other team in the California Collegiate Athletic Association (which in 1969 was renamed the Pacific Coast Athletic Association), but left open the possibility of swimming for a non-conference school. Despite the relatively unrestrictive nature of the letter, Mark's signing made quite a stir locally. In addition to television coverage, an article on the front page of the *Independent Press-Telegram* enthusiastically reported that he would be a 49er. Despite his qualms, Mark stopped actively looking at other universities.

‼‼‼

Because the Olympics ended in October, Mark planned to take the fall semester off and recharge his batteries before beginning classes in the spring of 1969. Good thing. He returned home from Mexico City feeling emotionally down, mentally frazzled, physically exhausted, and generally vulnerable. He was comfortable with the idea of heading to Long Beach, but was having his doubts. He didn't quite know what to do about it, and he knew he wasn't in the right frame of mind to make serious inquiries elsewhere.

In December, Mark spent two weeks touring and competing in South America with a group of U.S. Olympians, including former Arden Hills teammate John Ferris and current Santa Clara

Swim Club teammate Mitch Ivey. In contrast to his previous two trips as an Olympian—to Colorado Springs and Mexico City— Mark actually enjoyed this one. The trip was long, the food was bad, and the living conditions were only tolerable, but Mark summed it up in a letter to his mother by writing, "We are all sick with diarrhea but having a great time." The lack of pressure that pervades the atmosphere leading up to a Games helped the enjoyment factor immensely. But after enduring difficult relationships on his teams for the past several years, Mark found his travel partners to be friendly, honest, and supportive, and that emotional comfort more than outweighed every physical nuisance.

Among the topics of conversation included Ivey's choice of colleges. Unhappy at Stanford, he pondered aloud the idea of transferring to another school. The one he talked about most was Indiana University, expounding on the program's rich history, its recent NCAA Championship, its well-respected coach Doc Counsilman, and guys he knew on the team. Mark listened, curiously at first and then more intently. He remembered that the camaraderie of the Indiana swimmers at camp—Charles Hickcox, Chet Jastremski, Don McKenzie, and Dave Perkowski— impressed him, especially compared to the constant bickering, backstabbing, manipulating, and petty politicking of his own team. He also recalled hearing coaches and his father talk reverently about the coach whose research and technical expertise was revolutionizing the sport.

The conversations stayed with Mark, who said nothing but quietly began to consider abandoning Long Beach for the Hoosiers. His flight home included a day's layover in Miami. As fate would have it, the Indiana swim team was in the midst of its winter training camp at the International Swimming Hall of Fame pool in nearby Ft. Lauderdale.

Mark's limited knowledge about James "Doc" Counsilman barely scratched the surface of the foremost swimming scientist's contributions to the sport. When Mark found him in his hotel room that day, the man had already cemented his reputation as a creative, ingenious leader in the science of swimming. Doc, a nickname honoring his 1951 doctorate degree in physiology from the University of Iowa, had parlayed his childhood fascination with watching fish swim and two near-death experiences into a pioneering life. After a respectable career in which he won two national titles in the breaststroke, he had earned three degrees that focused on human movement. He had begun analyzing strokes using underwater photography after designing a case to protect the camera. He had helped prove that appropriate weight training benefited swimmers rather than leaving them muscle-bound and inflexible as conventional wisdom asserted. He had introduced the concept of interval training, followed shortly by inventing the pace clock so swimmers could keep track of their own splits. He had published articles on those findings and others, including one on the effects of altitude on swimmers, and had just written his first book, *The Science of Swimming*, that year.

In the coming 20 years, Doc would gift to the swimming world more than one hundred articles based on his meticulous research on biomechanics, specificity in dry-land training, optimal sculling movements, human propulsion in water, isokinetic and biokinetic exercise, hand-speed acceleration, and starts. He would write a second book, *The Competitive Swimming Manual*, in 1977, and he would expand his innovative ideas to swimming pool design and anti-turbulence lanes.

The more he'd thought about it, the more excited Mark had become about tapping into all of that knowledge like the rest of Doc's swimmers did. In eleven years at IU, his team had won eight Big Ten titles and finished in the top three at NCAAs in seven of the eight years they went. He had coached his first Olympic champion in 1948 and his second Olympic medalist in 1956 prior to building his Hoosier dynasty. In 1964, the year he served as head coach of the men's Olympic team, half of the Trials finalists in the 200 breaststroke competed at Indiana.

When Mark showed up unannounced at Doc's door that December, Doc's wife, Marge, answered his knock. Immediately recognizing him, she invited Mark in and explained that Doc was in the bathroom. While they waited, Mark told Marge about the tour and asked if Mitch Ivey had come by, thinking he may be doing the same thing, but Marge said he hadn't.

When Doc saw his visitor, he said "Hi, Mark. Nice Olympics." Mark instinctively recoiled at the comment, figuring everyone thought he bombed, but relaxed fairly quickly as he took in Doc's tone and expression. Somehow, coming from Doc, the compliment sounded sincere. Mark replied, "Not really," but felt valued and safe. Without pretense, he continued, "Doc, you know about me signing with Long Beach State. Well, I'm a cut to the chase kind of guy, and, well, I'd like to attend Indiana University."

Doc was a little taken aback. After all, one of the premier swimmers in the world, easily the most hyped from Mexico City and likely the most talented, had just asked him to be his coach. Doc, whose reputation for humor didn't let him down, quickly responded, "Gee, good thing I already went to the bathroom." After the laughter subsided, Doc also cut to the chase, telling Mark about Indiana and what he could expect out of school and the team. Doc said he'd put an application in the mail, which needed prompt attention so Mark could begin classes on February 3. If Mark was admitted, he would receive a full scholarship. Most emphatically, though, Doc told Mark to discuss his decision with Gambril immediately. Not only was it the respectful thing to do, but Doc didn't want his friendship with Gambril jeopardized when Gambril's number one recruit showed up on his team.

Mark reviewed the abrupt turn of events as he flew home and felt at peace with it. His only concerns were whether he could meet the university's admission standards, given his setback with

Stanford, and telling his parents. His father was usually involved in decisions of such magnitude, and Mark knew they felt a personal obligation to Gambril. While Mark was proud that he had taken such initiative and gone with his gut, breaking the news to his father and mother would be difficult. "Guess what," Mark told his mother when he got home, "I met with Doc Counsilman in Florida." Lenore cheerfully responded that she also met Doc in Mexico City and thought he seemed like a nice man. Mark then blurted out, "Well, I'm not going to Long Beach. I'm going to Indiana." Lenore's attitude instantly changed to anger. "You promised to go to Long Beach. Your father will not like this. Don't upset him," she pleaded.

Arnold also reacted negatively, but as the three sat in a hospital room the next day awaiting Mark's scheduled tonsillectomy, Mark carefully explained to his parents what changed his mind: the camaraderie among the Indiana swimmers; the full scholarship instead of a partial scholarship with a job at Long Beach; the availability of free tutors; his improved chances of being accepted to dental school with an IU education; and, most of all, the respect he felt for Doc's coaching methods and how at ease he felt around him. By the end of the conversation and impressed with their son's thought process and maturity, they agreed.

‼‼‼

Doc noticed on his application that Mark had taken the ACT entrance exam twice, scoring much higher the second time. Aware that testing procedures were somewhat loose, with "sit-ins" taking the test for many athletes across the country, and wanting to avoid any suspicion of wrong-doing, Doc quickly decided that Mark would have to take another exam. At that time, procedures allowed universities to administer the ACT entrance exam, so Doc arranged for Mark to take the test on his recruiting visit. Doc explained to Mark that he required a satis-factory score that confirmed no irregularities with his previous ACT scores and met Big Ten and NCAA standards before he would accept Mark's application.

Mark flew to Bloomington to take the test in mid-January, the same weekend Joe Namath led the New York Jets to the AFL's first victory in a Super Bowl over the heavily favored Baltimore Colts from the NFL. Doc and the team were competing in the Big Ten Relays at Michigan State, so team manager Mark Wallace picked Mark up at the airport and took him to the School of Education, where a test administrator put Mark in a room about the size of a closet and told Wallace to come back in two hours. When he did, she sent both Marks away for another two hours while she scored the test.

Wallace took Mark to eat at the school cafeteria, then to Royer Pool. They watched the freshman swim team work out, Mark hoping beyond hope to join them soon, before hanging out in Doc's office as time crept by. Finally, Wallace called for the results. Needing at least an 18 each on the math and language sections, Mark earned a 28 and 24, respectively.

"Let's call Doc!" Wallace exclaimed after shaking Mark's hand excitedly. When Wallace asked to speak to Doc, the atten-dant on Michigan State's pool deck hesitated. "You know, there is a meet going on here, and he's in the middle of coaching the team," the man responded over the significant background noise. Wallace countered, "Yes, I know that. But my name is Mark Wallace, and I'm the Indiana team manager. I guarantee you that Doc is going to want to take this call." After a few minutes, Doc picked up the phone, and Wallace animatedly relayed the news. Relieved, Doc exclaimed, "That's great! Put Mark on the phone." Doc congratulated Mark and expressed his own eager-ness for Mark to arrive before telling him he would pick him up for breakfast the following morning.

At the time, despite its recent domination in the conference, Indiana was losing the meet. Nothing seemed to be going right. Seizing on the opportunity to lift his team's spirits, Doc huddled his athletes on the deck and confirmed the rumors: Mark Spitz would join the team at the beginning of the spring semester. The team erupted, jumping up and down and cheering loudly. Everyone else at the meet looked at them with surprise, no doubt thinking, "They're losing. What do they have to cheer about?" Buoyed with the thrill that another Olympic star would be joining the team, they finished first in every remaining relay and won the meet. Mark's spirits soared even higher when he heard their positive reaction. After being treated poorly at SCSC, ostracized at training camp, and maligned in the press, Mark felt like he'd get a new start with his new team.

The next morning after breakfast, Doc took Mark to see Mrs. Aline Robinson, the head of admissions for the university and wife of Doc's colleague Sid Robinson, Ph.D., a faculty member and exercise physiologist of some repute. The Counsilmans and Robinsons were personal friends. Since this was Sunday, Mark's interview for admission was held at the Robinsons' house, a courtesy that would not be extended to "ordinary" applicants. The Bay Area native walked cautiously up the icy sidewalk, having spent very little time in a winter environment. It showed. He slipped and fell flat on his back. Rather than panic that his best athlete could have broken a bone or concussed his head, Doc chuckled, "It's easy to pick out the Californians."

When Mark returned home, he had one more difficult task facing him—telling Gambril. Doc wouldn't allow him on the team until he'd done so. He first wrote a letter and reported back to Doc, but that wasn't satisfactory. Doc told Mark the letter was nice, but the situation called for a personal conversation.

As he dialed Gambril's number, Mark silently hoped that he wouldn't answer, but Gambril picked up after the first ring. When Mark identified himself, Gambril quickly said, "Good to hear from you, Mark! We're expecting you next week. Everything is set to go." Mark's heart stopped. "Coach," he stammered, "I have to tell you something. I've changed my mind. I'm going to Indiana University." Stunned and momentary silent, Gambril regrouped to handle the news graciously. Deflated, he thanked Mark for calling and wished him the best. When Mark put down the phone, he felt bad about disappointing Gambril but relieved about where he was heading.

Ironically, Mitch Ivey transferred from Stanford, but not to Indiana. He decided to attend Long Beach State, where he could swim for Gambril in the spring and play water polo for Jim Schultz in the fall.

CHAPTER 7

Ψ Ψ Ψ

THE NCAA YEARS AND THE SPITZ-RUSSELL REMATCH

DOC'S INNOVATIVE blend of science with swimming intrigued Mark, to be sure. Ironically, one of Mark's most overt reasons for seeking out Doc—his technical expertise in analyzing strokes—wound up being for naught. It took Doc far less time to conclude that Mark's stroke didn't need improving than it did convincing the swimmer of the same. But what really drew Mark to Doc, perhaps instinctively, was the coach's flair for interacting with his swimmers individually and for fostering positive group dynamics. More important to Mark's final ascension as a swimmer than improving physical technique or fitness was experiencing Doc's affirming influence on a personal, social, mental, and emotional level. Watching the Hoosiers enjoy swimming and each other without fighting, cliques, or fierce rivalries offered his only clue he'd get that at IU.

Truly, the brilliance and beauty in Doc's coaching lie as much in his psychological approach as his physiological breakthroughs. Just as impressive as his scientific discoveries was his artful ability to infuse workouts with humor and lightheartedness while demanding an unwavering work ethic, to relate to each swimmer meaningfully, and to mold a revolving group of highly competitive all-stars into a cohesive, cooperative team.

He achieved such impressive results with positivity instead of intimidation, a tactic most took for granted in those days. Perhaps no anecdote illustrates that marriage of science and art more than the day his swimmers showed up in T-shirts that asked "What's up Doc?" It was usually something groundbreaking, and his swimmers demonstrated both their respect and affection for their coach with the clever attire.

Mark came to Indiana emotionally weak and mentally fractured. The brashness and arrogance exhibited in the past few years belied his insecurities and shyness. His unsettling experiences in Colorado Springs and the deflating results from the Games left his confidence shaken. Doc had heard of Mark's checkered past in the swimming community, but he also heard stories about how Mark had been treated by his club team, at camp, and in Mexico City. He knew Mark wouldn't achieve the greatness within his grasp until his self-esteem returned, and he humbly knew he could guide Mark back to the right path.

Despite his team's initial exuberance at the relay meet at Mark's forthcoming arrival, Doc had heard a few muttered misgivings about their new teammate. Wanting to clear the air and establish some ground rules before Mark set foot on campus, Doc called a team meeting. He acknowledged Mark's reputation but countered by describing his affinity for Mark. Finally, Doc instructed the team to give Mark a chance and cautioned that he wouldn't stand for anyone belittling, browbeating, or picking on another team member, much less Mark. His message was clear: Mark was to be given the benefit of every doubt.

Fred Southward, a sophomore All-American at that time, had witnessed the dysfunction among Santa Clara Swim Club teammates firsthand at several national meets and remembers having mixed emotions about Mark coming on board. "Listening to Doc, I was thinking, 'Great. If he can't get along with people he's known all his life, what's it going to be like here?' We had a close-knit team and had just won our first NCAA Championship the year before. While Mark was certainly a talent, I was concerned that he might disrupt the team chemistry." Besides, one might argue, did they really need him after winning the 1968 national title by almost one hundred points?

Displaying his wisdom in dealing with competitive collegians, Doc took additional measures to smooth Mark's transition in Bloomington and as a Hoosier. "Doc assigned freshman Canadian Olympian George Smith to be Mark's roommate and had his son Jimmy take Mark under his wing," teammate Gary Hall remembers. "Doc just wanted Mark to fit in. There was an unwritten rule that nobody was allowed to pick on him, but Ronnie Jacks, an upperclassman from Canada, somehow got away with it. He had a wry sense of humor, and his quips actually humanized Mark and helped endear him to the team," said Hall.

Jacks' approach with the newcomer managed to make Mark feel included because he was being picked on, rather than making him defensive or hurt. "Mark had a different personality," Jacks remembered. "He was certainly arrogant, but we included him on the team. It was important to joke with him to bring him down a notch. He was one of the best swimmers in the world, and we wanted to make sure Mark felt like he was one of us."

However, Mark's omnipresent competitive spirit amazed—and bugged—the sophomore Canadian who had competed in five events in Mexico City. "Everything he did and everything he owned or accumulated had to be the best," he recalled. "It seemed to prop him up and give him some inner strength. One day he drove on campus in a new Triumph TR6, with its British racing green paint glimmering. He was being quite arrogant about that damn car, so I told him that I had just read a report about the TR6 in *Consumer Reports* and that it had all sorts of problems. Of course I hadn't read any such article, but I just wanted to piss him off a bit."

Mark quickly developed a close relationship with Doc, reminiscent of that with Chavoor, only now as a young man instead of a child. They talked endlessly about photographic equipment and stereos, not to mention swimming. Doc hired Mark to work a few hours a week in his shop assembling and repairing his inventive pace clocks, which Doc sold nationwide as a sideline. With Doc as his new mentor, Mark began to feel more at ease about how his life was going than he had in a very long time.

The few bucks Mark earned each week helped pay off his losses in card games. The freshman joined the weekly get-together right away, happy to mingle finally with welcoming teammates. The group of mostly upperclassmen may have been even more excited about the new player, given that Mark, whose prowess did not extend to cards, rarely left with more money than he brought. He did develop a better poker face as the school years passed, though, and by his senior year Mark pilfered the pockets of wide-eyed freshmen unwittingly drawn into the contests.

!!!

Mark looked forward to his first meet as a Hoosier. He'd not competed in a meaningful event since the Olympics, more than four months ago. He was anxious not only to race but also to move on, to cover up those foul memories with more pleasant ones. But when he was handed a pair of Hoosier swim trunks, he balked. Why he hadn't put this together yet, he had no idea. Officially, Indiana University's colors are crimson and cream, but they were close enough to red and white to turn his stomach. He wanted to wear the suit with pride, but it was red and white, for heaven's sake! Red and white represented second and third place—failure—to him. Could he actually compete in the dreaded hues? Finally, he came to the psychological angle he needed. The colors simply served as a reminder to those swimming against him of the best they could do.

The Hoosiers waltzed through the 1969 dual-meet competition with an 11–0 record before easily winning the Big Ten Championship in Madison, Wisconsin. They looked solid to defend their NCAA Championship, and it certainly didn't hurt that it would be held in the Hoosiers' own pool in Bloomington.

Mark's foray into NCAA competition started with the 500-yard freestyle on the first day, pitted against Long Beach State's Hans Fassnacht, USC Trojans Andy Strenk and Greg Charlton, Stanford's Brent Berk, and Southward. Fassnacht had finished seventh in the 400 free in Mexico City but was somewhat of an unknown to the college crowd, having moved to California the previous fall from Germany. Although Mark had competed against him in the 4x100 and 4x200 free relays, George Haines nonetheless called Mark that morning to warn him about the foreigner.

Mark and Fassnacht dueled stroke for stroke through the first 400 yards of the final, albeit at a slower pace than expected. Mark pulled ahead by a half-body length at the 450 turn and maintained that lead over the final two laps, winning his first attempt at an NCAA event championship. Incredibly, the rest of the field lagged more than six seconds behind the duo's 4:33.48 and 4:33.57.

The next day in the 200-yard freestyle, Mark faced Peruvian champion and Michigan Wolverine Juan Bello. Bello had displayed his fortitude the previous December during the South American trip, beating Mark in the 200 free and 200 IM. Two Yale swimmers, John Nelson and Michael Cadden, Trojan Frank Heckl, and Minnesota's Martin Knight also made the final.

Bello came within two-tenths of Mark's American record, clocking a 1:40.70, but that wasn't nearly enough. A tight race at the 150-yard turn spurred Mark to a blistering finish and a new American record, outdistancing Bello by more than a second in 1:39.53. The young Hoosier had his second NCAA event in two tries.

His third came the following day in the 100-yard butterfly, besting Olympic teammate Ross Wales, 49.69 to 49.88. Wales swam his typical all-out race but couldn't hold off Mark's surge at the end. Jerry Heidenreich from SMU garnered third, with Arden Hills teammate John Ferris of Stanford fourth. Roger Lyon from USC and Leland Bisbee from Michigan rounded out the scoring.

Mark's three victories helped propel Indiana to its second consecutive NCAA crown. Indiana won nine of the fifteen individual events, including titles by Charlie Hickcox (200-yard backstroke and 200-yard IM), Don McKenzie (100-yard breaststroke), and Jim Henry (1-meter and 3-meter diving). Mark also anchored the 400 and 800 freestyle relays, in which the Hoosiers finished second to a very talented USC team. Some people argue that the 1969 Indiana team was the best ever.

Even though Doc protected Mark, the athlete wasn't immune to Doc's discipline. During one winter training trip in Ft. Lauderdale, Mark, Hall, and Jimmy Counsilman headed for the afternoon workout in the team-provided station wagon. "It was about a fifteen-minute drive to the pool, and the road paralleled the ocean," Mark eagerly recalled. "Gary and I noticed that the waves were really big, and both of us being from California, we just had to catch a couple. We had so much fun that we bodysurfed for an hour and a half without thinking about the consequences. When we showed up at the pool, Doc was really pissed off. He made us stay an hour late that day, putting us through grueling sets of swims. But that wasn't all. He also made us come in an hour early the next three days. Our hour-and-a-half soiree cost us an additional four hours in the pool, but you know what, it was worth it!"

IU's domination in the conference made the addition of Mark's services icing on the cake. After another undefeated dual season against twelve opponents in 1970, the Hoosiers again enjoyed the comforts of their own home for a championship meet when it won its tenth straight Big Ten title. Although the margin varied, Michigan took the runner-up position throughout the streak. In a nail biter, Indiana won its first by a mere 3.7 points, but starting in 1967, the margin hit triple digits—this time it was one hundred and seventy—and remained as much throughout Mark's career.

The University of Utah, some six thousand feet above sea level, hosted NCAAs that year. The altitude concerned Mark after not handling it well in Mexico City, but the return of his prime nemesis from the Games unsettled him even more. Doug Russell had skipped the 1969 NCAA season and the rivals' teams hadn't faced off in a dual meet, so the duo had yet to compete again. The UTA senior won the Division II title in the 100 fly to qualify for the Division I meet. Both advanced to the final, setting up the much anticipated rematch.

Almost all international meets are swum long-course, in 50-meter pools, so at the Olympics the 100 fly consists of two laps. By contrast, the NCAA Championships is a short-course meet in a 25-yard pool, doubling the number of laps. The short laps and additional turns favored Russell, whose fast-twitch muscles made him extremely quick off the wall. According to general consensus, the altitude also favored Russell, who had performed well in Mexico City.

The whole scene brought back horrible memories for Mark. Negative images, negative thoughts, and negative feelings welled up in him, and he struggled to put the race out of his mind. "It was the one event I knew I had to swim, but was also the one I didn't want to swim," Mark later admitted. "I wanted to redeem myself and show that his Olympic victory was a fluke, but on the other hand, I was afraid that if he won, it would prove that he was absolutely better than me. I felt like a law student who had just been handed his bar exam results. He wants to open the envelope but is afraid of what it might say."

Indiana and USC were in a pitched battle for the team title. When the 100 fly finalists marched toward the blocks, the Hoosiers started chanting, "Let's go, Spitz-O!" but USC quickly responded with, "Let's go, Russell!" Soon, almost every person in the packed natatorium joined in the cheer for the Maverick. The choice was easy for the Trojans, who needed a Russell win to take points away from Indiana. The crowd and other competitors jumped on the bandwagon, opting for the well-liked, street-smart, fair-haired boy from Texas over the demonized, insolent figure from the Olympic Games. Mark's supporters clearly comprised the minority. Except among his teammates, he still was not a sympathetic figure.

Peter Daland, the USC coach, remembers the scene vividly. "It was deafening. The crowd was so loud, you could hardly hear. Russell was the obvious favorite of the crowd and the swimmers. I can't remember many races in my life where there was so much excitement."

IU team manager Mark Wallace concurred. "That was the only time in my life I experienced such a tension-filled race. You could have cut the tension with a knife, to use an old phrase. When Mark stepped up to the block, his hands were clenched so tight, he had a hard time opening them in order to dive in and start his strokes."

Even with the masses demonstrably on Russell's side, the Indiana team's encouraging yells reached the grateful ears of Mark, who remembered his U.S. teammates plainly cheering for Zac Zorn in the final of the 100-meter freestyle at the Games. The decibel level, significantly favoring Russell, made the spirited Hoosiers that much more inspiring for Mark. "If you were in the stands, you probably only heard the yells for Russell, but I heard my teammates loud and clear," Mark said afterward.

Once on the blocks, the starter summoned the swimmers to their marks, but the fans were so loud the swimmers couldn't hear the directive. The crowd would not relent. If anything, the ear-splitting racket intensified. Finally, after two minutes with no abatement of the noise, Mark stepped off the blocks. Russell followed suit. The clamor diminished slightly, but when they returned to the blocks, the hysteria returned as well. All swimmers then climbed down and wondered if they'd ever get to swim. After a few moments, the starter called the swimmers back to their blocks, intent on starting the race despite the deafening roar.

Before the starter could pull the trigger, Mark intentionally false started. "I wasn't ready yet," he remembered. "There was too much tension, and I wasn't able to focus on the race. I swam slowly down the pool and back. It relaxed me, and I was hoping it would have the opposite effect on Russell. It was like a football coach calling a timeout right before the other team's field goal kicker sets to kick. I was hoping to mentally 'ice' Russell."

Finally, the gun went off. Curiously, Russell reverted back to his old strategy of going all out from the start instead of employing his winning tactic from Mexico City, when he laid back until the end of the race and blazed past Mark to victory. Unfazed by Mark's false start, Russell edged ahead and maintained the lead at the final turn. With twenty-five yards to go, Mark trailed slightly but began gaining ground. He then did to Russell what Russell had done to him in 1968. He held off ever so slightly and then with fifteen yards to go made his move. Stunning the crowd, Mark won by a fingernail.

The relief was palpable. "When Mark won, it was if an enormous weight had been lifted off his shoulders," Wallace recalled. Mark shed his burden, the win merely adding panache in the process. "I wouldn't have cared if I ended up fifth, as long as Russell was sixth," he said later.

Mark exorcised his demon. He won because of his ability to persevere and succeed in an ugly environment, something he hadn't mastered in Mexico City. After that, he felt he could overcome anything and began looking forward to Munich. According to Wallace, "That event is when the fire turned the rough steel into a samurai sword in his soul. There was nothing anybody could do to him after that to shake his confidence, because there just couldn't be any more pressure than there was at that race."

Indiana went on to win its third consecutive championship with the help of Larry Barbiere's win in the 200 backstroke, Hall's in the 400 IM, and Henry's repeat in the diving events.

❗❗❗

Doc's training logs were legendary. He kept every workout he ever wrote, endlessly scrutinizing them to determine their effectiveness in the long and short term. Based on his experimentation and research, he developed not only interval training workouts but also periodized workouts, meticulously planning specific training on specific days at specific times in the season. Diligently following the scientifically designed practice sessions brought the swimmer along gradually but precisely, allowed him to peak for a particular race at a defined time.

And then along came Mark, whose distaste for workouts matched Doc's fascination with and faith in them. Mark used a variety of blatantly obvious to barely concealed methods to dawdle during, cut short, or altogether avoid workouts. Periodically he asked Doc for a "get-out swim," his favorite technique, and Doc usually obliged. The rules were simple. Doc picked a stroke and distance, then set a time. If Mark beat the time, he got to skip the workout. These antics usually annoyed his teammates, as they did nothing for them but delay practice.

John Kinsella, though, fondly remembered an instance in which the whole team benefited. "One time when Doc was away from practice, Mark suggested a get-out swim to the assistant coach. We didn't like these swims because only Mark got out if he beat the time, and it disrupted practice. Knowing Doc usually accommodated him, the assistant coach agreed. But he smiled real smug-like and announced that Mark had to swim a 100 freestyle at close to American-record pace to get out. It was at the start of practice, and most of us hadn't been in the pool yet. Mark dipped his toe in the water, took a few minutes to psyche himself up, and told the assistant he was ready. We wildly cheered Mark on. When he beat the time, we instinctively cheered louder as we headed for the locker room before the assistant could do anything to get us back to workout. He lost control of us and stood there with his jaw dropped open."

During the fall, most members of the team kept in shape by playing pickup water polo matches in the pool. Even though Mark earned high school All-American honors in the sport, he rarely participated in the games, leaving his teammates to wonder about his commitment. As usual, Mark avoided the natatorium until reluctantly appearing for a team swim workout in December. He characteristically lounged around the pool, wasting as much time as possible. Doc yelled at him several times before Mark finally jumped in the pool and swam a few warm-up laps. Not feeling in the mood for a workout, Mark swam over to Doc and asked for get-out swim. Doc frowned, knowing Mark needed to get some yardage in. Grudgingly, he agreed to the proposal but set a tough standard: break 50 seconds in the 100-yard butterfly. Knowing the American (world records did not exist in 25-yard pools) record was 49.1, Doc figured his out-of-shape junior could not come close to succeeding. To his surprise, Mark accepted the challenge without balking.

Mark took several minutes to psyche himself up, pacing back and forth, shooting glances at the wall at the far end of the pool, closing his eyes, looking up at the ceiling, and shaking his arms to get loose. Doc kept telling Mark to get on the blocks, each time getting a litter sterner, but Mark kept delaying. "One side benefit of the get-out swims was that I tried to maximize my psych up time in order to miss as much of the workout as possible," Mark conceded.

Finally, five minutes after laying down the gauntlet, Doc said "That's it! Let's go." When Mark dutifully stepped onto the block, Doc pulled out his stopwatch and whistled Mark to start. Mark shot off the block but didn't take a stroke, gliding slowly to the surface. When his head broke the watery plane, there was a dead silence. Mark looked up at a stunned Doc and said, "I heard you click your stopwatch before I started." Some audible "ooohs" sprang from the other swimmers, a little shocked and amused that Mark would challenge Doc in such fashion. Doc simply smiled—aware that he'd been psyched out—and told Mark to get back on the blocks. After five more minutes of psyching up and numerous attempts by Doc to cajole Mark back to the block, he was ready. This time, Mark attacked the water with swift and flawless strokes. To the amazement of Doc and the other swimmers, his first three splits were near world-record pace. As promising as that sounded, everyone knew Mark's lack of training would result in a last-lap fizzle, leaving him well short of the time and with no option but to finish the workout. But when Mark hit the final wall, Doc couldn't suppress another grin. Mark had just swum an incredible 49.6, only five-tenths of a second off the American record.

Most of the Hoosiers pushed themselves on every set of every workout in an effort to reach their maximum potential. Mark, on the other hand, picked his moments. His obvious reluctance to work out hard sometimes created mild animosity with his teammates. One day Mark swam in a lane next to Jacks, Barbiere, and Hall. For most of the workout, the perpetual slacker gave minimal effort. But when Doc assigned a long set of 50-yard butterflies—Mark suddenly burned up the pool and, in the process, made everyone else look slow. Excited to see his protégé excelling,

Doc praised and encouraged Mark, which understandably irritated the laboring Jacks. The Canadian quickly devised a plan to put Mark in his place and whispered to Hall and Barbiere that the three of them would alternate going first. The one who went first was to go all out to beat Mark then go to the back of the line, where he could swim slowly and recover before the next time he led off against Mark. Mark welcomed the competition, but as hard as he tried, he couldn't beat the rotating trio. In frustration, he whined to Doc that they were changing the order just to beat him. Doc simply shrugged, and the trio hid their smiles, pleased at getting their point across.

But the message they sent was not the message Mark received. "Their effort to beat me that way only confirmed to me that I was the best," he explained. "You can take that as arrogance, but if you look into the minds of most champions, you will find, as a common denominator, self-assuredness. Champions know they can rely on themselves, and the stronger they get mentally, the more they do rely on themselves and the less they concern themselves with what others do."

Kinsella, two years Mark's junior, wondered whether Mark ever did one hard set. "If you didn't know who Mark was and you watched one of our practices, you wouldn't suspect that he was a world-class swimmer," he marveled. "He was content to be mediocre in training."

Mark knew full well of his malingering reputation, but it didn't bother him. "Some swimmers are the consummate workout swimmers, but they can't translate that effort to winning a race," he said, defending himself years later. "I didn't need long and hard workouts. I was a sprinter and didn't need to be in as good of shape as others. I was a racer, not a workout swimmer."

From Mark's standpoint, this behavior had reaped excellent success in the past and he saw no need to change. As for Doc, he knew that what Mark usually needed more than yardage was the ability to face and meet challenges. He also respected Mark's ability to read his body.

"Great swimmers usually have an innate sense of how they function," Cecil Colwin quotes Doc as saying in "The Talent Is the Call," an ode to the legend after his death in 2004. "They seem to know instinctively how hard they need to work, and when they need to ease off. There's no need for the slave-driver approach to coaching. By respecting the swimmer's perceptions about his swimming, and by good communication, a coach can develop the sensitivity to understand the swimmer's basic needs."

In addition to workout slacker, Mark also filled the role of team hypochondriac, equally susceptible to illnesses he imagined and those suggested by others. One time, Jacks took advantage of a situation to smite two of Mark's irksome habits with one hilarious prank. "One time we were in Ft. Lauderdale for a winter training camp. Mark had missed a couple of hard workouts. The rest of us were tired, but Mark was fresh and started ripping up the place, which annoyed me a bit. When the workout was over, I asked what was wrong with his ankles. He said, 'What do you mean?' and I told him that his ankles looked funny and suggested he had polio of the ankles. Despite the ridiculousness of this fake disease, Mark seriously began to examine his ankles."

Riding back to the hotel on the bus, Kinsella began talking about competing in open-water swimming, long-distance events held in lakes or the ocean. Mark and his teammates listened to Kinsella for a while before Mark blurted out, "I could never get into open-water swimming. My ankles are too weak." Jacks and the others close enough to hear shook their heads in dismay, barely able to conceal their chortles.

When the team reached the hotel, a sports reporter took Jacks and Hall to the side for an interview. When the reporter suggested they ought to win NCAAs again, Jacks, with a straight face, quipped, "We should if Mark's ankles hold out." The reporter asked what he meant, but Jacks simply shrugged and told him to ask Mark. The reporter cornered Mark, and Jacks could no longer suppress his laughter when he saw Mark showing the reporter his ankles. Doc ambled by, wondering what was so funny, and quickly dispatched the jokester to set the reporter straight. Doc guided Indiana to yet another undefeated dual-meet mark in 1971 and the Hoosiers' largest margin in the Big Ten Championship—an astounding 276 points. Many swimming enthusiasts thought the 1971 Indiana team rivaled the great Hoosier team from 1969, but at the 48th annual NCAA Championships at Iowa State University, strong teams from UCLA, Stanford, Long Beach State, and Tennessee threatened IU's string of titles.

Before the meet began, Mark's hypochondriac tendency backfired. On the plane to Ames, Doc noticed a red blotch on Mark's neck. With sophomore Gary Conelly in the recovery stage of the German measles, Doc figured his star swimmer had contracted the disease. Although minor in severity compared to full-blown measles, they nonetheless jeopardized Mark's ability to score points. Knowing Mark's inclination to enlarge his dubious conditions beyond the boundaries of medical truth, Doc knew he had to take action. If Mark knew he had the measles, he would insist on scratching from his races. So, when the team arrived at the hotel, Doc told his swimmers to shave down immediately. Some were surprised—the shave down came a day earlier than normal—but they obeyed their coach without question.

Mark's overabundance of body hair made the ritual more difficult and time-consuming for him than for most of his teammates. When he finally finished and critiqued his effort in the mirror, he noticed a red spot on his chest. He also thought his face looked pale, and his joints ached. He went to tell Doc about his symptoms, saying, "Doc, I don't feel so well." Doc peered intently at the red spot, deliberately paused for a moment, and replied, "You aren't sick. You shaved too close—you have razor rash!" Mark protested that he hurt all over and his ears itched, but Doc convinced Mark he was probably just jittery and predicted he would have a great meet.

On the first day of competition, an ailing Mark loosened up but felt cold in the water. He began shivering but didn't think much about it when he heard others complain about the frigid water conditions. He managed to qualify for the final of the 50-yard freestyle behind Tennessee phenom Dave Edgar—who many thought was the fastest sprinter in the world—Edgar's teammate John Trembley, and UCLA's Barry Townsend. Dean Jerger from Florida State and Martin Pedley of Stanford qualified behind Mark.

After a false start, Edgar ripped through the water and won by a body length, an incredible margin at that distance. Mark finished a disappointing fourth behind Townsend and Trembley, but the points were helpful. "The 50-yard freestyle is an all-out event," said Mark later. "I wasn't feeling that well, and that was definitely a distraction for me. But even healthy, at that time in my career, I doubt I could have beaten Edgar. He was incredible."

Mark rebounded the next day in the prelims of the 200-yard butterfly to qualify second behind Rob Dickson of Southern Illinois. He hadn't swum well and was encouraged that his time trailed Dickson by only about a tenth of a second. Mark's former Arden Hills teammate, John Ferris of Stanford, qualified third, followed by UCLA's Robert Clarke, Steve Craven from New Mexico, and Charles Orr from USC.

Dickson, a sophomore in his first NCAA final, wilted under the pressure of the final. He started out fast but couldn't hold off Mark and Clarke. "Razor rash" and all, Mark bested Clarke by a full second. Dickson managed to finish third, ahead of Orr, Ferris, and Craven. According to Mark Wallace, this was an incredible performance by Mark. "Before the race, Mark was lying on his back on a massage table in his sweatsuit, and I was very lightly massaging his chest to relax him. He was trembling like a leaf with the chills. I tried not to let my concern show. I knew he had the measles, but didn't say anything. Given his condition, and the physical demands of the 200 butterfly, this, for me, was one of his greatest victories."

That same night, Mark, Conelly, Kinsella, and Hall hoped to dethrone USC in the 800-yard free relay, an event the Trojans had won the previous two years. Mark led off with a respectable 1:41.24, but NCAA 200-yard freestyle champion Jim McConica touched first at 1:39.76 for a full body-length lead. Southern Cal maintained that advantage through the end of the third leg, leaving Hall to make up the distance against two-time AAU short-distance champ Frank Heckl. Hall ripped the first hundred in 46.74 to draw almost even, but Heckl staunchly held on down the stretch for the win.

Overcome with emotion about his teammate's valiant effort, and in an uncharacteristic mental lapse, Kinsella leaped into the pool to congratulate Hall before the third-place team finished. The spontaneous celebration breached a clear and long-standing rule at every level of competition—no swimmer can reenter the pool until all teams have finished. Caught up in the excitement, Mark also jumped in. The moment his toes touched the water, he realized the race wasn't over and immediately climbed back out, hoping no one saw him. The mistake disqualified the Hoosiers, depriving them of the twenty-six second-place points.

On the third and final day, Mark faced the 100-yard butterfly, the "chills," and more red splotches. Doc somehow—gamely exploiting the trust he'd fostered in the past few years—convinced the medical neurotic he was okay, that the razor rash should clear up in a day or two. Ferris battled hard in the final, ahead at the turn, but Mark won by an arm's length. Climbing out of the pool, Mark knew something was wrong. He shivered constantly, and the aches were getting worse. But he atypically ignored the obvious signs of illness and focused on the final 100 yards to swim as anchor of the Hoosier's 400-yard freestyle relay. Nearly exhausted from the rigors of the meet and physically weakened by his yet unknown disease, he mentally readied himself for the final event.

Three schools, Tennessee, USC, and Indiana, had posted qualifying times within three-tenths of a second, ensuring a thrilling conclusion to the meet. Tennessee coach Ray Bussard altered his standard procedure of anchoring with his fastest swimmer and instead led off with Edgar, who opened up a two-body-length lead for the Volunteers. It quickly became a question of whether USC or Indiana could catch up over the next three legs. Mark hit the water slightly after Heckl, who trailed Tennessee by about one and a half seconds. Mark and Heckl closed on the Vols, but the order didn't change. Heckl surged ahead a stroke from the wall to take second, and third was the best the Hoosiers could muster. They did receive a "consolation" prize, though: their fourth-straight NCAA Championship trophy.

On the plane ride home, Doc deviously grinned at his wife, Marge. He was about to break the news to Mark that he had the German measles and said she should watch what was sure to be a dramatic reaction. Doc worked his way up the aisle discreetly and found Mark playing cards. Without pause, Doc gingerly whispered to him, "You know those red spots you have? I think you have the measles." Mark immediately gasped, "I knew it! I've got to lie down!" Mark's mental state led to a physical collapse so complete that his teammates had to help him off the plane. A trip to the campus clinic the next day verified Doc's diagnosis.

Mark predictably recovered and laughs about the incident. "I knew from that day forward that as great as he was as a mentor, Doc was a lousy physician," Mark said. "I wasn't about to take any more medical advice from him."

Despite that "near-death" experience, Mark felt things were going well for him at Indiana. Doc, ever the scientist, confirmed that perception by giving Mark a psychological test similar to one he'd administered when Mark joined the team. In 1969, it showed the swimmer was "overly tense," no big surprise. In the spring of 1971, it disclosed a vast improvement—the tenseness was practically gone.

Mark entered his senior year in good spirits. He won the 1971 AAU Sullivan Award at the end of the year, he learned in January of 1972 that he'd been admitted to the Indiana University Dental School, and he and Hall were named co-captains of the team. Mark enjoyed the camaraderie of his IU teammates, the fraternity parties he attended as a member of Phi Kappa Psi, and interaction with the sorority girls.

Furthermore, the Hoosiers hadn't lost a team championship since he'd been on board, and he intended to do his part to keep it that way. IU kept alive their undefeated streak in dual meets—in fact, Doc's teams had lost only two duals since 1960—and won the league by another landslide of two hundred and fifty points. The 1972 NCAA Championships, however, would not be so easy.

The meet, held at the new Crandall Pool at West Point's U.S. Military Academy, didn't start out too well for Mark. In his first event, the 50-yard freestyle, he placed third behind the formidable Tennessee sprinters, Edgar and Trembley. He regained his form the next day in the 200-yard butterfly, sustaining a fast start throughout the race for a 1:46.89, an NCAA and American record. IU teammate Bob Alsfelder finished a distant second, more than four seconds back.

Prior to Mark's final individual event, USC took a surprising twelve-point lead in the team competition. The Hoosiers found their streak endangered for the first time after winning the past four titles by an average of one hundred points. But with no Trojans in the final of the 100-yard butterfly, Indiana stood to regain the lead. Prior to the race, Doc Counsilman thought Mark capable of a 49-second race and predicted a win for him. Mark exceeded those expectations, searing the middle lane in 47.98 seconds—the first time in history anyone broke 48 (or 49) seconds—to set another pair of NCAA and American records. SMU's Jerry Heidenreich finished a distant second in 49.51.

Those points put the Trojans out of the running for the championship barring another bizarre disqualification in the final event, the 400-yard free relay. The Hoosiers didn't win the race—Tennessee took that crown—but they managed to stay within the rules during their fourth-place finish to seal the team title, topping the Trojans by nineteen points.

In four seasons at Indiana, Mark turned in some impressive results. He racked up eight individual NCAA titles, sweeping the 100 fly and winning four more in the 200 free, 500 free, and 200 fly. In three Big Ten Championship meets, he swept the 100 fly and 200 fly and won the 50 free twice. More significant, though, Mark thrived under Doc's leadership. "Doc was a father figure to me and everyone who swam at Indiana," Mark fondly recalled. He was not just interested in how fast we could swim; he was concerned with our academics and how we developed as people. He was a great person to look up to."

CHAPTER 8

CHANGE FOR
THE BETTER

". . . it is my decision to drop the entire Spitz family
from the Santa Clara Swim Club membership."
— George Haines, August 14, 1969

WHEN MARK returned to California after the 1969 collegiate
season and spring semester at Indiana, he knew he was burnt out.
His career had begun a decade earlier at age nine rather by de-
fault, without knowing exactly what lay before him. Within a year
he had been swimming about ten thousand yards a day over two
workouts, a routine he more or less had continued for the next
nine years. After competing in local and regional meets in the
first half of his career, he'd spent the next five nation- and globe-
trotting, winning and setting records at the high school, NCAA,
national, international, and Olympic levels. He'd also endured
three moves, five coaching changes, and the tremendous stress
surrounding the Olympic Trials, training camp, and Games.

What he didn't know was that the tension between him and
George Haines would flare up one more monumental time,
resulting in a separation between arguably the world's best
coach and the world's best swimmer.

Once back in Sacramento, Mark took the break he knew his
body needed, lounging around the house and relaxing before

jumping back into a rigid workout schedule. His sister, Nancy, on the other hand, attended workouts religiously and unfailingly gave them her complete focus and effort. The fifteen-year-old thrived in Haines' program, becoming a contender on the national scene as a freestyler. One day when Haines asked her why Mark wasn't at practice, she shrugged and said he'd have to ask Mark.

That night, Haines made a rare exception to his standard procedures and stopped by the Spitz home to speak with Mark and his father. Haines' foremost objective was obtaining a commitment from Mark to compete at the upcoming Santa Clara Invitational. ABC contracted to televise the event and justifiably wanted the world's most recognizable swimmer to participate at his home club's major meet. Mark explained to his coach that, exhausted physically and sapped emotionally from the Olympics, international trips, and the collegiate season, he needed time off. After considerable discussion, Mark reluctantly agreed to enter the meet but made no other assurances.

Arnold also told Haines that the one trip holding Mark's interest that summer was to Israel to compete in his second Maccabiah Games. When Haines questioned their logic, given the journey's difficulty and the swimmer's supposed lack of energy, Mark described the event's importance to him because of the rare opportunity to return to their homeland and the fellowship with other Jewish athletes. He would say afterward, "I will never forget the opportunity Israel gave me through the Maccabiah Games to participate in a world-class event early in my career, and the excitement of meeting Jewish athletes from around the world and sharing with them the universal spirit of sports competition was a matchless opportunity." Arnold added that Mark wanted to be the first person to set a world record at those Games. Haines didn't seem to understand but grudgingly accepted the effusion.

The trio failed to discuss Mark's participation in the AAU national long-course championships in Louisville, Kentucky, at the end of the summer. They should have. Haines assumed his star would obligatorily contribute his annual and indispensable points toward the team's championship. In Mark's mind, the issue remained open.

VVV

The 1969 Santa Clara Invitational drew stars from sixteen countries that July, living up to its reputation as an important annual meet. East German backstroker Roland Matthes, the two-year world-record holder who swept the two strokes in Mexico City, set one of three world records during the three-day event; Gary Hall added another in the 400 IM. About ten thousand spectators filled the International Swim Center during the three-day meet, including more than four thousand for Sunday's finals.

As promised, Mark competed in the televised meet, contributing to the festivities by tying the world record in the 200 freestyle. Mark also easily won the 100 free, with runner-up Frank Heckl almost two seconds behind him, and the 100 fly. At the close of the meet, Mark felt that he had more than fulfilled his obligations. Little did he know that he would never swim for Haines or Santa Clara again.

In late July, Mark and sixteen other U.S. swimmers, including Nancy Spitz, departed for Israel and the Eighth World Maccabiah Games in which athletes from twenty-seven countries competed in twenty-two sports. Mark didn't set the world record he had hoped for, but he dazzled the crowds with six gold medals in the 100- and 200-meter freestyles, 100-meter butterfly, and three relays. Nancy turned in her finest performance to date, winning the 200, 400, and 800 freestyle events.

Mark dreaded returning to California to tell Haines he wouldn't be going to Nationals. "I made my mind up before I left Israel that I was through for the summer," Mark later explained. "Worldwide and collegiate competitions had worn me out, and

I needed a rest. I knew George wouldn't be happy, but I wasn't prepared for his reaction."

The confrontation came quickly. Haines called Mark not long after the plane touched down in Sacramento to discuss what events he would be swimming at Nationals. Mark's declaration that he was taking the rest of the summer off came out of left field from Haines' perspective. Haines took great pride in his club winning the team title at Nationals—by the end of his twenty-four-year tenure, SCSC won an unprecedented forty-three AAU national championships—and never considered he'd be without Mark's services in maintaining the club's glory.

Initially, Haines remained calm and collected, using logic and remarks about "dedication to the team" in an effort to change Mark's mind. When that tactic failed, he blew up. Yelling into the phone, the headstrong coach informed Mark of his responsibility to participate as a member of the Santa Clara Swim Club and gave a vague warning about how his skipping the meet could impact his membership at the club. Mark, finally aware of the difference an enjoyable team atmosphere makes, fueled Haines' threatening outburst with bold indifference by retorting, "I have other options." Haines slammed down the phone after a vengeful, "We'll see."

Mark's decision didn't seem to affect Nancy, who accompanied the team to Louisville. However, Haines had secretly prepared a handwritten letter on club stationery notifying the Spitz family of their expired welcome. Greedy for a team victory, though, he waited until after the meet and the return to Northern California to deliver the letter to the Spitzes.

Word of the termination quickly spread. Haines defended his action to a *Swimming World Magazine* reporter by saying, "For the good of the team, for morale, I thought he should have gone to Nationals. There is no way I can condone this and maintain the type of teams and tradition we have had in the past. I have great respect for Mark. He's one of the great talents. I respect everything he has done for this club. But I'm afraid I haven't taught him the little things, like what a team means."

Haines' decision devastated Nancy, but Mark appeared relieved. Arnold, who never got along with Haines, angrily decried the harsh verdict. "Everybody recognized that Mark wasn't going, except George. He wouldn't accept it. Mark knew this summer would be his only chance to rest, to have a vacation, before 1972. He's been swimming for 10 years."

But Haines' wrath had not yet run its course. Citing a vague bylaw on team loyalty, he filed a complaint with the AAU to ban Mark from future competition. Shocked by Haines' latest missive, Arnold sought advice from his uncle, who referred him to prominent antitrust lawyer and mayor of San Francisco, Joseph Alioto. Alioto wrote a letter to Haines implying that anti-Semitism factored into his harsh treatment of the Spitzes. He further noted that it seemed odd for a coach to be expounding moral platitudes about team loyalty while at the same time retaining Nancy a few more days solely to benefit from her points. At the end of the letter, Alioto suggested that the grievance be dropped. Faced with pressure from the legal ace and the obvious inconsistency of his behavior, Haines quietly dropped the matter.

Nancy didn't talk with Haines for about four years. "I was really angry," recalled Nancy. "Years later, I was swimming in a pool at UCLA. George had become the coach of the UCLA swim team and he saw me. He came over and apologized for what he had done. He said that at the time, he thought he was doing the right thing, but looking back, he knew he had made a big mistake."

It would be years before Mark and Haines spoke again. They saw each other at major meets, but Haines always avoided contact with his former star, and Mark did nothing to break the icy silence. Haines served as assistant coach for the women's Olympic team in 1972, forcing their close proximity a few times, but Haines painstakingly evaded Mark. When Mark worked as a television commentator at the 1976 Montreal Olympics, he saw Haines at the swim venue, but neither moved to end the standoff.

Their first real contact after the 1969 falling-out occurred in 1984, just prior to the Olympic Games. The Los Angeles organizing committee had arranged a luncheon to honor all former Olympic coaches and, oblivious to the fifteen-year quarrel, asked Mark to present Haines an award. Mark's initial reaction was to decline, but then he thought better of it. "A lot of time had passed, and I knew George had done a lot for me, so I smiled and said that I would be happy to give out the award," Mark recalled. "When I presented it to him, he came up to me and smiled. He shook my hand, and it was clear that he felt relieved. I did, too."

They bumped into one another from time to time over the following few years but usually limited their conversations to general pleasantries. But when the city planned an event in June 2000, at which it would rename the Santa Clara International Swim Center to the George F. Haines International Swim Center, Mark informed them that he would attend to pay tribute to the legendary coach. The gesture of forgiveness meant so much to Haines that he called Mark to express his happiness and appreciation. Unfortunately, business called Mark out of the country the day of the dedication. "I was disappointed that I had to miss the ceremony, but George and I had made our peace," Mark said. Sadly, the two never spoke again. Haines suffered a severe stroke in 2002 and passed away on May 1, 2006.

¡¡¡

After the acrimonious split, Arnold moved his children back to the friendly fold of Arden Hills and Sherm Chavoor. Unlike with Haines, Chavoor got along well with Arnold. In his 1973 book, *The 50-Meter Jungle: How Olympic Gold Medal Swimmers Are Made*, Chavoor wrote that he enjoyed Arnold and often visited the Spitz home to consult on Mark and Nancy's development. He considered Arnold to be a member of his inner circle.

Even though Mark was happy to be back with his old coach, the older and more experienced swimmer questioned Chavoor's overtraining methods and constantly complained about the daily mileage. By contrast, Mike Burton, winner of the 400 free and 1500 free in Mexico City and two-time national champion in the 200 fly in 1969, thrived on Chavoor's workouts. The two achieved tremendous success as swimmers but with extremely different approaches to their training. Burton swam every workout as if it was his last. Mark looked for ways to avoid training.

One day Chavoor assigned a set of three 800-meter freestyles. Mark stopped on the first two without finishing even half of the distance. When he pledged to Burton prior to the last swim that "this time I'm going to finish all of the laps," Burton could only shake his head in disbelief.

Although Burton felt disdain toward Mark's work ethic, he respected the relationship between Mark and Chavoor. "He [Chavoor] and Doc Counsilman turned Mark around," Burton asserted. "Sherm became Mark's close friend. If Mark got into stereos, Sherm did. If Mark got into photography, Sherm followed. They had a special relationship. At Arden Hills, Mark didn't suffer the animosity he experienced at Santa Clara."

Just as he did at Indiana, Mark sometimes skipped entire practices. Whenever he didn't feel like working out, he called his cousin Sherman and said, "Let's go rafting!" They loaded into the car the two large truck tires Arnold secured for that very purpose and headed to the Sacramento River for a relaxing day in the sun.

Mark admits he didn't train as hard as others, but he also contends it wasn't out of laziness but rather because of a phenomenal understanding of his body. He knew that as a sprinter, he didn't need the excess yardage of Chavoor's workouts. "I could feel if I was benefiting from the workout," he explained years later. "If a set had marginal benefit to me, I wouldn't take it seriously. On the other hand, I would work out very hard on portions of the workout that made me a better sprinter. I don't recommend this to other swimmers, but it worked for me."

Mark trained with Chavoor at Arden Hills the rest of that summer but had already promised to swim for Gatorade, Doc's Bloomington club, during the 1970 long-course season. Mark competed in only two major meets that summer of 1970: the Santa Clara Invitational and AAU Nationals. Entering his old stroking grounds for the first time since being kicked off the team didn't bother Mark. "It was just another swim meet for me," he said. "I was still friends with a lot of guys from Santa Clara, like Mitch Ivey and others, and it was good to see them."

Nancy was only fifteen years old at the time Haines kicked the family off the team and her parents tried not to involve her in the dispute. When she learned what had transpired she was very angry with Haines. When she walked on the deck for the SC Invitational, she was motivated. "I swam well at that meet and that was all that counted. The best revenge is success and that is what I showed them," recalled Nancy.

Mark wasn't in the best of shape, but he managed to take second in the 100 freestyle behind Dave Edgar. In that race, Mark normally laid low behind the leaders and then surged the last ten meters to win. This time, though, he went out too fast and turned first. Mark's lack of conditioning caused him to falter at the end, allowing Edgar to catch and pass him for the win. Recognizing the oddity of the situation, Edgar remarked to *Swimming World Magazine*, "I had no intention of coming from behind. You have to think that's a freak to catch someone like Mark."

But Mark redeemed himself the next day, winning the 200 butterfly—his first time to swim the event in two years—and beating Frank Heckl by two and a half seconds in the 100 butterfly. Excited with the margin of victory in the shorter race, Mark told *Swimming World Magazine*, "I'm excited. When I go to

CHANGE FOR THE BETTER 125

Nationals in August, I'll be in shape, and this will be my first event. I want to start winning right off the bat."

※ ※ ※

Los Angeles hosted the 1970 AAU Long-Course Nationals, and despite good results, several of Mark's performances left him disgruntled. True to his prediction, he won the 100 butterfly, beating out John Ferris and Heckl. His time of 56.12 missed the world record by only a half-second, but Mark groused, "I was disappointed in my time. It would have been nice to have Doug Russell in there. I'm in the best shape of my life, and I was expecting a better time."

The next day, Mark came from behind to edge out Mark Lambert and Heckl in the 200 freestyle, but Mark didn't think he swam a good tactical race. "If I'd have gone out faster, I might have broken the world record," he told *Swimming World Magazine.*

The 400 medley relay offered unusual allure, pitting Mark's current team, Gatorade, against his former. Mitch Ivey gave Santa Clara an initial lead over Larry Barbiere, which Brian Job increased in the breaststroke leg as Gatorade fell back to third behind Santa Clara and Phillips 66 of Long Beach. Mark's powerful butterfly stroke made up the ground on both teams to touch the wall first, giving rise to a tense battle between Gatorade's Gary Conelly and Santa Clara's Martin Pedley in the final leg. With the crowd cheering loudly, Pedley overtook Conelly to give SCSC a narrow victory. Haines' team didn't need the points to win the meet, but the none-too-pleased coach certainly didn't want to lose to Mark. He acknowledged after the race, "I really wanted this one."

To Mark's surprise, he broke a world record the next day in the prelims of the 200 fly, his least favorite stroke. In the final, he battled Hall, Burton, and John Ferris from the outset but in the end lost to all of them, finishing a disappointing fourth. "I took it out too hard in the prelims," Mark admitted. "I didn't have anything left in the finals that night. Taking fourth place did nothing for my confidence in the 200 fly. I really don't like this event and am seriously considered not swimming it anymore."

On the last day of competition, Mark excited the early morning crowd by breaking yet another world record, this time in the 100 freestyle prelims. Conserving energy in the final so as not to suffer a repeat of the 200 fly, Mark took the first lap a little slow. Edgar, Heckl, and Jack Nelson beat him to the turn. Mark caught the pack with twenty-five meters to go and locked in stroke for stroke with Heckl, but the USC Trojan seemed to have a longer reach at the end and stretched for the title.

Even though he only competed in two major meets, Mark vaulted to the top of the 1970 world rankings, with the fastest long-course time in three events: the 100 fly, 100 free, and 200 free. He also tallied a third-place ranking in the dreaded 200 fly.

❢❢❢
○ ○ ○

After two summers of relative rest in 1969 and 1970, Mark annihilated any doubt in 1971 as to the identity of the world's best swimmer. The long-course season began, again, with the Santa Clara Invitational. Mark waxed the field in the 100 free, beating out Jerry Heidenreich, Heckl, Russia's Vladimir Bure, Ed McCleskey, and Joe Bottom. He followed up by winning the 100 butterfly for the fifth straight year, beating Ross Wales by a full body length. Although entered in the 200 butterfly, Mark scratched and watched as Hans Fassnacht broke the European and German records. "I hate that event and wasn't mentally prepared for it," Mark recalled. "I was pleased with my performance in the other events and looked forward to Nationals in Houston."

Rain and humidity greeted Mark and Chavoor in Texas's largest city at AAU Nationals. Swimmers joked that they didn't need to warm up because in Houston "you are always loose." Mark stunned the crowd in his first swim when he set a world record in the prelims of the 100 butterfly. In the final that night, it was all Mark. He started out slower than his morning split, but everyone was slower. Mark left the field with twenty-five meters to go, finishing with a flurry to win by a second and a half. But he made headlines for another reason, bluntly telling *Swimming World Magazine* afterward, "The pool is terrible. I tried for the record in the prelims and just to win in the finals."

On day two, Mark led all qualifiers in the 200 freestyle. Right before the final, Steve Genter amused the crowd with unusual body twitches and jigs behind the starting block in lane eight. He then used the manufactured adrenaline to lead at the final turn, with Heidenreich and Mark close behind. But neither challenger could match Mark's speed down the stretch, ripping through the water to win by a stroke.

He continued his tremendous effort on the third day, setting a global mark in the preliminaries of the 200 butterfly, but his outlook appeared dim at the last turn in the final with Hall leading by two strokes and swimming strong. Mark began to close, but Hall still maintained a one-stroke lead with fifteen meters to go. Only a furious close allowed Mark to sneak past a dying Hall to win in another world record time of 2:03.89 to Hall's 2:03.91. Robin Backhaus, a sixteen-year-old from Redlands, California, gave notice that he could contend the following year at the Olympic Trials with a surprising third-place finish.

On the final day, Mark established himself as the best swimmer in the country, if not the world. Heidenreich, Mark's longtime foe, qualified first in the 100 freestyle to set himself up as a potential spoiler. In the final, the field was so tight at the turn that nobody seemed to have an edge. Halfway back home, though, Mark opened up a lead with a surge to win by a stroke over Heidenreich.

Mark's four individual wins in one AAU Nationals made history, but he had little time to celebrate. The next day, he and a select group of twenty-three other male and female swimmers boarded an eighteen-hour flight to Leipzig for a dual meet against the German National Team. The U.S. squad crushed their counterparts from Deutschland, 221–123, winning twenty-five of the twenty-nine events. Mark narrowly beat Matthes in the 100 butterfly and then electrified the crowd on the opening leg of the 4x200 freestyle relay. His lead-off 1:53.5 broke the world record for 200 meters, and Heidenreich, Fred Tyler, and Tom McBreen followed with fast times to help set a world record in the relay.

The tour continued when the team traveled to Minsk for a three-way meet with the Soviet Union and Great Britain. The Americans proved even more dominant, losing only two of the twenty-nine events to overwhelm both teams. In the final trip of the year, the Japanese Swimming Federation invited Mark and seven other swimmers to compete in Osaka and Tokyo.

Exhausted but satisfied at the end of his extraordinary year, he began accepting awards. The editors of *Swimming World Magazine* selected Mark as the male Swimmer of the Year, and he earned the coveted James E. Sullivan Trophy as the nation's outstanding male amateur athlete. It would have been hard to justify selecting anyone else, given that Mark posted the fastest times in the world in three events—the 100 fly, 100 free, and 200 free—and the second-fastest time in the 200 fly. So far in his career, he had set an amazing twenty world records in eight events. As of January 1, 1972, Mark led the world in the number of all-time, year-end, first-place rankings with twelve. Don Schollander and Roland Matthes were tied for second with ten.

!!!

Even after that success in 1971, or perhaps because of it, Mark expressed ambivalence about competing in what would become his legacy-defining meet. On a rafting trip with Sherman one spring day in 1972, their conversation ranged from girls to family to sports in general before Mark stupefied Sherman by announcing that he was considering skipping the Olympics. "I already have Olympic medals, world records, and the Sullivan Award," he rationalized. "I want to start dental school in the fall. What are the Olympics going to do for me?" His stunned cousin replied, "Well, if I had your talent, I'd go, but it's your decision," knowing not to push Mark or badger him into doing something. The idea went no further in speech or action.

Mark's last stop before the Trials was the Los Angeles Invitational, three weeks before the Olympic qualifying event. Mark entered in only one event—the 100-meter butterfly. CBS televised the meet and had purchased Mark's plane ticket, hoping to boost ratings with the possibility of a world record. His performance, however, was not an impressive prelude.

In the prelims, Mark set a meet record and, to CBS's glee, announced that his goal in the final was to set the world standard. The starter called the eight finalists to the blocks. The large crowd quieted. Mark, in lane four, bent down for a grab start. But before the gun went off, he dove into the water for a false start. At that time, rules allowed two false starts unless the race official determined that the swimmer intentionally jumped. As Mark approached the block again, the starter disqualified him because of his supposed deliberate intensions. "Are you sure of that, sir?" Mark asked. "Yes," the starter replied. "Gee whiz. Then I suppose you can tell us who's going to win the race today," Mark responded, obviously upset that the man could somehow look into his mind and see a premeditated infraction. It was not a total loss for CBS, though. The drama took up more airtime than if he had swum the race.

Despite the fluke at the L.A. Invitational, Mark entered Chicago as the swimmer to beat in the 100 fly, 100 free, and 200 free. The only question that lingered in Mark's mind was whether to enter the 200 fly. He hated the event, but it wasn't obvious by his results. He'd set more world records in the 200 fly—six—than any other event.

‼‼‼

CHAPTER 9

PRESSURE AT THE 1972 TRIALS

THE MEMORY of the 1968 Olympics smoldered in Mark's psyche ever since that final, disastrous race in Mexico City. He dreamed repeatedly of the pool, the crowds, and, above all, the disappointments. His medal count—two gold, one silver, and one bronze—would have elevated many U.S. Olympians to national hero status and thrilled all but the most elite of athletes. But the public compared Mark to his audacious aspirations, not to his actual accomplishments, and viewed him as a failure and a fraud for daring to dream huge. Some of his teammates reveled in—a few in some way contributed to—his vexation, and most alienated him, unable to get past his immaturity, personality defects, and irritating habit of beating them. For Mark, those Games literally became a nightmare. Not one memory, not one individual performance, pleased him.

The penultimate obstacle to Mark's liberation from that haunting chapter in his life was the 1972 USA Olympic Trials, but that's like saying a struggling tightrope walker must traverse the line backward and blindfolded in front of a packed big top before getting off the wire. The process, the participants— even the pool that year—all added to the suspense of the nerve-wracking event.

The 1972 U.S. Olympic Swim Trials were held August 2–6 at the Portage Park Pool, an outdoor facility near the Chicago

O'Hare Airport. By today's standards, the pool was inferior. The depth of the water varied, tapering to three and a half feet at the shallow end. Now, USA Swimming requires at least a two-meter, all-deep pool, in part because the reduced wave action of deeper water produces faster times. The conditions at Portage Park were not ideal, especially for swimmers hoping for ultra-fast times in a speedy pool. But, of course, the situation was the same for all swimmers. Besides, order of finish easily ranked ahead of time as the most important result at the Trials.

As in 1968, the athletes had to equal or beat stringent times established by the AAU Men's Swim Committee just to qualify for the meet, and it got tougher from there. An average of thirty-four—and as many as forty-eight—of the nation's best swimmers competed in each event, with only the top three finalists earning the right to participate individually in Munich. Although a few would make the trip as relay members or alternates, in several cases the fourth-place finisher watched the Olympics on television, just like the millions who hadn't sweated and sacrificed in self-administered pain to mold their bodies and minds into peak condition. There were no second chances, no do-overs, no committee who overrode the results if a favorite swam poorly, no formula to account for past performances. If someone bonked during the Trials—a world-record holder, a national-record holder, a former Olympian, an NCAA champion, anyone—he didn't make the team. It was as simple as that. You either performed in the pool during that race or you didn't advance. The difference between making and not making the team often measured in tenths of a second, and sometimes only by a few hundredths. Hearts could be broken in less than a heartbeat.

Worse was the knowledge that the fourth-fastest American just might be the fourth-fastest in the world, or at least among the top eight. The United States had dominated the swimming competition in the past two Olympiads. In 1968, the U.S. squad won twenty-six of forty-five medals, including ten of fifteen gold.

Of the thirty-six individual performances, thirty-two resulted in a finals appearance. In 1964, they took home fourteen of thirty medals—seven of fourteen gold—and finaled in twenty of twenty-one individual events. That meant a potential Olympic finalist could be sitting stateside, missing the biggest moment of his career. Swimmers often either rose valiantly to the daunting task of achieving their towering goals or collapsed spectacularly under the tremendous weight of intense desire and world-class competition. U.S. men's Olympic coach Peter Daland described it best: "This is a meet filled with triumph and tragedy." Most swimmers from the 1972 Trials felt the meet was more competitive and pressure-packed than the subsequent Olympic Games.

Any U.S. Olympic Trials is full of drama, tension, and a certain amount of heartache, but the '72 version was especially cruel. Take Charlie Campbell for example. The Princeton junior from Pasadena, California, was a tough, ferocious backstroker who arrived in Chicago after a very strong year. In 1971, he won the 200 backstroke at the Pan Am Games and the national long-course championships, and swam the third-fastest time in the world in the 200 backstroke behind German Roland Matthes and Gary Hall. He also clocked the second-fastest 100 backstroke in the world for an American record, just tenths off Matthes' world standard. According to his long-time coach, Don Gambril, Campbell was a lock to make the Olympic team in both events. He didn't in either, finishing an inexplicable seventh in each. His Olympic dreams vanished.

Don Havens suffered a headache. Havens won four national titles in the 100 free between 1967 and 1969, brought home gold medals in the event from the 1967 World University Games and the 1969 Pan Am Games, and helped set a world record in the 4x100 freestyle relay in 1970. Havens drew a spot in Mark's preliminary heat. Because he had plenty of speed to make the final, Daland suggested that he watch Mark during the race to see if he could learn anything that might help him beat Mark in the final. From lane one, Havens watched Mark in lane four so intently that he failed to notice the wall and cracked his head on it. He didn't qualify.

Kurt Krumpholz felt the tease of the Trials. The nineteen-year-old UCLA freshman brought with him modest credentials but even more raw talent as a "country-club swimmer" for Balboa Bay Club in Newport Beach. He won the CIF Southern California high school 100-yard freestyle as a senior, but he turned more heads as a water polo player. After earning first-team All-CIF honors his junior and senior years, Krumpholz earned a full scholarship to play at UCLA. He competed on the Bruin swim team merely to stay in shape, but he was no slouch, placing seventh in the 500-yard freestyle at the NCAA Championships and finaling in two relays.

After witnessing his potential and enjoying his friendship for a year, UCLA swimmers Steve Doyle and Carl Thomas encouraged Krumpholz to join them at the Santa Clara Swim Club and train with George Haines. In late June, after lining up housing with a few San Jose State water polo players, Krumpholz moved to Northern California and focused on qualifying for the Trials in the 100 free, 200 free, and 400 free. Meeting the marks in the two shorter events came fairly easily because of his experience at those distances, but he had never swum the 400 before that summer. He missed the time his first try at the Santa Clara Swim Meet and had just one last chance at the Los Angeles Invitational. Swimming in his heat was Gunnar Larsen, a Swede attending Long Beach State who had already made his country's Olympic team and knew what was on the line for Krumpholz. "What time do you need for the U.S. Trials?" he asked. When Krumpholz replied 4:08, Larsen offered, "Stick with me and you'll make it." He did. The water polo player qualified for the Trials in three events.

A week later, when Krumpholz was training back in Santa Clara, his father died after a long illness. His family delayed telling him to keep from disrupting his training for too long, and after the funeral they encouraged him to return to Santa Clara. Krumpholz ached for his father's presence and support, but his goal remained the same: to place in the top six in the 200 free. That would make him an alternate on the 4x100 and 4x200 freestyle relays, which was as much as he dared to expect. He felt his chances to final in the 100 free and 400 free were unrealistic.

The 200 free brought disappointment when he missed the finals by five hundredths of a second. The next morning, before the 400 free prelims, Krumpholz didn't have a care in the world. "I thought my shot at the Olympic team was in the 200, so as far as I was concerned, I had ten more laps to swim and I was done," he said, referring to eight laps of the 400 and two of the 100. His Santa Clara coaches weren't projecting Krumpholz to make the finals but were hoping he would swim a personal best under 4:04.

Krumpholz was dispensed to an outside lane in the second-to-last preliminary heat, next to reigning Olympic gold medalist Mike Burton from Arden Hills. At the end of six laps, Krumpholz saw Haines and Schollander jumping up and down, but he wasn't sure why they were so excited. As he began the final lap, he could hear the crowd roaring but still didn't know for whom. When he glanced to his right and didn't see Burton, Krumpholz realized the cheers were for him. Krumpholz was winning his heat! Finishing with a flourish, the water polo player shocked the swimming community with a world record of 4:00.11. In just his third time to swim the event, he almost became the first human to break the four-minute barrier. His closest competitor, the veteran John Kinsella, posted a 4:01.36. No one was sure who Krumpholz was, but they were sure they just saw the next Olympic champion.

Back at the hotel, Krumpholz called his mother to share the news, but she thought he was joking. It wasn't until Jerry Kirshenbaum, a reporter for *Sports Illustrated*, made the operator break in so he could ask Krumpholz a few questions that his mother finally believed him. The next six hours before the final dragged mercilessly for Krumpholz, who spent most of the time relaxing alone in his room. "None of my family was there, so I had a lot of hours to savor breaking the world record and psyche myself up for the finals," said Krumpholz. "But I don't think I was mentally prepared for it."

Almost every athlete swam slower in the final, not unusual at the longer distances when the prelims are swum on the same day. Tom McBreen broke ranks, winning in 4:00.70 after his 4:02.11 in the prelims. Rick DeMont took second in 4:01.20, and Krumpholz's UCLA teammate and friend Steve Genter bagged the final Olympic spot in 4:02.03. Krumpholz finished a distant sixth at 4:03.82. His only consolation was beating eighth-place Burton, but it meant nothing.

Genter watched Krumpholz's agonizing plummet from ecstasy to anguish, and hurt for his buddy. In a quiet and selfless act, he approached fourth-place finisher Doug Northway and offered his own spot to Krumpholz if Northway and then Kinsella would also step aside. If both agreed, the world-record holder would swim in the Olympics. "I thought Kurt deserved it and only lost the finals because he hadn't swum the event enough times," recalled Genter. "But Doug said no, which I understood." Krumpholz didn't final in the 100 free, either. His world record held through the Munich Olympics, but he was unaware of Genter's gesture until thirty-five years later.

"Every once in a while, an athlete turns in a spectacular performance that nobody expected or can explain," said Peter Daland, head coach of the 1972 U.S. Olympic men's team. "Kurt's world record in the 400 free was one of those breakout events. It's also a reminder that the favorites can't take success for granted at the Trials. There may be a Kurt Krumpholz looming in the race."

The schedule accommodated Mark's strengths much better this time around. Instead of choosing events strategically based on the timetable, Mark was able to enter the four in which he excelled: the 100 freestyle, 200 freestyle, 100 butterfly, and 200 butterfly. With each event contained to a single day—the prelims in the morning and final in the evening—and only one event per day, the concern about fatigue in swimming several races on one day was not an issue like it was in 1968.

Frank Heckl emerged as Mark's most daunting opponent at the Trials and Games. The Los Angeles native's schedule matched Mark's with the exception of the 200 fly, which Heckl would not swim. That meant their three overlapping races could lead to a position on the three relays: 4x100 free, 4x200 free, and 4x100 medley. In other words, a potential six gold medals in Munich lay in the balance between the two.

Heckl, a big, strong athlete and blazing fast swimmer, competed collegiately for Daland at the University of Southern California and as a club teamer with the Los Angeles Athletic Club. His star had risen to prominence and ushered in heightened expectations after his performances at the 1971 short-course national championships in the spring and the Pan Am Games later that fall in Cali, Colombia. After capturing one national title each in 1969 (200-yard freestyle) and 1970 (100-meter freestyle), Heckl claimed three in 1971: 100-yard freestyle, 200-yard freestyle, and 100-yard butterfly. In Mark's absence at Pan Ams, Heckl won the 100 free, 200 free, and 100 fly; helped the three relays to golds; and finished second in the 200 individual medley.

Some considered Heckl the toast of the U.S. swimming community despite Mark's dominance during a seventeen-day stretch starting at the long-course championships two weeks after Pan Ams and ending in Europe. At nationals, Mark won his four specialties, lowering his three-year-old world record in the 100 fly final and his one-year-old global standard in the 200 fly prelims, which he equaled in the final. In Leipzig, Germany, it was his 200 free mark that fell, along with the 4x100 medley relay. Six days later in Minsk, he beat his newest 200 free time and helped the 4x200 lower the record that Heckl and company set in Cali. The message to other swimmers was clear: swimming faster than either of them would be tough.

Mark's most grueling event came first: the 200 fly. Of the other thirty-one entrants, Gary Hall, Mark's friend and teammate at Indiana, posed the biggest threat, followed by Mike Burton. Hall had won the 200 fly at the 1970 long-course and 1971 short-course national championships, the former being the last time Mark had been beaten in the event. Burton had won both in 1969, when Mark shied away from the distance, though his forte was the middle-distance freestyle. Robin Backhaus, a high school junior from Riverside, California, was a dangerous up-and-comer who had posted the fifth fastest time in the world in 1971.

In the fourth preliminary heat, Backhaus basked in a few minutes of glory when he broke Spitz's American record in 2:03.84. Five minutes later, though, in heat five, Mark upped the ante—or lowered it, rather—with a 2:01.87, his first world record at the Trials. Hall qualified third in 2:04.54, but Burton's 2:06.40 missed the cut by thirty-two hundredths of a second. Swimming exactly three seconds slower than Mark was Robert Alsfelder from Ohio, followed by Scott Lautman with the Husky Swim Club, Michigan State junior Kenneth Winfield, Murphy Reinschrieber with Coronado, and William Furniss from Huntington Beach, California.

Mark's strategy in the final was to be close to Gary Hall at the 100-meter mark, reasoning that Hall would be first to the wall and that Mark could beat anyone in the second half of the race. Mark surprised himself by leading Hall by half a body length at the midway point, with Backhaus third. Mark carried on with his plan, blistering the final two laps to post yet another world record of 2:01.53. Backhaus passed Hall down the stretch, swimming faster than his short-lived American record that morning, but was almost two seconds back in 2:03.39. Hall held off a closing Alsfelder to earn the last spot in 2:04.09.

The committee assigned lanes based on qualifying times, with the three fastest entrants drawing lane four in each of the last three heats. The minimal wave action and optimal vantage point for keeping track of other swimmers gave them the best shot of advancing to the finals. In the 200 freestyle, Heckl qualified third-fastest behind Mark and Jerry Heidenreich, the 1972 NCAA champion in the event and part of two world records on the 4x200 freestyle relay the previous summer. The exceedingly strong field included Fred Tyler, John Kinsella, and Jim Mc-Conica, three other swimmers who'd helped the U.S. set world records in the 4x200 and had at least one national or Pan Am title in the 200 free; Tom McBreen, another relay member; and Steve Genter, who won the short-course title earlier that year.

Genter, from Lakewood Swim Club in Southern California, seemed to be the most dangerous and, depending on preference, either the most fun or most odd. The gangly swimmer became known for his regular pre-race spectacle of violently shaking his arms and legs in all directions. As if that didn't attract enough attention, he also shaved every hair off his body except his eyelids just before the competition. Spectators warmed up to the gyrating Genter, and an unofficial but rabid fan club emerged. Genter had never beaten Mark in the 200-meter freestyle, but many of the previous races had been very close.

Stormy weather accompanied the 200 freestyle swimmers and fans to the outdoor pool that day, as thunder and dark clouds threatened the event. Mark watched Heckl swim a 1:56.25, third-best after four heats, and wondered how long it would hold up against such a talented cast. Mark believed at least three others in heat six would swim faster than that trying to keep up with him. For Heckl to make the final under that scenario, only one swimmer could advance out of heat five. The odds weren't good. As Heckl walked by after his race, Mark indiscreetly said, "Gee, I hope you make the finals." Not words Heckl wanted to hear. Mark's prediction played out when he qualified first in 1:54.02 and pulled Kinsella from McDonald's (1:54.58), McConica of the Los Angeles Athletic Club (1:54.71), and Genter (1:54.99) with him. Heckl fell to tenth on the list and out of the final. Incredibly, it took a 1:55.91 to advance, a time surpassed only twice in all of 1971.

The fast times from the prelims carried over into the evening session. Mark's 1:53.58, just eight hundredths off his own world record, barely defeated Genter, who came within a finger length of an upset in 1:53.79. Genter's fan club erupted over his second-place finish. When he responded with a wild celebration befitting his warm-up act, one boisterous and quick-witted fan yelled out, "Way to go, Curly!" Fred Tyler earned the third Olympic berth in 1:54.21.

Mark acknowledged the strength of the field afterward in a visible sign of his growing maturity. He told *Swimming World Magazine,* "This meet here is the toughest. At Munich, there are just two other Americans competing against me. Here, there are guys like Kinsella, McBreen, Heidenreich, and many more. This is real tough competition." He surmised later, "Our 200 freestylers were so good that we could have taken first and second at Munich in the 800-meter free relay."

Mark's specialty, the 100 fly, filled day three. His premacy in the event could not be overstated. Since he was sixteen, Mark had set four world records anu won two state high school titles, the 1967 Pan Am Games, and the 1968 Olympic Trials. He'd also placed a near stranglehold on the short- and long-course national titles, winning ten of thirteen during that stretch. Of the three other national champions, one had been Doug Russell (1969 long course), who upended Mark at the Games in Mexico City. The other two were in the '72 Trials field. Wales won the 1969 short-course title, as well as the 1966 short-course title just before Mark took over, and Heckl took the 1971 short-course crown.

Residual heartache from the mind games and subsequent loss to Russell in Mexico City lingered, but Mark's confidence from the ensuing years of support and the week's strong performances seemed to make his win a lock . . . just like Heckl's berth on the Olympic team. In the prelims, Mark shot out with a 25.84 fifty-meter split and cruised home in 54.68, another world record and more than two seconds ahead of Dave Edgar, a 100 free standout from Florida. Less than a half second separated Edgar from Christian Noll, the eighth qualifier. Ross Wales, the bronze medalist from the '68 Games; Joe Bottom from SCSC; John Trembley out of California; Heidenreich; and Patrick O'Conner with Gatorade finished in between. Heckl won his heat but was a quarter second slower than Noll in tenth and missed the finals for a second straight event.

Mark swam even faster that evening, making the turn in 25.7 and lowering his global standard to 54.56, another two-second cushion over Edgar. Heidenreich improved three spots to nab the third spot on the team. "I wanted to send a message that this event was mine," Mark reflected. "I lost it in 1968 when I was the world-record holder and it just wasn't going to happen again. At the time, I believed I was capable of breaking 54 seconds."

!!!
∘ ∘ ∘

The final event for Mark and Heckl was the 100 freestyle, the most volatile and unpredictable race in swimming at the time. A slow start, bad turn, or brief loss of focus can doom a champion, as can a great start, fast turn, and zone-like performance of a dark horse, of which there were many among the Trials-high forty-eight entrants.

Mark's routine of setting world records in the preliminaries continued with a 51.47, bettering his own standard by more than four-tenths of a second. Predictably, given the strong field, competition to advance was intense. Heidenreich, winner of heat five, swam just more than a second slower than Mark but only a quarter-second faster than the formidable 52.79 posted by Kenneth Knox, one of five swimmers separated by a tenth of a second. This time Heckl benefited from swimming with Mark in heat six to qualify with the sixth-fastest time. They were joined in the final by a "who's who" of American sprinters: Gary Conelly of Bloomington Gatorade, John Murphy with McDonald-Hinsdale, Arden Hills teammate David Fairbank, and Edgar.

Fairbank turned first in the final, three-tenths ahead of Mark, which may have surprised Fairbank and the crowd, but not Mark. His game plan was to take the first 50 fairly easily, then sprint hard to the finish to ensured he had enough gas in the tank to cap his busy meet with one more win. The tactic worked. Mark outsprinted the field down the home stretch in 51.91, tying his world record entering the meet. Only three athletes lowered their prelim times, and each earned a spot on the Olympic team: Heidenreich (second) and Murphy (third) as individuals and on the 4x100 free relay, and Edgar as the fourth relay member. Conelly and Fairbank made the team as relay alternates with the lamentable chore of swimming the prelims in

Munich, without the prospect of a medal, so that two teammates could save their energy for the final.

Heckl, in his best event of the Trials, touched last. A tested champion with a legitimate chance to win three to six Olympic medals failed to make the team in a single event. Daland believes that Heckl's decision to quit his job to focus on qualifying for the Olympics backfired. Heckl's time-management skills enabled him to thrive at the 1971 Pan American Games despite holding a job, but Daland thought Heckl had too much time on his hands that summer. One month before the Trials, Heckl had "lost it in his head," Daland remembers. "I told him it was a bad idea to quit his job. When he got to Chicago, he was finished."

At the other end of the spectrum, the Trials could not have gone better for Mark. Four victories gave him a chance at an incredible seven gold medals, including the three relays. To put this in perspective in the pre-Spitz era, Don Schollander was lauded as the greatest swimmer of all time after he won four gold medals in 1964. Mark could almost double that count.

But there was another training camp to survive first, no small task considering Mark's torture at the 1968 camp in Colorado Springs. Twenty-five swimmers boarded planes for the East Coast to train in the recently built Crandall Pool at the United States Military Academy at West Point.

1. Robin Backhaus, 17, Riverside Aquatics, 200 fly
2. Tom Bruce, 20, Santa Clara Swim Club, 100 breast
3. Mike Burton, 27, Arden Hills Swim Club, 1500 free
4. Mark Chatfield, 19, Pasadena Swimming Association, 100 breast
5. Rick Colella, 21, Cascade Swim Club, 200 breast
6. Gary Conelly; 20; Bloomington Gatorade; alt 400 free, 4x100 FR, and 4x200 FR
7. Rick DeMont; 16; Marlin Aquatic Club; 400 free, 1500 free
8. Dave Edgar; 22; Jack Nelson Swim Club; 100 fly, alt 4x100 FR

9. Dave Fairbank, 17, Arden Hills Swim Club, alt 4x100 FR

10. Steve Furniss; 19; Huntington Beach Aquatics Club; 200 IM, 400 IM

11. Steve Genter; 21; Lakewood Aquatic Club; 200 free, 400 free

12. Gary Hall; 21; Huntington Beach Aquatics Club; 200 fly, 200 IM, 400 IM

13. Jerry Heidenreich; 22; Dallas Swim Club; 100 free, 100 fly, 4x100 FR

14. John Hencken; 18; Santa Clara Swim Club; 100 breast, 200 breast

15. Mitch Ivey; 23; Santa Clara Swim Club; 100 back, 200 back

16. Brian Job, 20, Santa Clara Swim Club, 200 breast

17. John Kinsella, 20, McDonald-Hinsdale (IL), alt 4x200 FR

18. Tom McBreen, 20, Golden Gate Aquatic Club, 400 free

19. Tim McKee; 19; Suburban Swim Club; 200 back, 200 IM, 400 IM

20. John Murphy; 19; McDonald-Hinsdale (IL); 100 free, 100 back

21. Doug Northway, 20, Pima Co. Dolphins, 1500 free

22. Mark Spitz; 22; Arden Hills Swim Club; 100 free, 200 free, 100 fly, 200 fly, 4x100 FR, 4x200 FR

23. Mike Stamm; 20; Coronado-Navy Swim Association; 100 back, 200 back

24. Fred Tyler, 18, Canada Dry Jets, 200 free

Mark and sisters Heidi and Nancy at Foothill College, 1962.

Mark displays stopwatch with winning 50-meter butterfly time at 1960 age group championship in Fresno, California.

Mark, Nancy, and Heidi at Foothill College, 1963.

Mark stands atop the podium at 1963 age group swim championships in San Mateo, California.

Arnold and Mark display Pacific Association and National record banners, 1964.

George Haines presents Mark with high-point trophy for 1965 Santa Clara Valley Swimming Championships.

George Haines and Mark pose in 1966 after Mark missed the world record in 1500 freestyle by two tenths of a second.

Mark on podium after winning 100-yard butterfly at 1967 National AAU Championships in Dallas, Texas.

June 1967 cover of Swimming World Magazine *after Mark set American record for the 100-yard butterfly as a high school junior.*

Mark Spitz and Debbie Meyer grace the December 1967 cover of Swimming World Magazine *after being selected World Swimmers of the Year by the publication.*

George Haines and Mark after Mark set another American record in the 100 butterfly in 1968.

High school graduation picture, Santa Clara High School, 1968.

Cover of July 1968 Sports Illustrated.

Mexico City Olympics U.S. gold medal 4x200 free relay team (Don Schollander, Mark Spitz, Steve Rerych, and John Nelson).

Doc Counsilman, Charlie Hickcox, and Mark at 1969 NCAA Championships in Bloomington, Indiana.

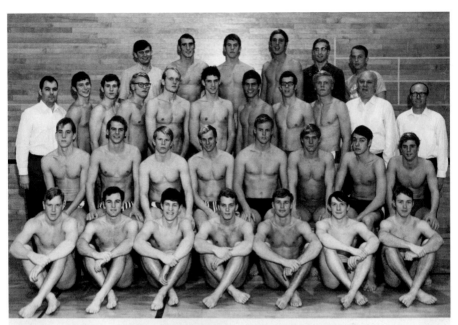

· BIG TEN AND N.C.A.A. CHAMPIONS · 1969 ·
INDIANA UNIVERSITY

Gary Hall, Roland Matthes, and Mark on the August 1969 cover of Swimming World Magazine.

Winter of 1970 at Indiana University.

Charlie Hickcox and Mark listening to Doc Counsilman, 1970.

Cover of September 1970 Swimming World Magazine.

Mark joins Jerry Heidenreich, Charlie Campbell, and Peter Dahlberg after setting a world record in the medley relay, Leipzig, East Germany, 1971.

Heidi, Lenore, Nancy, and Arnold Spitz in Sacramento, California, 1971.

Cover of August 1971 Swimming World Magazine.

Mark swims butterfly at the 1971 NCAA Championships at the U.S. Military Academy.

Cover of April 1972 Swimming World Magazine.

Cover of October 1972 Swimming World Magazine.

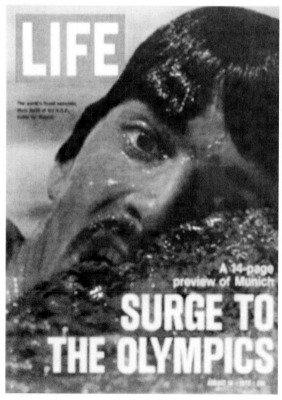

Cover of August 1972 Life *magazine.*

Mark (center) leads a preliminary heat into the water in his first race at the 1972 Munich Olympics.

Mark near the finish of the 200-meter butterfly at the Munich Olympics.

Mark is relieved to win the 200-meter butterfly in Munich.

Seven golds and seven world records.

Tom Bruce and Mike Stamm hoist Mark after his seventh gold medal in Munich.

Team arena publicity shot. Back row: Steve Furniss, Klaus Dibiasi, Mark Spitz, Don Schollander, Gary Hall, and David Wilkie. Front row: Shirley Babashoff, Ullrich Knab, Novella Calligaris, and Micki King.

Cover of Time *magazine, September 1972 issue.*

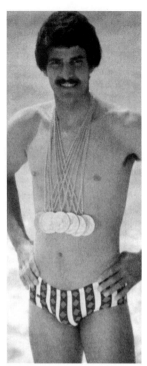

A 1973 publicity shot— Mark and seven gold medals.

Mark and Suzy on cover of Sports Illustrated.

Suzy Spitz on honeymoon in Hawaii, 1973.

Mark and Sherm Chavoor, 1972.

Mark is interviewed in 1977 after induction into the International Swimming Hall of Fame.

A 1978 photo of the Spitz family: Mark, Lenore, Heidi, Nancy, and Arnold.

Mark interviews swimmers at NCAA Championships for ABC Television.

Mark and parents at his 40th birthday party, 1990.

Mark poses with wax figure of himself (he thought it looked more like Robert Goulet).

A 2005 photo of the Spitz family: Suzy, Matt, Mark, and Justin.

Mark is presented with a trophy for "Athlete of the Century" in Vienna, Austria.

CHAPTER 10

‼‼

ON THE ROAD
TO REDEMPTION

PHYSICAL, MENTAL, and emotional duress lined Mark's path to Mexico City, creating a perfect storm of calamity. But that same trio of humanistic elements, which produce a greater whole than their sum might suggest, shifted in the four interim years to place Mark in perfect form for the 1972 Olympics. His eight world records, eleven national titles, eight NCAA crowns, thirteen Big Ten championships, and multiple dazzling performances at the Trials restored his faith in his ability. His fellow Hoosiers and Arden Hills swimmers resurrected his standing as a desirable teammate. But most importantly, his coaches—Doc Counsilman at Indiana and Sherm Chavoor at Arden Hills—rehabilitated the genuine self-assurance that had deteriorated into the brash confidence that insecurity often breeds. The positive mojo continued at West Point.

The 1972 camp lasted only fourteen days compared to the five weeks of dysfunction in 1968, when ample time and pressure allowed minor personality conflicts to fester and erupt into bitter exchanges. This time, although the athletes again endured intense training alongside their toughest competition for Olympic medals, the shorter time frame softened its severity. Two weeks of subjugation simply was much easier to take than five.

In 1968, the influential cliques were at best Spitz-neutral and at worst anti-Spitz. Four years later, Mark enjoyed the allied protection of six Indiana teammates (Gary Conelly, Gary Hall, John Kinsella, John Murphy, Mike Stamm, and Fred Tyler), two Arden Hills teammates (Mike Burton and Dave Fairbank), and a buddy from Santa Clara (Mitch Ivey). That group also yielded four of the five at West Point who had been in Colorado Springs. The supportive brotherhood created an enjoyable environment in which Mark excelled.

But perhaps the most significant difference between 1968 and 1972 was Mark's maturity. Just out of high school going into his first Olympics and one of the younger members of the team, Mark's raw personality and overzealous confidence was offputting. It didn't help that he almost always backed up his boasts. However, Doc Counsilman's team policy of prohibiting harassing or teasing Mark in any way—even clumsy but sincere guy-like attempts at inclusion or showing affection—and Sherm Chavoor's focus on his star athlete shepherded Mark to a much better place than where he was leading up to and in Mexico City.

"Sherm Chavoor and Doc Counsilman did a lot for Mark between '68 and '72," recalled Ross Wales, a Princeton grad and 1968 Olympic bronze medalist who later became vice president of FINA. Burton agreed. "In 1972, Mark seemed to have an inner confidence that was missing in 1968. It was disappointing to see him sitting next to Don Schollander, who was the god of Olympic swimming, and brashly predict he was going to smash Don's record of four gold medals. In 1972, he was more humble and mature. When he was asked about whether he could match or exceed Don's record, Mark was respectful and said he would take it one event at a time."

All of that, though, could not keep the old memories at bay. Vivid nightmares reminded him of his 1968 failures, as huge balloons emblazoned with "Mexico 68" interrupted his sleep in the United States Military Academy dorm room. They rolled toward him in a slow-but-sure suffocation march, but he jolted awake each time just before they overtook him. Staring into the darkness, the balloons transformed into images of the 1968 debacle—the camp, the eighth-place finish in the 200 fly, the episode with Doug Russell and his medal. Finally, he drifted back to sleep vowing to turn the agony into glory.

Three-time Olympian Gary Hall, one of the nicest, most honest people to emerge from the ranks of U.S. swimmers, described the '68 camp as bitter and fierce, easily the most divisive of the three he attended. "Mark was very blunt. He said what he meant, but he should have watched out who he said things to. Pretty soon, he had crossed the line and it got pretty ugly." In contrast, the most disturbing event Hall recalled from West Point involved a cat and 100 freestyler and backstroker John Murphy. "Murphy scared the coaching staff by climbing up a tree to rescue a cat trapped in the branches. I think John had total control of the situation, but it put Don Gambril in a state of panic. John was built like a tight end, and with one wrong move his huge body could have come crashing to the ground. Fortunately, nothing happened, except that John did rescue the cat."

On the last night of camp, the team staged a show to thank their hosts. The athletes competed in a series of mostly 50-meter races, some swimming their normal strokes and some not. "I was amazed at the excitement that night," said Gambril. "The facility had a capacity crowd, and Mark just tore through the water. He won everything he entered. Incredibly, he even beat the backstrokers in their own event."

A paper airplane contest highlighted the evening. It no doubt was designed to take the edge off the pervasive competitive mood at camp, but that's hard to accomplish with a bunch of Olympians. Swimmers toiled that day perfecting their aircraft, endlessly testing their flight patterns and making miniscule aerodynamic changes to increase their chances of victory. The rules of engagement were simple. Swimmers tossed their handiwork off the ten-meter diving platform. The longest flight time won. The crowd got into it as well, emitting oohs and aaahs as the announcer broadcast the running time for each plane pitched from the tower. Mark spent little time on his glider, opting for the elementary design he recalled from his boyhood days. Jokes and snickers ensued when Mark displayed his craft with a smile. To everyone's surprise, except probably Mark's, his plain model easily surpassed the more complicated creations. Gambril's daughter, Kim leaned over to her father and whispered, "Too bad there isn't a car raffle tonight. Mark would win it, too!"

Prior to packing their bags and departing for Munich, the dreaded but obligatory vaccination process reappeared. This time, though, Mark took a different approach. "I never liked needles and didn't handle the situation well in 1968," Mark admitted. "I didn't know if anybody else thought about what happened then, but I knew the shot was inevitable. I decided to take the bull by the horns and volunteer to go first. The last thing I recall is the nurse swabbing my arm. I guess I fainted, but when I woke up, the next two guys in line were on the floor, too. The result wasn't pretty, but it was much more tolerable."

The 200 butterfly loomed as Mark's first event in Munich. Storming into the '68 Games as the world-record holder and Trials winner had done him no good, succumbing to the altitude and seven other finalists. But Mark disliked the race even before that doomed day, and he left Mexico City unable mentally to commit to swimming the dreaded metered version of the event again.

"There is no way to make a 200-meter butterfly easy," Mark explained. "It doesn't matter if you swim it slow or fast, it beats you up. The 200-yard event is much easier to accept from a mental standpoint. It is typically swum in pools with gutters, so you can grab them and pull yourself up to make the turn. Plus, the pools are twenty-five yards long, so there are seven turns that help break up the swim. But the 200-meter version is swum in fifty-meter pools. There are only three turns, so each lap is long, and there are no gutters to pull up on, just touch pads. You literally get no support from the touch pads like you do with gutters. You just touch them quickly, like you would a hot plate, and twist your body to complete the turn."

That Mark even swam the 200 fly in Munich was a textbook case of artful psychology on the part of Sherm Chavoor. Sherm knew Mark hated the 200-meter fly, but he also knew Mark was the best butterflyer in the world. Sherm believed nothing could stop Mark from standing on top of the Olympic podium if he would only embrace the possibility. Forcing him to swim it wouldn't work. Somehow, the coach surreptitiously had to break Mark's mental block and get him to *want* to swim it.

After almost two years of Mark avoiding the race, Sherm hatched a plan in the summer of 1970. He imposed set after set of 200-meter butterflies on the entire Arden Hills team, preaching ostensible benefits for all swimmers but in reality targeting Mark's psyche. Debbie Meyer, a three-time gold medalist in Mexico City, was not fooled. "Sherm told the team that swimming 200-meter butterfly sets was good training for all strokes and distances, but it was pretty clear his attention was on Mark," she recalled. "He made the team swim 200-meter flies until they were dead."

While most of the swimmers viewed the workouts as sheer drudgery, Mark, John Ferris, and Mike Burton became engaged in a fierce competition as they peeled off lap after lap. All three were master butterflyers and could handle the regimen more easily than their suffering teammates. Their practice sessions were so intense Sherm decided to enter all three in the race at the 1970 AAU Nationals that summer at the Coliseum Pool in Los Angeles.

The 2:05.70 Mark swam in Berlin in 1967 still stood as the globe's fastest time, and Sherm thought Mark was well on his way to mentally accepting the race when his 2:05.04 broke the three-year-old world standard. Ferris was close behind in 2:05.87. German Hans Fassnacht, who trained with the Phillips 66 Club in Long Beach, qualified third, with Hall, Burton, Ken Winfield, Duncan Scott, and Robert Alsfelder rounding out the top eight.

In the final, Mark led at fifty meters, but Burton and Hall passed him on the next lap. At the third turn, Burton maintained half a body length lead until Hall drew even with twenty-five meters to go, the pair matching each other stroke for stroke. Hall prevailed, breaking Mark's hours old world record in 2:05.01. Burton took second, a tenth back, touching out Ferris. Mark finished a disappointing fourth in 2:05.79. Sherm winced. The first three swimmers bettered the meet-opening world record, and Mark's performance was exceptional given his hiatus from the race, but the loss would impede his rehabilitation project.

Sherm somehow managed to convince Mark to try again the following year at Nationals in Houston. Mark responded well, swimming 2:03.91 in the preliminaries to annihilate Hall's world record by more than a second, then breaking it again in the final with a 2:03.89. With the crowd still cheering him, Mark abrasively told a stunned press, "This pool here in Houston is the worst I've ever competed in." Technically, he may have been right. The pool was shallow, causing extra waves that slowed swimmers, and the blocks had been built out of plywood a few days before the meet. But that didn't make spewing his opinion during a post-race interview the best of choices. From that point on, the Texas fans booed Mark. Sherm wondered if the dark clouds hovering over Mark and the 200 fly would ever dissipate, especially after another psychological blow came just four days later. In Sweden, Fassnacht shattered Mark's world record with a 2:03.3, six-tenths faster than Mark had swum in Houston.

Mark began to wonder out loud if he should risk swimming the 200 fly in Munich. Six gold medals had a much better ring to it than six golds and one silver. That rumor reached Daland early in the summer of 1972. Two months before the entry deadline for the Trials, Daland implored, "Sherm, you have to get Spitz entered in the 200 butterfly. You've got to talk him into swimming it. We *need* him in that event in the Olympics. The country needs him. Otherwise, we lose it to the German." Sherm pursed his lips at the thought of the onerous undertaking and said he would keep trying.

Time was of the essence, and Sherm was out of inspiration, so once again he made the whole team swim long sets of 200 butterflies, hoping for a breakthrough. When Mark complained one day, Sherm saw an opportunity and challenged him to swim one for time. He told Mark if he could swim a 2:07 from a push start, the whole team would be excused from the rest of the workout. Mark loved such challenges, having spent his career using them to get himself out of training sessions. But the twist in this test—excusing the entire team—played an integral role in the scheme.

Sherm poured on his natural showmanship, enthusiastically telling the rest of the swimmers about the deal. They erupted in cheers. Some jumped in the water to pump up Mark. Others chattered in eager anticipation of being saved from the remaining workout if Mark was successful. Mark basked in their attention and buoyancy. Nobody noticed Sherm turn off the pace clock. After a few minutes of frivolity, Sherm asked Mark if he was ready. Mark nodded and prepared for push-off. Sherm chanted, "Ready, set, go!" At each split, Sherm dramatically called off Mark's time as if he had just won the lottery. With each lap, the swimmers on deck became more animated in their encouragement and excitement. When Mark finished, Sherm shouted out, "I can't believe it! A 2:05!" The swimmers descended on Mark in pure joy, caring about little else than that they were done for the day. When the chaos subsided, Sherm looked Mark in the eye and said, "Look, you nut. You just came within two seconds of Fassnacht's world record. If you can do that after a hard practice, and with a push-start to boot, Fassnacht will be looking at your feet at the Olympics." Mark, still high from his teammates' adulation, became serious and replied, "You think so? Maybe I ought to swim it in the Trials." Sherm smiled. It had worked.

The seasoned Debbie Meyer was on deck that day and had her doubts about the veracity of the ruse. After all, she'd been the beneficiary of Sherm's motivational tactic of claiming she had recorded extremely fast times in practice, and she'd often wondered if she was as fast as Sherm wanted her to believe. She didn't know if Mark actually swam a 2:05—no one ever would, because Sherm had the only stopwatch—but she knew it didn't matter. Like Sherm had done dozens of times with her, he had accomplished his goal. Mark swam the 200 fly in Chicago.

The IOC entrusted Germany with the Olympic Games for the third time in history. The VI Games of 1916, awarded to Berlin, never materialized because of World War I. Berlin did host the XI Games of 1936, but under the oppressive eye of Adolf Hitler, who played a major role in the instigation of World War II. With that dubious history, Germany approached its bid to the XX Games in 1972 very seriously and deliberately, obtaining political assurances that their bid would be accepted and making it a priority to stage a Games that centered on peace and the Olympic ideals. Ironically, one of the contravened Olympic principles the Germans decried was the increase in commercialism, yet Munich was the first to create a mascot—Waldi the dachshund—to help promote and raise funds for the event. But their commitment to a lighthearted affair carried over into everything from architectural design to the official motto, "The Happy Games," and unofficial billing as the "Games of Peace and Joy."

Among Munich's favorable characteristics in its selection as the host city included its size (at 1.3 million, large enough to accommodate the visitors but not overwhelmingly so), its history and tradition as an arts and cultural leader, and its physical beauty. It did not have much already built in the way of facilities, but an area near the Munich city center—Oberwiesenfeld, or "upper meadow field"—emerged as the logical site for the hub of Olympic activities. The desolate area was mostly flat, save a hill that formed from the wreckage of World War II. The Olympic Park sprouted amid landscaped lawns, trees, shrubbery, and a man-made lake about the size of nine football fields. Included in the complex with the Olympic Village, the Olympic Stadium, and several sports halls, stadiums, and training areas was the swimming hall.

More than seven thousand athletes from over one hundred and twenty nations, and approximately one hundred and fifty thousand visitors, descended on Munich for seventeen days of festivities, starting August 26 with the opening ceremonies. Fans, snatching up tickets at a smart clip, witnessed competition in twelve of the twenty-one sports on the first day. The wait for swimming races was short, with the eight-day schedule beginning on day two. Their first image of Schwimmhalle, from an entrance plaza shared with Olympiastadion and Olympiahalle likely was its roof. The architects somehow married a traditional Bavarian look with a futuristic design that resembled a cross between a steel tent-like awning and a large sailboat's masts and ropes. Other unique aspects of the structure benefited swimmers, fans, and post-Olympic users of the facility. The west side of the main pool featured permanent seating for sixteen hundred. Temporary bleachers on the east accommodated forty-six hundred spectators sitting and twenty-eight hundred standing. After the Games, removal of the temporary stands created the impression that the primary pool flowed into the outdoor lake. Specific design elements of the pool helped minimize wave action, and the suspended ceiling dissipated the chlorine odor that often plagues aquatic centers.

!!!

Mark's performance in his "psych out" event—the 200 fly—
could very well dictate how the rest of the Games went for him.
A great swim could validate his emotional state; anything but a
gold medal could shatter it. But Mark saw its placement as first
on his to-do list in Munich as a positive. There was no sense in
putting off "getting back on the horse," and it allowed him to
focus on it the most leading up to the race. "Since it was my first
event, I had time to mentally prepare for it," Mark explained. "I
knew that winning could springboard me to great swims in the
rest of my events and failure could stop me in my tracks."

The distaste for the 200 fly didn't stop with Mark. Only
thirty-one others qualified for the event, the smallest field in
the men's swimming competition. Hall, Backhaus, and Fassnacht represented Mark's primary threats, but two finalists from
1968, Volkert Meeuw of Germany and Viktor Sharygin of Russia, also made the field. Fassnacht proved the previous summer
he was capable of swimming extremely fast. Backhaus' powerful
stroke and Trials times made the teenager dangerous despite
his inexperience, and Hall believed he had a legitimate shot at
the gold. "I had beaten Mark in 1970 at Nationals and nearly
beaten him the next year in Houston," recalled Hall. "I was not
willing to relinquish the race to him."

Mark's great respect for Hall extended beyond his abilities in
the pool. The two had become friends during their careers at
Indiana. Although they rarely swam the same race, Hall's versatility—he won fourteen national IM titles and the silver in the
400 IM at Mexico City—occasionally pitted him against his
friend. When they did compete head to head, both valued their
friendship and refrained from introducing head games into the
mix. As collegians, they usually roomed together at away meets.
In the Olympic Village in Munich, the sliding door separating

their adjoining rooms stayed open as they settled into their rooms and routines before the Games began. Two days before the 200 butterfly, though, Mark closed the door. "Stakes were high for both of us," Mark acknowledged. "I didn't want to have to censor myself around Gary, and I didn't want to wonder about what he was doing. My focus for that race was intense. I told Gary it was nothing personal, and we could open the door again after the race. He said 'No problem' and went about his business."

The three Americans stole the show in the preliminaries, swimming in separate heats from each other and Fassnacht. After lowering the world standard by more than five seconds in the past four years, Mark "only" set an Olympic record of 2:02.11 for the fastest time of the morning. Backhaus won his heat by more than three seconds and exactly a second slower than Mark. Hall's 2:03.70 was a full second and a quarter ahead of the fastest non-American. Fassnacht cruised to a 2:05.39 to qualify fifth behind András Hargitay, Hungary's finest swimmer. Barely more than a second separated Fassnacht from East Germany's Hartmut Floeckner, Ecuadorian Jorge Delgado, and Meeuw. By all indications, Mark was on top of his game, and the Americans could dominate the race.

But as the athletes paraded from the holding area to the pool in front of the nine thousand spectators packed into Schwimmhalle, the Mexico 68 balloons suddenly bobbed toward him, breaking his concentration. A mild panic attack set in, but he quickly regained his composure. "I closed my eyes for a minute and forced myself to settle down, willing those stupid balloons out of my mind," Mark remembered. "But I had to permanently erase those images, and I knew the only way to do that was to win."

If anyone would have noticed his momentary lapse, it would have been his coach. But sitting among the screaming fans, Sherm only saw his protégé's confident gait and seasoned focused as he approached the blocks. The thin, smooth-faced schoolboy of 1968 was gone, replaced by a man with a chiseled body, bushy mustache, mop of dark curly hair, and sun-drenched complexion, à la film star Omar Sharif. His stunning good looks mesmerized millions of women young and old around the globe that night as he shed his warm-ups to reveal his red, white, and blue Speedos. He loosened his arms with huge forward and backward swings and, at one point, gave a sort of boxer's one-two punch. The anticipation and frenzied atmosphere spiked his adrenaline. Flanked by his teammates in adjoining lanes, he was ready.

The ABC network televised the Games. Lead commentator Keith Jackson and color analyst Murray Rose, Australia's most decorated Olympic swimmer with four golds, a silver, and a bronze, set the stage for the importance of the 200 fly. Jackson commented that if Mark could live up to expectations, he would be one of the super athletes of the 1972 Olympic Games. Rose agreed, and pointed out that it was important for Mark to get past his first event, the 200 yard butterfly, an event he dreaded. Rose went on to say that U.S. men's team head coach Peter Daland had predicted that Mark's success in that event would set the tone for the entire men's team.

Mark immediately took control of the race. At fifty meters, he already led Backhaus by three-quarters of a body length. Hall, Floeckner, and Fassnacht battled for third. At the halfway mark, he extended his lead to about six feet and was about a second ahead of world record pace. At the third turn, Hall passed Backhaus while Fassnacht bravely struggled to close, but no one could match Mark's fast, smooth stroke. Jackson and Rose became animated at the finish as Mark won in a world record time of 2:01.53. Hall fought off Backhaus for second, as the Americans swept the event.

Mark raised his arms in triumphant relief and soaked in the moment. In 1968, his demon was Doug Russell. In 1972, his demon was the race itself, and he vanquished it. He didn't just win. He demolished the field and the record. As the crowd roared in appreciation, he closed his eyes, leaned his head back, and vigorously slapped the water, as if metaphorically popping those blasted balloons.

Hall had finished in 2:02.86, more than two seconds behind Mark and four-tenths ahead of Backhaus, who completed the U.S. sweep by pulling away from Delgado and putting almost a second-and-a-half cushion between the Americans and the rest of the world. Mark and Hall, both gasping for air and too tired to smile, met at the lane line to congratulate each other before Mark did the same with Backhaus.

As many times as he'd seen Mark's mind-numbing feats, the record still astounded Hall. "I thought a 2:01-plus would win the Olympics," he reflected. "I never thought anybody would be around two minutes flat. I swam the race I wanted to swim, but it just wasn't good enough. And, unfortunately for me, I concentrated a little too much on that race and wasn't mentally prepared to swim the 400 individual medley two days later [when he finished fifth]. But everybody knew Mark hated that race. If he had lost, I don't think he would have swum well the rest of the Olympics."

For Mark, though, the weight was lifted, the struggles resolved, the doubts erased, the confidence repaired. "The relief of that first gold medal was so great that if I had quit then and there, I would have considered my years of hard work worth it."

But instead, as he slowly warmed down with a relaxed backstroke, he thought to himself, "I think I can win everything."

Dave Fairbank, Gary Conelly, Jerry Heidenreich, and Dave Edgar set a world record of 3:28.84 in the 4x100 freestyle prelims that morning, when the major casualty had been Australia. With bronze medals from 1964 and 1968 at home and defending 100 free Olympic champion, Michael Wenden, in their lane, they were strong medal contenders. Like the Americans did with their top athletes, the Aussies rested Wenden in the prelim, but the strategy backfired. They missed the final eight by more than one and a half seconds, a fact the openly disgruntled Rose belabored during the evening broadcast. "A surprise omission from this final tonight [. . .] Australia. They didn't qualify. The reason is that Mike Wenden didn't swim in the heats. They have a rule here where you are allowed to swim a different team in the heats to the finals, and Australia gambled they could make it through to the final without Michael and they didn't. If they had, they could have won a medal," complained the proud champion from Down Under. The Soviets qualified second, followed by East Germany, Canada, France, Brazil, West Germany, and Spain.

As planned, Mark and John Murphy replaced Fairbank and Conelly in the final even though Conelly recorded the team's fastest split that morning with a 51.69. The Russians opened with their fastest swimmer, Vladimir Bure, hoping he would benefit from the calm waters and invigorate his team by handing over a rousing lead. He did, out-touching Edgar, but it didn't last. Murphy responded by catching Viktor Mazanov and turning over a half-body length lead to Heidenreich. Heidenreich scorched the third leg, raising more than a few eyebrows with a 50.78. Mark anchored the relay with a 50.91 split. The Americans set the fourth world record of the night, but Rose could not avoid mentioning that Heidenriech was faster than Mark.

Mark, of course, didn't hear Rose's comment, but it didn't take long for uncertainty about the 100 free to enter Mark's mind. He knew that Heidenriech was blazing fast and Mark began to wonder if seven gold medals would be that much better than six.

CHAPTER 11

!!!

WHAT IF?

SWIMMING ENTHUSIASTS eagerly anticipated the 200-meter freestyle on August 29, the final of which would almost certainly pit Mark against fellow American Steve Genter. Although the lanky UCLA junior had never defeated Mark in that event, a few signs indicated he could be the one to derail the gold-medal train at the third station.

A middle-distance freestyle specialist, Steve came within a finger length of winning the event at the Trials a few weeks earlier, qualifying for his first Olympics in the 400-meter freestyle as well. His 200-meter freestyle berth also placed him on the 4x200-meter freestyle relay with Mark. Steve's rise in the swimming world germinated four years earlier at the 1968 Olympic Trials with a solid showing in the 400-meter freestyle. He missed advancing to the finals by four spots in Long Beach, but his respectable time and performance, especially for a seventeen-year-old high school junior, forecasted a bright future. Since that time, the Southern Californian accumulated a trio of silver medals at the 1970 World University Games and the 1971 Pan American Games and helped UCLA finish among the nation's top four teams in each of his three years, earning All-American honors in 1971 and 1972 in the process.

Steve's progression in the pool wasn't as quick as Mark's, nor had he accomplished as much, but the paths of their journeys converged to place them side by side in a delicate and unenviable position. They were teammates in the relatively broad sense that they represented the United States of America as swimmers at international meets. They were also teammates more tangibly each time they joined forces with two others on a relay, relying on each other's strengths and trusting in each other's maximum effort in competition. But, most palpably, they were competitors. Both had set an ultimate goal—to be the fastest individual in the world in the 200-meter freestyle—and so it is not surprising that their relationship, while mostly amiable, had its share of tension.

About a year before the Olympics, Mark played off Steve's last name to dub his rival, in sophomoric style, "Genitalia." The nickname served no other purpose than to get inside Steve's head, to irritate him just enough to lower his concentration when they squared off in the same race. Steve didn't like the nickname, but he knew better than to fall for the obvious bait, made all the more apparent because only Mark used it.

Head-to-head in the pool, Mark's domination over Steve was as slim as their bodies in the handful of times they swam the same race if you considered only their times. Steve established the bulk of his reputation in the 400-meter and 1500-meter races, not the shorter distances which Mark owned, but the sprinter out-touched Steve only by a finger length at the Trials, by a second at the 1971 NCAA Championships, and by a body length at the 1972 NCAA Championships. In five attempts, Steve had come away with just one victory. That lone triumph at the AAU National Short Course Championships in Dallas added another layer of lore to the pair's mounting rivalry.

Steve's long-time coach since his days as an age-group swimmer at Lakewood Aquatic Club was Jim Montrella, a 2005 inductee in the American Swimming Coaches Association Hall of Fame. A character in his own right, the successful and seasoned coach developed a reputation among highly competitive individuals for being highly competitive. It didn't matter if he was coaching an athlete in an international swimming championship or playing miniature golf with his family, Jim did anything within the rules to win. To that end, he always angled to give his athletes an advantage, especially in races he knew would be close. In the 200-meter freestyle preliminaries at nationals that April, Steve had qualified for the finals with the second-fastest time behind Mark. Jim knew that, on paper, the odds favored Mark. But he also knew his talented swimmer had an upset in him if only they could disrupt Mark's mental equilibrium ever so slightly.

"Psych outs don't work if one swimmer is overwhelmingly faster than the other," Jim explained, looking back on the situation. "But if the swimmers are close in physical ability, as Steve and Mark were at the time, they can be effective. I knew if Steve could do something just slightly out of the norm to crack Mark's concentration right before the race, he might be able to affect the outcome."

With that theory in mind, Jim hatched an innocuous but wily plan, implemented when the public-address announcer introduced the competitors. The finalists would be standing beside their starting blocks, the large crowd would respond to each name with applause, and the swimmer would reciprocate with an appreciative smile and wave. No ovation would be as long or loud as that for Mark, who, as the fastest qualifier, would be introduced last. After Steve was introduced, he moved behind the timer sitting directly behind Mark's block to get in position.

"I told Steve that as Mark was waving to the crowd, he was to walk up to him, look him right in the eye, shake his hand, and say, 'I want to wish you good luck,'" Jim recalled. "But the key was he had to turn his back on Mark immediately, without acknowledging any response from him whatsoever. Just turn around, walk to his starting block, and not look back."

The ploy worked—immediately, according to one timer. "Steve had that race won before it started," Jim remembered him saying. "I don't know what he said to Spitz, but you should have seen the look on Spitz's face. He was stunned."

Steve proceeded to seal the deal, leading from start to finish as Mark, never really in the race, remained fixated on the bizarre encounter. The incident shattered Mark's mystique in Steve's mind, providing evidence and confidence that the growing legend was beatable.

A finger-length separating them at the Trials . . . a seedy moniker by one . . . a psych out by the other . . . this had all the makings of a physical and psychological thriller on the sport's grandest stage, a drama unfolding in the water at the Olympic Swimming Center and, for those with a keen eye for nuance, perhaps a bit of drama out of the water as well.

And that was before Steve's lung collapsed in Munich.

❗❗❗

The United States Olympic Committee chartered several flights to get most of the 3,105 American athletes to West Germany that summer. The men's and women's swim teams, together with numerous athletes from other sports, boarded a plane the night of August 21 in Washington, D.C., for a red-eye flight to Munich.

Not leaving in-flight romances, territorial disputes, or chaos to chance, the USOC, in its infinite wisdom, assigned seats, using the middle aisle to segregate the sexes. The resulting configuration meant that the male—and, for the most part, larger—athletes were crammed uncomfortably on one side of the plane, while their female counterparts by and large enjoyed spacious environs. Steve, and, by proximity, his row-mates, were further impacted by the freestyler's high fever and constant cough.

"That was the worst flight of my life," Steve said later, reliving the agony. "I was sick, I was squeezed in a middle seat between two big guys, and I just couldn't get comfortable. I'm sure they weren't too happy to be sitting next to a guy hacking up his lungs all the way across the Atlantic Ocean."

When they landed, it was seven days before the 200-meter freestyle, and exhaustion and general misery understated Steve's condition. His body was breaking down from the combined lack of sleep, jet lag, and an infectious-feeling mild chest pain. But the team headed straight to the pool for an easy workout, and he convinced himself that loosening up would kick-start his adrenaline and jolt his body back into good health.

It didn't. Steve felt terrible in the water. He couldn't generate any speed. His breath was labored. His chest was tight. Anxious, he pulled one of his coaches aside to describe his symptoms and was sent to the medical clinic in the Olympic Village. The pain intensified as he rode the athlete shuttle bus, but he masked his discomfort in case any opponents or snitches saw him. He didn't want to give any opportunity for competitors to assume a physical advantage—or manufacture a mental one—over him.

But the truth was, if he couldn't walk from the bus stop to the Village without sitting down because of total fatigue, which he couldn't, he was not going to pose much of a threat to forty-five of the best swimmers on the planet, and he knew it. Finally making his way to the clinic, a U.S. doctor poked and prodded him for a few minutes before asking if he was in pain. "Only when I breathe," Steve replied sarcastically, at least hopeful that if the doctor couldn't tell he was hurting, then maybe any fellow freestylers who had happened to see him couldn't either. The doctor said and did little else besides hand Steve some pills and tell him to come back the next day, seemingly a real-life but ill-timed "take two aspirin and call me in the morning" remedy.

Steve felt uneasy about the doctor's cursory examination and wondered about the medic's credentials. He tried to determine what type of pills he had been given, exceedingly vigilant about the dangers of accidentally ingesting a substance banned by the International Olympic Committee. Such a transgression could result in disqualification after the race, assuming he would be able to race in the first place. But the nondescript pills came in a generic bottle with no label noting their name, dosage, or purpose. Not wanting to take any chances, especially given his dubious instinct about the doctor, he decided not to take the pills.

The next day Steve returned to the clinic feeling no better but thinking clearly enough to keep his disregard for the medication quiet. The two went to the University of Munich Medical Center for X-rays, after which Steve noticed the German and U.S. doctors talking in a somewhat panicky fashion. Now, in addition to breathing discomfort, he had a full-on case of nerves. Then came their verdict when they finally did include him in the discussion.

Steve had experienced a pneumothorax, a collection of air or gas in the chest that causes part or all of a lung to collapse. It also causes significant pain. Most collapsed lungs are the result of a penetrating injury—a knife wound, for instance—or a blunt trauma, such as a bad fall or a car accident. Occasionally a lung will spontaneously collapse, most commonly in tall, lean males like Steve, whose one hundred and eighty-five pounds were thinly spread across his six-foot, five-inch frame. The doctors hypothesized that his slender build, persistent cough, and recent flight had combined to rupture a small air- or fluid-filled sac in the lung.

This was exceedingly bad news for a man needing every bit of the extraordinary lung capacity he'd spent years developing to win a gold medal. But it got worse. The German doctors wanted to keep Steve under observation for a few days to see if the condition self-corrected. If it didn't, they would have to release the air by carving a small hole in his chest and inserting a plastic tube, connected on the other end to a suction device. One physician ventured that Steve would be unable to train or compete for six months.

Steve listened with dismay. His goal of being an Olympic champion literally was about to be sucked out of him. Tears streamed down his face. How in the world could this be happening to him? His chest pain now paled in comparison to his heartache. Gearing up for years for this specific week in time meant waking up way before dawn, swimming miles daily, and forgoing "normal" teen and college shenanigans, among other things. Having even a minor cold imposed a certain cruelty on a swimmer. But despite the seriousness of his condition, Steve would not—could not—go down without a fight. He pleaded with the doctors to speed up the process. "My first race is in six days!" he reminded them, as if they had overlooked that key piece of information in their initial diagnosis.

The German and American doctors argued. The hosts thought it not only foolhardy but also a cruel tease and somewhat medically irresponsible to give the athlete any hint of hope that he could actually compete in Munich. Under their care and at their hospital, they insisted on taking the more conservative approach. The U.S. doctor considered the situation less serious and wanted to perform surgery immediately, giving Steve as much of a chance to recover and compete as possible, remote as that may be. In his view, the outcome of a ball game should not be decided by the officials, and an athlete's destiny should not be determined by doctors as long as the aggressive approach is not dangerous. The operation was not dangerous. The American doctor prevailed. Steve would have surgery the following day.

Befitting his situation, Steve had difficulty sleeping that night. His mind raced with questions: How had his lung—his huge, superhuman, finely tuned, highly developed lung—collapsed? Why now? Did the doctors know what they were doing? How much would the surgery hurt? Will the anesthetist give me a banned substance? Is there any way I can recover in time? I wonder when my coaches, teammates, and opponents will find out?

The questions slowly turned into memories: The endless hours of training. The sacrifices he'd made. The sacrifices his family had made. His coaches. His races. His victories.

Gradually, the memories morphed into hope: He was determined. He was tough. He was strong. He was willing to swim through pain. The question that kept resurfacing was, would they let him, or would they deny him the opportunity of a lifetime?

Doctors performed the surgery on August 24. The procedure enabled Steve's lung to expand back to normal, but it wasn't designed to repair the thoracic organ. Normally the healing process takes several days. Until the lung fully mends, any physical activity would be risky and potentially fatal. A recurrence can cause escaping air to push against the heart and other lung, constricting the ability to breathe.

The surgery was relatively minor, unless you consider that Steve was scheduled to make his Olympic debut in five days. Drained from the surgery, the accumulation of restless nights, and the uncomfortable flight to Munich, Steve slept much of the day. A hospital rehabilitation nurse came to his room after dinner to begin Steve's therapy, which consisted of no more than extending his right arm and raising it up until his hand pointed toward the ceiling. Steve was so stiff and sore from the new hole near his right underarm that it took him more than a minute to do the simple maneuver. After a few repetitions, the nurse told him she would be back the next morning. Steve wasn't satisfied with his progress or her dedication. Clearly she was not on as tight a deadline as he was, so Steve asked if he could continue the exercise on his own.

"She thought I should wait for an hour and do it a few more times, but that's it," he remembered. "But I couldn't sleep after sleeping all day, and I couldn't just lay there wasting time, not doing anything to help myself, so I did the exercise in five-minute intervals all night. By morning I could move my arm up and down easily, with no pain at all."

At eight o'clock the next morning, the doctors examined their handiwork and hardheaded patient. The tube, one end still in Steve's chest, acted as an escape route for the trapped air, which in turn kept the lung at its normal size and shape. The real test would be how quickly the lung collapsed again under the pressure of air seeping back into the cavity when the tube was removed. The larger the hole in the lung, the more quickly the collapse.

To gauge the damage, doctors clamped off the end attached to the suction machine, waited a few minutes, and took X-rays. To their immense surprise, the lung remained totally inflated. They waited several more minutes and took more X-rays. Still, the lung maintained its full shape. Somehow, against immeasurable odds, he had mended overnight.

"One of the doctors told me that my recovery was something of a miracle, because a punctured lung takes days to heal," Steve said. "I didn't tell them about doing rehab all night, but I knew it made the difference. The only down side was I had to stay in the hospital three more days to make sure it really was OK."

Thirteen stitches later, he was in pain but essentially back to normal, save his status as a detainee in a foreign medical facility. While doctors still thought his chance of swimming in Munich remote, Steve now truly believed he would be ready to race in four days.

In the meantime, Jim Montrella, at the Games as an assistant coach for the Colombian swimming team, noticed Steve wasn't at the Americans' morning practice, but no one seemed to know why. Finally, a swimmer quietly approached Jim, revealing that Steve had checked into the hospital but wanted to keep it under wraps. Dumbfounded and not a little alarmed about how his star athlete could have been sick or injured, diagnosed, and potentially treated without his or the U.S. coaches' knowledge, Jim rushed to the hospital juggling dual personalities of a concerned parent and empathetic friend to find Steve freshly stitched.

After being briefed on his condition, Jim automatically and without pause shifted into the role which had benefited both men so well: coach. His swimmer had a race on Tuesday, the biggest race of his life, and he needed to continue preparing for it, just as he'd done for the past ten years. His confinement to a hospital bed was inconsequential to the task at hand.

Jim knew for two reasons that Steve would be fine physically. In the months leading up to the Olympics, Steve swam an average of sixteen thousand yards a day, about nine miles. In the past few weeks, though, Jim decreased his yardage gradually but significantly, to the point that the primary reason for pool time in Munich was to stay loose and relaxed in the water, do a bit of kicking, and swim a few sprints. This part-science, part-art training concept of tapering allows a swimmer's muscles just enough time to recover from the months and years of difficult training without losing any conditioning, packing the athlete with the triple threat of power, speed, and endurance. When timed properly, the swimmer is ready to explode off the blocks or wall as a finely tuned bundle of energy—a racehorse chomping at the bit to burst from his stall and attack the ground in an efficient blur of limbs.

The coach also knew Steve had a tremendous capacity to deal with pain. A few years earlier, Steve had been playing water polo, a rough-and-tumble sport in which athletes tread water or swim the entire game while fighting off opponents who either are allowed to or manage to get by with punching, kicking, grabbing, pulling, and who knows what else to obtain or maintain control of a ball in order to score. Think rugby in the water, because that's what the game's inventors did when establishing the first set of rules. In the middle of such a contest, Steve took a kick so hard to his torso that a few of his ribs broke. But, the game wasn't over, so Steve forced himself to ignore the excruciating injury and continued playing.

Kurt Krumpholz, Steve's college friend and one-time world-record holder in the 400-meter freestyle, stated the obvious. "Steve was so tough mentally, there is no way he would have let the pain affect him."

No, Jim wasn't worried about Steve being physically primed to compete, even if he had to drag a hospital bed behind him. It was Steve's mental and emotional readiness that concerned the coach. The inactivity might have a slight negative impact on Steve being optimally loose and smooth in the water. But, with seventy-two hours to do little else than fret and doubt, it could have a huge effect on whether Steve *perceived* himself ready.

Knowing he had to keep Steve mentally and emotionally optimistic about his fitness level, Jim wondered how he might achieve this placebo effect without Steve recognizing it as such. Looking around the room, his eyes lit on some plastic tubes, probably the same type the doctors inserted into Steve's chest. Jim's imagination took over, quickly devising an exercise that he believed would make Steve feel he was continuing to train and prepare for his races. Squeezing several tube openings into each other, Jim created a six-foot straw then tied off one end. Steve was to exhale slowly into the straw until there was no more air in his lungs and then inhale slowly. In addition to this somewhat aerobic exercise, Jim also positioned a traction bar over Steve's bed for supine pullovers to work his upper body muscles at various angles by altering the traction bar to different locations in relation to the bed.

Steve didn't much like the modified pullovers, but did them when his coach was around. Conversely, though, and incredibly, he blew into the huge straw four hours a day. When asked how he had been able to focus so long on such a boring exercise, Steve responded, "Don't tell me what boring is. I swim up and down a pool in a straight line for nine or ten miles a day. I looked at it as a challenge, so it didn't bother me. The thought of beating Mark kept me going."

Improbably, Steve recovered nicely. There didn't appear to be any loss of lung capacity, and damage to the lung seemed to have healed. The U.S. doctors thought he could swim. In character, the German doctors believed otherwise and fretted about their legal accountability if they released him. The U.S. doctors prevailed again, agreeing to take full responsibility for Steve's health and well-being, but only if Steve, in turn, agreed that they could refuse to let him participate if they thought he was at risk. Steve realized it was as good as he was going to get, so he signed the waivers and headed straight for the pool. It was Monday, the day before the 200-meter freestyle.

Jim asked Steve to swim fifteen hundred meters slowly while he and the U.S. doctor observed from the deck. The pain had changed but was still present. The doctor speculated the breakup of scar tissue on the incision caused the discomfort and should dissipate. Jim then told Steve to swim another fifteen hundred meters, this time covering each three hundred meters faster than the previous. Steve finished powerfully, with unmistakable joy written on his face.

"I started feeling better during the second 1500," Steve recalled with renewed delight. "The soreness was gone, and I felt great in the water by the end of it. When I finished, I swam straight to the doctor, shook his hand, and said, 'Thank you!'" He then began his normal pre-race workout, ecstatic that he had conquered—not dodged—that bullet. In an unexpected benefit, the incident bolstered him as well: If he could defeat a collapsed lung, he presumed, he could defeat Spitz.

¡¡¡

By this time, word was finally out about Steve's ordeal, and Mark was concerned. "I talked to Steve and Peter Daland (the head U.S. coach) about the danger that competing posed to Steve's health," Mark explained. "As great a thrill and honor as it is to compete at the Olympic Games, I didn't think it was worth a legitimate risk to his life."

Steve took Mark's comments as a feeble attempt to psych him out, but there was no way he was falling for the scheme. Steve told the *Los Angeles Times* then, "I think he was the big psych out of 1968. Everyone worked on him then, and so I think he tried to work on me." But Steve simply wasn't a guy who caved to mental games. "I've disciplined myself to ignore the problems involved," he'd told the reporter. Jim would later call Steve the most focused and mentally tough athlete he ever coached.

Looking back, Steve expounded on those earlier thoughts. "Mark's comments made me more aggressive toward beating him. If someone tries to psych me out, I'm a dangerous person. I told Mark that there was only one gold medal, and I was going to get it."

Steve climbed on the starting blocks for the prelims the next morning needing to post one of the top eight times to make the final. Psychologically, he was ready. The question remained whether he would be physically ready after spending five days on his back in a hospital bed. Steve swam in the sixth of seven heats. Incredibly, he won in a time of 1:55.42, about a second and a half slower than his time at the Olympic Trials but the second-fastest qualifying time behind Mark, who swam only thirteen-hundredths of a second faster. Steve felt renewed confidence that he was poised and ready to beat Mark in the final that evening.

Only about one and a half seconds separated Mark's prelim time from that of the eighth qualifier, Ralph Hutton of Canada. Two Germans, Klaus Steinbach and Werner Lampe, joined Steve in the striking-distance range of less than seven-tenths of a second back, and fellow American Fred Tyler qualified just slower than Lampe in fifth. Vladimir Bure from Russia and Australian Michael Wenden rounded out the field, their great sprinting ability making them unpredictably dangerous. Wenden's speed was of particular concern; he was the 1968 Olympic champion in the 100- and 200-meter freestyle events. The final was shaping up to be a barnburner.

Mark's plan was to get an early lead, reasoning that Steve and the rest of the field could deflate early if they saw him out ahead at the first of three turns. The tactic was well-executed. After only fifty meters, he led Steve by more than a half-second and Hutton, who was the last to touch the wall, by almost one and a half seconds. But his psychological strategy failed. By the halfway point, Steve caught and passed him. The medical marvel's lead was small, only thirteen-hundredths of a second, but it was a lead, something no one in the aquatics center believed was possible except Jim and him. Steve felt strong. Shortly after the second turn, some of his stitches ripped open. The sharp pain disturbed him momentarily, but he blocked it out. At the third turn, one hundred and fifty meters into the race, Steve maintained his slim lead, touching at 1:24.28 to Mark's 1:24.44. Only a few inches separated the two. Lampe and Wenden were about a second behind Steve in a virtual dead heat for third.

With twenty-five meters to go, though, Steve's miraculous recovery and performance began to falter with his form. His father, watching the race on television at the family residence in Lakewood, noticed the sudden shift in his son's stroke. "It just deteriorated," he would later say. Steve's past week was catching up with him. During that slight deviation in technique, that barely perceptible glitch in an otherwise almost perfect race, Mark shot past Steve. Recognizing Mark was just too fast on that day, Steve turned his attention to Wenden and Lampe, who were quickly closing the gap. Almost blacking out from pain and exertion, Steve gritted his teeth and resolved not to concede another spot.

Mark smashed his own world record—set a year earlier at a USA/Soviet Union dual meet in Minsk—by three-quarters of a second, finishing in 1:52.78 to grab his third gold in two days. Steve was about a body length back at 1:53.73 (a personal best) holding off Lampe by about a quarter of a second. Wenden faded to fourth, followed by Tyler, Steinbach, Bure, and Hutton.

Steve's story has been wildly embellished in some accounts, such as the bestseller *Friday Night Lights*, the true story about a Texas high school football dynasty. In an attempt to motivate a team that had been subjected to its own share of adversity, coach Gary Gaines invoked a semblance of Steve's ordeal. H.G. Bissinger wrote:

> The night before the game at the private team meeting behind locked doors, Gaines told the story of a swimmer named Steve Genter, who had been set to go to the Munich Olympics in 1972 in the two-hundred-meter freestyle when his lung collapsed. He was cut open to repair the lung and then sewn back up. Doctors said there was no way Genter could swim unless he took painkillers, the use of which was illegal under Olympic rules. But Genter, who had dreamed of going to the Olympics since the age of nine, decided to swim anyway—without medication. In the silent locker room, Gaines told what happened next, for he clearly saw a message in Genter's actions.
>
> "His face was ashen-white because the pain was so excruciating. He hits the water, he makes the first lap, does a spin turn at the other end and pushes off, and comes up for air, and lets out a blood-curdling scream. Because the pain is so intense, the sound just echoes off the walls of the swimming arena. He makes a split turn at the end of the second lap, pushes off, and he breaks his stitches, his stitches split apart and he starts bleed-

ing. They said he lost a pint and a half of blood over the course of the next two laps.

"I guarantee you, I'd want him in my corner," said Gaines of Genter, who ended up losing the gold medal to Mark Spitz by the length of a finger. "When the chips were down, I'd want a guy with that kind of character in my corner, I promise you, 'cause he's a fighter."

When Steve heard the excerpt, he laughed hard and long. "That was a bit of an exaggeration," he acknowledged. "I lost by a body length, I didn't lose an appreciable amount of blood, and I certainly didn't let out a bloodcurdling scream." What was not an exaggeration, by his own account, was his effort. "I could not have gone any faster. At the Olympic Games, you are really psyched. When the race started, I couldn't feel the pain."

In Mark's mind, though, the outcome was unquestionable by the third turn, if not before. "Steve's swim was remarkable in any situation, much less considering what he'd just been through. But at the third turn, Steve and I were almost dead even. When I was even with anybody with fifty meters to go, I was going to win," he explained bluntly. "I had the ability to turn up the speed whenever I needed to." Perhaps a bit brash, but Mark knew he had the talent to back up such statements.

Nonetheless, historians and fans of the sport will debate both sides of the "What If?" question for as long as people reminisce about that special week. What if Steve's lung hadn't collapsed? What if he had been healthy? Would Mark still have made history? Steve himself is uncertain. His response when posed the question honestly reflects the impossibility of predicting the outcome based on an alternate scenario. "You have to understand that Mark was an incredible athlete. He had so much speed," he admitted. But with a hint of confidence in his voice even still about his own ability, he continued, "All I can say is, if my lung had not collapsed, Mark would have had to swim a little faster to get the gold medal."

Indeed, contrary to the 1968 Olympics, Mark was in rare form—utterly unique form, as it turned out—and had a great attitude to match. On top of his game physically and mentally, the ominous adversary firmly believed his competitors could do no better than second place. Mark could shift into another gear virtually at will. The incredibly gifted athlete possessed, more so that week than at any other time in his career, the impenetrable defense of supreme talent, perfect training, emotional stability, and an unfaltering belief in himself.

The persistent questioning is a waste of breath for another, more simple reason than Mark's prowess: He won. Unless you are playing Frisbee in a 1960s-style hippie commune, there is only one winner, and an athlete's hardship doesn't matter. It just adds to the drama. Although some people pontificate on whether the outcome might have been different under other circumstances, events aren't postponed because conditions aren't perfect for an unlucky or unprepared contestant. You win in the pool, on the track, and in the arena on the day of competition. There is no "feel good" committee to award medals or advance athletes to the winner's podium if they had a bad moment, a mistimed taper, or a medical emergency. Would Mark have done better in 1968 if he didn't have tonsillitis? Probably, but no one suggested that the swimmers who beat him had tarnished medals. Would Steve have swum faster but for his medical condition? Maybe, but no one knows how much faster, or if the faster time would have been enough to disrupt destiny.

No one can deny that Steve accomplished an amazing feat. International Hall of Fame swimmer Murray Rose, an Australian working as a commentator for ABC, called the swim heroic. Indeed, it is hard not to look at Steve with admiration. He badly wanted to beat Mark. It was a great performance, just not a gold medal performance.

♥♥♥

Mark had bristled at the assertion that he tried to use Genter's difficult circumstance to gain an advantage. Although they had been competitors for years, he generally liked Steve and felt bad about his untimely setback. Further, as almost everyone knew, Mark was a bit of a hypochondriac, and such matters were of great interest to him.

Wanting to clear both his conscience and the air between the swimmers, Mark found Steve after the race to defend his prerace comment that it was medically risky for Genter to compete. Steve accepted Mark's explanation, later telling a reporter that he had misunderstood Mark's original sentiment. Many thought Steve was just being diplomatic, but without another word spoken between the two about the matter, the door was shut on that controversy in the minds of its two primary subjects.

The drama surrounding the 200-meter freestyle, however, was not over. Still left was the awards presentation, known more for pomp and circumstance than for scandal and contention. The scene rarely changes: the top three finishers dress in their country's warm-ups and climb the podium, waving to the adoring crowd, accepting their medals, listening to the gold medalist's national anthem, and taking a victory lap around the pool deck. The ceremonies are almost never controversial, but the events surrounding this one almost eradicated Mark's golden streak.

Following his two finals that night, Mark warmed down, stretched, relished his accomplishment, and gathered his thoughts for about twenty-five minutes before receiving his medal. On this night, though, the timing was unexpectedly altered, and the presentation took place almost immediately after the race. When Mark eased out of the pool, a staff member rushed him to the holding area to retrieve his clothes—an official USA sweatsuit and a pair of Adidas shoes. As Mark hurriedly put on his sweats, he noticed three young German girls walking toward the podium carefully holding the medals perched on top of small pillows. Without time to close the ankle zippers on his pants, let alone put on his shoes, he grabbed the Adidas and joined the procession to the platform, behind which he placed the sneakers out of the spectators' sight.

The crowd cheered loudly when the public address announcer, with his thick German accent, identified the winner as "Machk Schpitz." With three quick gold medals, Mark was becoming the star of the Olympics, and Germany, ruled just a quarter century earlier by the world's deadliest anti-Semite, was beginning to embrace this Jewish-American champion.

Following the ceremony, FINA president Dr. Harold Henning paraded the medalists around the pool for fans to celebrate one last time. In front of the main stands, Henning stopped, grabbed Mark's right hand, and raised it in a victor's salute. When the crowd erupted with roaring cheers and thunderous applause, Henning looked at Mark and said, "Acknowledge your fans." Mark raised his left hand, again holding the shoes he had yet to find time to put on, and waved in appreciation. That simple act of following the instructions of the sport's highest official in the world unleashed a maelstrom that became Mark's most formidable opponent at the Games.

The next day, after seeing photographs of Mark and his shoes in the newspapers, the Russians filed a grievance questioning Mark's amateur status. They claimed his shoe-clutching wave was an overt attempt to advertise for Adidas, which they believed had paid Mark under the table to shake his sneakers and their distinctive three-stripe logo for an impromptu advertisement and thus an implied endorsement by a very popular and successful athlete. While this would not warrant a second thought in this era, when superstar athletes earn more money through endorsements than they do through winnings, it was a huge issue in 1972. Athletes at the Munich Olympics were expected to be pristine amateurs. The IOC enforced simple but strict rules on sponsorships and acceptance of money. Athletes could do nothing to cash in on their athletic fame. The consequences—being stripped of their medals and banned from future Olympic competitions—were harsh and virtually immutable.

Mark was stunned and frightened. He knew there was nothing to the charges, having purchased the well-worn shoes in California nine months earlier. His only experience with any shoe company was accepting free Adidas and Puma sneakers that had been openly distributed at the Olympic Village with the IOC's apparent approval. However, rumors were swirling that those companies had been quietly stuffing cash into the pockets of track athletes, and Mark was concerned he would be made a scapegoat.

"It didn't make sense that a track shoe company would pay to be associated with a swimmer," Mark reasoned. "But I was becoming one of the better known athletes at the Games, and I was afraid that group of old men who ruled the IOC wanted to make a strong statement by nailing a highly visible athlete."

Mark was called before the IOC Eligibility Committee, accompanied by Ken Treadway, the U.S. Swimming team manager. Reminded shortly before the hearing that IOC president Avery Brundage had stripped Austrian skier Karl Schranz of his gold medals at the recent 1972 Winter Olympics because Schranz had a consulting agreement with a ski company further tested Mark's nerves. Most of the top skiers had such contracts, but Brundage had wanted to make an example out of Schranz and singled him out.

Mark presented his case, recounting when and where he'd purchased the shoes and presenting them to the committee to show their wear. When asked why he was not wearing the new red shoes Adidas had passed out, the color-conscious fanatic replied in true fashion, "Blue represents winning. Red represents second place."

Once he had submitted the evidence, Mark abruptly switched from defense to offense. Addressing the Australian, he challenged, "Shane Gould held up a koala bear after she won an event. Isn't that the mascot of Qantas Airlines?" Confronting the Swede, he questioned, "Gunnar Larsen held his shoes above his head when he won. Wasn't that an endorsement?"

Brundage seemed to be the least pleased member of the panel, even after the pointed defiance. The eighty-four-year-old patriarch knew corporations put great pressure on athletes to jeopardize their medals for money, increasing friction regarding the sanctity of amateurism in the Olympic Games. Looking directly at Mark, he revealed, "You may not realize it, but these companies would have paid you $100,000 for what you did." The tone of Brundage's statement indicated the committee would reluctantly clear Mark of any wrongdoing, but that wasn't the message Mark focused on at that moment. "All I could think of was, 'Wow! A hundred grand? That's a lot of money. Maybe I'll take a deal. They can have the medals back.'"

After the ruling, some committee members switched roles from powerful, authoritative administrators to star-struck autograph-seekers. Mark appeased their requests, but when asked by reporters how the hearing went, he replied insolently, "I don't know. I think they just wanted to meet me."

When Mark went to bed that night, his last thought was about Brundage's comment. The stuffy old man had made Mark wonder whether any deals would come his way should he keep winning gold medals. Suddenly, it was Mark thinking "What if?"

CHAPTER 12

!!!

HUMP DAY

BEFORE MARK could cash in on unprecedented success, though, he had to win at least two more races. Don Schollander's quarry of gold from the 1964 Tokyo Games set the bar at four, and Mark's collection in Munich totaled three. Hump Day, then, arrived on a Thursday. August 31 was the fourth of seven days on which Mark would swim, and he would be attempting to collect his fourth and fifth of a potential seven gold medals. A win in either the 100 fly or the 800 free relay would tie his boyhood idol and adolescent adversary. A win in both would make history. Schwimmhalle fans, Olympic journalists, and the hundreds of millions of people watching on television around the world buzzed at the possibility.

Mark enjoyed swimming the 100 fly more than any other race. The stroke was his forte, the distance his favorite. At 100 meters, it's an obvious sprint. But with the world record three seconds slower than the 100 free, it's less frenzied and stressful, producing fewer flukish results. But the event would be taxing. Thirty-eight other qualifiers would join Mark in the preliminaries on Wednesday morning, with the top sixteen advancing to the semifinals that evening. The fastest eight would swim for the medals in the evening session on Hump Day.

In 1968, Mark's nemesis in the race was Doug Russell. Russell's retirement in 1970 after the NCAA Championships, at which Mark avenged the Olympic loss, eliminated that threat to Mark's historic run. But East Germany's Roland Matthes took his place as the athlete who gave Mark most pause. Matthes was best known as a backstroker—he hadn't lost an international backstroke race at any distance since 1967—but he was also a superb butterflyer, almost upsetting Mark at a U.S.-Germany dual meet a year earlier. "Matthes had a very smooth butterfly stroke, and I remember being surprised at how much speed he could generate," Mark recalled. "I really had to finish hard beating him at that meet. I won, but he sent me a message."

In the Munich preliminaries, Mark and Canada's Bruce Robertson both posted a 56.45, almost two seconds slower than world-record pace but more than four-tenths faster than Heidenreich's 56.86, the only other athlete under 57 seconds. Matthes took his 57.16 into the semifinals as the fourth qualifier, with Edgar next in 57.30. Each of the top five won his heat, and it took a fairly fast 58.37 to make the first cut, a time that would have placed fifth in Mexico City.

The semifinals proceeded true to form. Matthes won the first semifinal, lowering his time by about half a second to 56.51, and Mark followed suit in the second with a 55.98. Heidenreich gave Mark no breathing room, taking advantage of his placement in Mark's heat to post the second-fastest time in 56.18. Robertson qualified fourth in 56.86, with Edgar, East Germany's Harmut Floeckner, Canadian Byron MacDonald, and Australian Neil Rogers completing the field of finalists. Mark swam a leisurely lap to warm down, alternately swimming backstroke and breaststroke, then got out of the pool, done for the day.

Mark's prospecting for gold captured the public's intrigue and imagination as to the heights to which one athlete could rise. Mark's star status made the swim finals the hottest ticket at the Olympics, with scalpers peddling the $12 tickets for three to four times the face value. But another athlete competing at the same time captured their hearts as well. Belarus gymnast Olga Korbut captivated the worldwide audience during the team competition, her gritty performance on the uneven parallel bars accompanied by genuine joy unseen in other Eastern Bloc athletes. The seventeen-year-old, in her first major international competition, led Belarus to the team gold and appeared ready to storm the all-around competition on August 30. The sudden popularity played havoc on her nerves and focus, though, and she stumbled to seventh, due in part to the same event that catapulted her to fame. Ironically, the loss only intensified the public's fascination with her, again because of her inability or unwillingness to bottle her passion, weeping after that performance.

In many ways, Korbut and Mark stood at opposite ends of the spectrum. The gymnast came into the Games a relative unknown and became an overnight sensation. The swimmer's gigantic legacy preceded him. She charmed the world with her expressiveness despite few credentials, helping bridge the gap of tension between conflicting countries during the Cold War. At her age, he exuded polarizing arrogance and brashness as a loner, an image his high-profile accomplishments hadn't completely overcome.

But they were also quite similar. Both entered their first Olympics in their late teens. Both spoke their minds, although Korbut's had only been heard as an insistent—or, rather, inevitable—revolutionary of the sport, at odds with a static-minded Belarus gymnastics system. And both delighted crowds on Hump Day. The four-foot, eleven-inch, eighty-five pounds of effervescence finally broke through to win golds on the balance beam and floor exercise, adding a silver in the uneven parallel bars. Mark, meanwhile, faced a packed, highly expectant crowd at Schwimmhalle waiting to catch a glimpse of history.

That the German public and local press so genuinely embraced the Jewish swimmer perhaps provided a subtle sign that the country's rehabilitated image wasn't merely governmental theatrics at work. It would have been hard to mandate and then manufacture that level of authentic excitement only twenty miles southeast of Dachau, home to the Third Reich's longest-running concentration camp and the prototype for many others. From 1933 to 1945, the infamous camp imprisoned about two hundred thousand men, women, and children from more than thirty countries—direct and theoretical political opponents, Jews, gays, gypsies, priests, and deported prisoners from other European countries. One third of the prisoners were Jewish, and between twenty-five thousand and thirty thousand perished from disease, malnutrition, suicide, and execution. The second camp liberated by British or American troops, Dachau became the face of the Holocaust after journalists reported firsthand the torment and anguish that occurred there. Replacing that image of Germany in the world's collective mind with peaceful festivities ranked high as a major goal of the "Happy Games."

That perfectly described the atmosphere at Schwimmhalle on Hump Day, the crowd chattering enthusiastically before the race. Even though Heidenreich shadowed Mark in the semifinals, Matthes still concerned him more. Heidenreich certainly had impressive speed, but Mark had grown a bit complacent about him, having defeated him dozens of times in the past. Mark would later say after Heidenreich's death, "There is always somebody that makes somebody else great, and Jerry Heidenreich was the reason I was great."

The spectators quieted respectfully as Mark and the seven other finalists climbed up on the starting blocks but then erupted the moment the starter's gun sounded. Matthes got off to an incredibly slow start, immediately losing half a second to Mark, who only got a decent jump. Edgar, however, shot to an early lead. Halfway through the first lap Mark ratcheted up the speed, reaching the turn first with a 25.38 split and a half-body lead over Edgar. Heidenreich in third set up a potential American sweep.

Shortly after the turn, Matthes, Rogers, and Edgar made short-lived moves, but all three faded to various degrees in the end. With ten meters to go, Robertson closed with a brilliant sprint to overtake Heidenreich in the race for the silver, but nobody could catch Mark, who finished with a new world record of 54.27. Matthes, unable to overcome his poor start, finished fourth, followed by Edgar, MacDonald, Floeckner, and Rogers.

‼‼‼

Mark had only an hour to absorb tying Schollander's record of four golds at one Games before the 800 free relay final. In the preliminary heats that morning, the U.S. team of Gary Conelly, Tom McBreen, Mike Burton, and John Kinsella lowered the Olympic record, but of that grou, only Kinsella would swim in the final with Mark, Fred Tyler, and Steve Genter, the comeback kid of the Games. Like in the 4x100 relay prelims, Conelly was the fastest American, this time by more than three seconds. But under U.S. rules, once an alternate always an alternate, unless another swimmer is unable to swim.

Days earlier, the possibility of competing in the final not only of the 800 relay but also in the 200 freestyle seemed great because of Genter's collapsed lung, and Conelly had understandably gotten excited. Afterward, though, he was upset with himself for having such opportunistic thoughts at the expense of Genter's misfortune. "Nobody wants to win a medal that way, and if I had won a medal because of Genter's medical condition, I would have never felt good about it," Conelly said. So, instead of celebrating a gold with his relay teammates and what could have been an individual bronze based on his prelim time, Conelly watched from the stands empty-handed. Years later he was philosophical about his Olympic experience. "Ultimately, you swim for your own satisfaction and sense of accomplishment. In the morning, when I dove in, I was borderline depressed and not focused. The first 100 meters was mediocre, but when I hit the 100 mark, I had a bit of an epiphany about why one really swims, so I swam a pretty good back half. In the end, I learned a great deal about myself and was happy with my Olympic experience."

In 1984, Robert Helmick instigated a rule change that recognized the importance of swimmers who competed in the relay prelims. As president of the United States Olympic Committee and secretary of FINA, Helmick convinced the organizers of the 1984 Summer Olympic Games to award those swimmers medals if their team finished in the top three in the final. Four years later, FINA formally approved the rule change before the Seoul Games. Ross Wales, a bronze medalist in Mexico City who subsequently became secretary of FINA, felt the policy was long overdue. "The athletes who swim in the morning but not in the finals contribute to the medal just like the basketball player or water polo player who gets in the game for only a few minutes to give a starter some rest," Wales reasoned. "The prelim swimmer's contribution is important. They must swim fast enough for their country to qualify, and they allow the swimmers in the finals to rest. Unfortunately for the Gary Conellys of the world, the rule change was not retroactive."

!!!

The crowd stirred restlessly during the early stages of the relay. Russian Igor Grivennikov edged out John Kinsella in the first leg, with West Germany's Klaus Steinbach just inches behind. Werner Lampe, bronze medalist behind Mark and Genter in the 200 free, quickly passed both Tyler and Viktor Mazanov of Russia to put West Germany up. Lampe looked strong the first 100 meters, his shaved head leading the way down the pool. (Out of the pool, he donned an obvious wig that heightened his odd appearance.) The Germans' lead was a bit surprising, even though they had been swimming well in front of the partisan crowd all week. Tyler made a valiant effort to catch Lampe, hanging right by his shoulder, but the Floridian couldn't catch him and Lampe finished a half body length ahead, allowing Hans Vosseler to dive in ahead of Genter. By that time, it was a two-team race, with Russia and Australia battling for third. When the Australian team did not challenge for the lead, Murray Rose concluded that they had "overtrained and were swimming tired."

Genter wasted no time pushing ahead of Vosseler and taking control of the race. Stroke by stroke, he lengthened his lead over the German so that by the time he gave way to Mark, the Americans led by more than two body lengths. West Germany's anchor, Hans Fassnacht, had no chance to catch Mark, whose long, smooth strokes put even more distance between the U.S. and the host team. With fifty meters to go, ABC's Keith Jackson and Murray Rose knew they were calling a momentous occasion.

> *Jackson:* Of course, right now the whole story is Mark Spitz. The fact that we might get a new world record, the fact that we're almost certain to get a new Olympic Record, they almost become incidental to Mark Spitz, who now leads the German, Hans Fassnacht, by at least three body lengths. The story on Mark Spitz: If he continues to lead and the American team wins, Mark will win his fifth gold medal. Only one man has won four gold medals in one Olympic Games. That was an American swimmer, Don Schollander, the blonde bullet from Oregon. But here is Mark Spitz, suave, sophisticated, and in the opinion of some, outright arrogant, but supremely gifted as an athlete, supremely confidant as an athlete and as a person.

And here he is cruising easily, way out in front, headed for what will be history in the Olympic Games. He leads Hans Fassnacht, the German, by about three body lengths, or roughly twenty feet.

Rose: And he is a confident man, but I don't think Mark was always that way. It's only in the last year or two that we've seen Mark Spitz confident as a swimmer.

Jackson: He was maligned, no question about it, after what happened to him in Mexico City, but only because youthful enthusiasm had put him into a corner. He wasn't quite ready for it, but here he is. As his coach at Indiana, Dr. James Counsilman, says, now he comes to the Olympic Games as a man, and oh my, is he ever proving it!

The crowd erupted. The Americans finished in 7:35.78, crushing the world record by an incredible eight seconds. West Germany finished in 7:41.69, which would have been a world record but for the American feat. Genter's 1:52.72 bettered his 1:53.73 time in the open 200 free a few days earlier. While the two races aren't comparable because of the rolling start in the relay, his was the fastest swim of the evening by more than three-quarters of a second over Lampe. Each of his teammates clocked a 1:54-plus to outpace every other swimmer in the final. The Russians won the bronze, holding off a late Swede surge, followed by Australia, East Germany, and Canada.

As Mark caught his breath during a few warm-down meters of the breaststroke, reality slowly began to seep into his consciousness. He just topped his idol, Don Schollander. Before the race, Mark had allowed himself to consider what it would be like to break the record. "Don was the god of Olympic swimming, and it seemed odd to be on the verge of passing him," he remembered feeling. "It seemed almost sacrilegious to think about it." Mark stopped, leaned on the yellow lane line, and stared into space, lost in the overwhelming enormity of what he had just done. He blocked out the crowd's cheers. He blocked out the other swimmers. He blocked out the feel of the water. For an instant, he was alone with his thoughts. After winning his first four medals in Munich, he had immediately raised his arms in triumph as a smile dominated his mustachioed face. This time, though, it was different. Rather than exaltation, he felt subdued and reflective. It was as if he knew instinctively that he had changed, that his place in the world of swimming had changed, and his demeanor as a brash, insolent adolescent had completed its transformation into a respectful man to be revered for decades to come as the greatest Olympic champion ever.

After a few moments, he regained his consciousness and raised his arms to celebrate and acknowledge the crowd. He finally had caught up to his own legend.

CHAPTER 13

❗❗❗

HISTORY IS MADE

JUST TWO EVENTS remained on the program in Mark's pursuit of perfection. The 100 freestyle and the 4x100 medley relay accounted for up to four races over the next four days. Even taking Friday—his only day off—out of the equation, the rest of Mark's Olympic schedule was pretty light after starting the Games with nine races in the first four days. The 100 free prelims and semifinals were Saturday morning and evening, with the final Sunday evening. The relay prelims were scheduled for Monday morning, though Mark wouldn't swim them, and the final wrapped up the entire competition on Monday night. While the relaxed timetable gave Mark's body its first opportunity to rest and restore some of its energy reserves, it had the opposite effect on his mind.

For more than three days, Mark's focus on the races at hand had driven out a nagging concern about the 100 freestyle. The least predictable race in swimming also happened to be Mark's weakest. He'd set "only" two world records in the event entering the Games, compared with three in the 200 free, six in the 100 fly, and eight in the 200 fly. Nationally, he owned fewer 100-meter freestyle titles (two) than in the other races, with three in the 200 fly, four in the 200 free, and six in the 100 fly.

He'd taken the bronze in Mexico City, and at these Olympics, the field was threateningly stacked. Defending champion Michael Wenden of Australia hoped to avenge his fourth-place finish in the 200 free, which he'd won in 1968. Russia's Vladimir Bure showed capacity for speed in the 400 freestyle relay earlier in the week, turning in a 52.26 split in the final. Most unnerving, though, was teammate Jerry Heidenreich. Mark couldn't shake from his mind Heidenreich's own relay performance in which the SMU Mustang outswam Mark for the first time ever. That breakthrough and Heidenreich's mounting discontentment at losing to Mark over and over again caused memories of Doug Russell to bubble to the surface of Mark's consciousness. Heidenreich was really dangerous. A minor mistake at any stage of the race could leave Mark with a silver medal, or worse.

As he walked toward Schwimmhalle Friday morning with nothing but a brief workout to occupy him, Mark's confidence wobbled so much he seriously considered sitting out the race. He'd cemented his reputation as the most successful Olympic swimmer ever the night before, and America's overwhelming domination in the 4x100 medley relay virtually assured him of a sixth gold medal. A clean slate of gold sounded better than risking the supposed tarnish a silver or bronze medal would inflict on his 1972 collection.

After the workout, Mark shocked fellow Hoosier Gary Conelly during a conversation on the pool deck by blurting out that he might not swim the 100 free. "Mark looked at me with a smile and said, 'Boy, can you imagine how the press would have a field day if I didn't swim tomorrow,'" recalled Conelly. "I looked him in the face and told him that skipping the 100 would be an incredibly dumb thing to do. His only response was 'Yeah, maybe.'"

Later that day, Mark casually mentioned to head coach Peter Daland that he might not enter the event's prelims. Daland somehow contained his astonishment and calmly asked why not, to which Mark replied that he'd hurt his back on a racing car simulator installed in the Olympic Village for the athletes' amusement. Suspicious but not wanting to grovel or give Mark the impression he was more special than anyone else, Daland replied, "Well, I guess you have the right not to swim, but having come all this way, I think you should."

The feigned nonchalance ended when the two separated. A concerned Daland rushed to find Sherm Chavoor, again needing a quick intervention to keep Mark—and the U.S. team's goals—on track. "Sherm approached me about it, and he wasn't pleased," Mark said with a chuckle. "First he challenged me, asking why I didn't want to prove that I was the best athlete in the history of the Olympic Games by winning seven gold medals. I told him I'd already beaten Schollander's record and six was fine. Then he asked me if I was afraid to swim against Heidenreich. I told him I wasn't, but in my heart, I knew that if I had a bad turn or slow start, Heidenreich would be on top of the podium instead of me. Sherm got me, though, when he said the whole world would think I was a chicken if I didn't swim. I knew then that I had no choice."

Mark easily qualified for the semifinals, but his effort in the prelims did little to boost Chavoor's confidence in his protégé. Wenden (52.34) and Heidenreich (52.38) both posted times faster than Mark's (52.46), and Wenden's victory over Mark in the seventh heat was the first time Mark hadn't touched the wall first in Munich. Bure, Klaus Steinbach of Germany, and France's Michel Rousseau lurked within striking distance less than a half-second back.

That evening, Mark again swam more than fast enough to advance to the final with a 52.43, but not fast enough to ease Chavoor's anxiety. Wenden out-touched Mark in the second semifinal, recording a 52.32, and Heidenreich won the first semifinal a fingernail faster in 52.31. Bure and his countryman, Igor Grivennikov, posted times within seventeen-hundredths of a second of Mark's. Rousseau, Steinbach, and American John Murphy rounded out the field less than a second behind the leader.

All eight had a chance of being the fastest man in the world. Seven had a chance to break Mark's golden streak. And

Chavoor thought one wasn't taking the event seriously. "After the semifinals, Sherm came up to me and told me to stop fooling around," Mark remembered. "He complained that Heidenreich was swimming faster than me and wanted to know how in the world Wenden beat me again. I smiled and said, 'It's one thing to win in the heats, but it's the final that counts.' I think it gave Sherm some comfort to know that I didn't go all out in the heats. I had swum a 51.5 at the Olympic Trials, so I knew had the speed to win."

In reality, it seemed Mark was playing cat and mouse with Wenden and Heidenreich. Both had outswum Mark in the prelims and the semifinals, but neither seemed too confident in the ready room before the final on Sunday evening. Nobody else did, either, for that matter, except Mark. Everyone whirled their arms to warm up for the race, but nobody looked directly at Mark, their eyes darting everywhere but at him. It reminded Mark of baseball players not discussing their pitcher's possible no-hitter for fear of jinxing him. In this case, it appeared as if they believed by not making eye contact, he simply wouldn't exist.

What a difference four years makes. In 1968, Mark's first experience in a ready room before a final in an individual event—coincidentally, the 100 free—unnerved him. Now, in his last staging room before a final in an individual event, Mark enjoyed the tension. "For me, the ready room was like an execution chamber for the other swimmers," Mark explained. "Every time I left that room, they died, I won a gold medal, and my load got lighter. I was also very aware of the fact that every time I swam a race, it would be the last time I swam that event," having determined before the Games that this would be the end of his storied career, regardless of the outcome.

As the eight finalists paraded to the starting blocks, Mark hardly heard the roaring crowd. His focus centered on Chavoor's race instructions, which called for a different tactic than normal. "He told me that Heidenreich always got to the wall first, but this time he wanted me to use my speed to lead from start to finish," recalled Mark. "That made a lot of sense to me, because I'd been swimming in the Olympics for about a week and didn't think I had the stamina left to finish really fast." Chavoor also told Mark to swim the last lap toward the left side of the lane so Heidenreich couldn't draft in Mark's wake.

The crowd noise subsided as the announcer began what might have been the oddest introductions of the meet. Steinbach was identified as the swimmer in lane one, and his wave to the crowd was the last normal act for several lanes. Bure, in lane two, bent down, scooped up two handfuls of the chlorinated pool water, poured them in his mouth, looked to the ceiling as if gargling, and then gulped the water after he was introduced. When Mark was called to lane three, he absentmindedly began to walk to lane four, reserved for the fastest qualifier. He quickly realized his mistake and altered course, then nervously smoothed his thick mustache with his fingers as if that would make him more hydrodynamic. A jittery Heidenreich acknowledged the crowd quickly before immediately jumping in the diving pool behind lane four to ease his tension. Wenden simply stood stoically behind the block in lane five when his name was called. "I may have looked impassive, but it was a mixture of concentration and worry. I was concerned that I was tired and may have taken it out too hard in the prelims and semifinals," said the defending Olympic champion. Grivennikov, Rousseau, and Murphy responded in unassuming ways from lanes six, seven, and eight.

Even though Heidenreich and Wenden were the top qualifiers, all eyes and cameras focused on lane three as the swimmers mounted the blocks. Mark and Heidenreich started well, but Mark set the pace after fifteen meters. By the turn, he had a quarter-body length lead over Heidenreich and Bure. At seventy-five meters, Bure held the second position, with Heidenreich, perhaps surprised that Mark beat him to the wall, in third.

Although Bure had slipped to about a half-body length behind, he had also drifted to the right side of his lane to take advantage of Mark's draft and stroked furiously in an attempt to close the gap. With fifteen meters to go, Heidenreich and Murphy rallied desperately as Mark realized Bure's tactic and quickly moved toward the center of the lane to eliminate the Russian's free ride. Murphy, who could be mistaken for a tight end in football, recalls his surge. "There is obviously a lot of tension being in an Olympic final, but not so much for me. I was just happy to be there. On the final lap, I looked to my left and saw that I was in the race, so I went all out. I didn't quite have the speed to catch Bure or Heidenreich, but it was exciting," he said.

All the drafting, surging, and eccentric pre-race girding, though, did the seven challengers no good. Heidenreich's last-second expenditure came up short. Bure failed to seriously threaten without the benefit of Mark's wake, despite his pre-race mouth-washing technique. Wenden swam as dispassionately as he responded to the crowd. "I had overtrained, and the workout regimen for the Australian team was really more beneficial for the middle-distance swimmers than us sprinters," Wenden recalled.

Destiny, not to mention talent, sided with Mark. Setting his sixth world record in as many events with a 51.22, Mark added another notch to his historic week. His six gold medals set an Olympic record as the most won by any athlete at a single Games, surpassing Italian Nedo Nadi's five gold medals in fencing at the 1920 Olympics in Antwerp. Heidenreich finished second in 51.65, holding off Bure (51.77). Murphy settled into fourth place with a 52.08 after qualifying seventh out of the prelims and eighth out of the semifinals, while Wenden barely managed fifth, touching three-hundredths of a second ahead of Grivennikov. Rousseau and Steinbach battled to keep from finishing last, a race won by the Frenchman by two-hundredths of a second.

Mark's low-key reaction paled in comparison to the animated Bure, who ecstatically celebrated his bronze-medal performance by repeatedly slamming his fists on the water, lane line, and pool wall in rapid succession. After two Olympics in which he'd won three relay medals, this was his first individual medal. When Mark looked over at the exuberant and frenzied outburst, Bure lunged toward him with his right hand outstretched in congratulations and his left shaking three fingers to indicate his place. Nonplussed, Mark nodded his head and quickly turned to his right, accepting Wenden's hand and complimentary comments. Mark then shook hands with a disconsolate Heidenreich, who personified frustration.

"Winning the race was a big relief, but it wasn't as big of a moment as winning the fifth gold medal, because that was the one that surpassed Schollander," Mark relived. "To me, six was just one more than five."

❗❗❗

On Monday, September 4, the final day of swimming competition, noisy spectators jammed Schwimmhalle to capacity to witness the final chapter of Mark's incredible saga. Lenore, Mark's mother, quietly sat smiling next to actor Kirk Douglas and his wife, Anne. Arnold stood confidently next to her, a smile advertising his swelling pride over his son's accomplishments and his confidence that Mark would cap the week victoriously. Like 1968, Nancy and Heidi watched the Olympics on television at home. "My parents couldn't afford for all of us to go. Many people think the Olympic Committee pays for family members to attend the Olympics, but they didn't," recalled Nancy. "Still, it was incredible to watch my brother win race after race. Heidi and I would scream and jump up and down each time he won."

Johnny Weissmuller, the most popular Tarzan and an Olympic legend in his own right, sat a few seats down with his sixth wife, Maria. Both looked a bit "Hollywood," wearing oversized, blue-tinted sunglasses in the indoor facility, but broad smiles exposed their anticipation of a historic race. Mark's triumphs prompted the media and public to discuss Weissmuller's exploits. The original golden boy of swimming had won three gold medals in 1924 at the Paris Games and two more four years later in Amsterdam. A bronze medal in water polo in 1924 and his vigor in Tarzan's make-believe jungle confirmed his tremendous athleticism. The sixty-eight-year-old liked the renewed attention, but drawing accurate comparisons between Mark and him is difficult. In an era in which records could be set in a myriad of distances, Weissmuller broke sixty-seven world standards and won fifty-two national championships. Also, when Weissmuller swam, workouts typically consisted of less than a thousand yards, as opposed to the ten thousand or more of the seventies.

After waiting politely through the finals of the men's 1500 freestyle, women's 200 butterfly, and men's 200 backstroke—in which no Germans competed for the hometown fans to cheer—the crowd roared to life just after seven o'clock. The final of the medley relay would be the last event for the Games and for Mark. "I kept thinking, 'Four laps to go, four laps to go, and my swimming career is over," said Mark. "We were heavy favorites. The Russians and East Germans were definite threats, but if we didn't do anything stupid to get disqualified, the race was ours."

Indeed. In the prelims that morning, the Americans swam three and a quarter seconds faster than second-place East Germany, a rather impressive margin. What made the performance astounding is the fact that the U.S. swam with four alternates against East Germany's four starters. Only three other teams made changes to its lineup for the final, and none more than two. The United States replaced the entire team with swimmers theoretically even faster than Mitchell Ivey, John Hencken, Gary Hall, and Dave Fairbank, who set an Olympic record eight hours earlier.

East Germany's Roland Matthes, the king of the backstrokers who won both individual events that week, smoked two-time silver-medalist Mike Stamm by more than a second and a half to lead off with a world-record-tying swim. Tom Bruce, who earlier had won silver in the 100 breaststroke, made up the time and then some with the fastest breaststroke split of the night against a solid effort by Klaus Katzur. Bruce handed Mark a slim, unexpected lead entering the butterfly leg, effectively reducing the race for gold to two teams. Butterflyer Hartmut Floeckner turned in the second-best fly of the race but was no match for Mark, who outpaced him by more than two seconds. The lead was a body and a half and the team was well under world-record pace when Mark gave way to Heidenreich, who added a body length and two seconds to the cushion for a world record of 3:48.16.

The standing ovation began for Mark's incomparable week. Seven swims, seven gold medals, seven world records. Keith Jackson described the feat as one that may never be broken again. In the stands, Kirk Douglas turned to Lenore and predicted, "Your lives will never be the same." Mark jumped out of the pool with only one train of thought: "No more swims! No more workouts! No more psych outs! I'm done!" Twenty minutes later, the crowd finally sat down.

That night, two *Sports Illustrated* representatives—photographer Heinz Kluetmeier and writer Jerry Kirshenbaum—treated Mark to a celebration dinner at Käfer-Schänke. The *SI* duo had earned a reputation for their excellent taste in restaurants, making them among Mark's favorite dining companions, and they did not disappoint on that landmark occasion. Anita Verschoth, a long-time *Sports Illustrated* reporter, who specialized in the Summer and Winter Olympics, and Kluetmeier's girlfriend joined them. The fashionable eatery bustled that evening when they arrived around 9:30 P.M., and virtually every patron immediately recognized the guest of honor. Some simply pointed out the Olympic hero to their dinner mates, while others offered congratulatory tributes. Mark didn't drink alcohol, but on that night, as the toast of the town, he needed no stimulants to enjoy the revelry.

After a long, leisurely, festive dinner, Kirshenbaum and Kluet-meier dropped Mark off at the Olympic Village around two o'clock in the morning. Nothing seemed out of order, but in the space of two hours and about a hundred yards, the first in a chain reaction of events would occur that made September 5, 1972, the most cataclysmic day in Olympic history.

‼‼‼

CHAPTER 14

"THEY'RE ALL GONE"

A NEAR-GIDDY mood enveloped the first week and a half of the largest, most elaborate, and most media-saturated Games ever staged at that point. West Germany brainstormed long, planned hard, and worked meticulously in an effort to cleanse the embarrassing stains that the 1936 "Nazi Games" had left on their nation. That overarching goal sprouted many tentacles. Organizers wanted every aspect of the Games to communicate and facilitate a carefree, harmonious atmosphere by embodying the public's desire for an uncomplicated world. They strove to break through the impersonal and overwhelming nature of the emerging electronic age, a quaint notion by today's standards but valid at that time. They sought to re-establish the Olympic ideals of an apolitical, commercial-free, amateur Games in which athletes competed for the pure pleasure of sport and countries accommodated those aspirations without seeking excessive nationalistic prestige.

The application of those goals manifested in a number of details obvious and subtle, benign and risky. Artists created pictograms, banners, flags, and personnel uniforms with happy colors and festive designs. Committees created ample leisure activities for athletes in the Olympic Village, including game rooms, movie and live arts theaters, and a disco. Architects designed the buildings—individually and as a group—to promote the relaxed socializing found in small communities rather than the bustling sprawl of suburbia. Gardeners transformed the deserted, debris-filled Oberwiesenfeld from a useless eyesore to a "natural" environment. In between sporting events, spectators could enjoy strolling through the hills and dales, relaxing at lakes and lawns. They even relegated roads and motor traffic to underground tunnels so as not to spoil the setting.

Experts disputed and derided the daring integration of landscape and architecture, but organizers were determined to give visitors an intimate, blithe experience with their surroundings, the feel of walking through a park, not a military institute. Aiding in that ambiance was the plan for security at the Games. In an idealistic effort to erase the image of Hitler's troops extolling German superiority, demanding deference, and overseeing the execution of six million Jews, organizers opted instead to trust that safety would grow out of a trusting milieu. In other words, they reasoned that facilitation of their anticipated mood would create a self-fulfilling prophecy. To this end, security personnel blended in with the crowd. Most patrolled the grounds unarmed, and many could be hoodwinked or sweet-talked into allowing unauthorized entrance. Some unlocked access points went unguarded because they were designated exits only, as if signs alone would keep miscreants out. The fence that enclosed and protected the athletes' village rose only six feet from the ground with no deterrents such as barbed wire on top or well-placed cameras on the perimeter. Athletes often scaled the wall during the night to avoid being caught out past curfew while security officers turned a blind eye.

World events at that time underscored the strategy's naiveté. Radical groups were using increasingly brutal means to support their political causes, and the Olympic Games offered a worldwide stage on which to attract attention. The Baader-Meinhof Group, a combatant leftist organization based in Frankfurt with links to radical Palestinian terrorists, had attacked American targets and public buildings in protest of the Vietnam War. The Red

Brigades, a terrorist group in Italy formed in 1969, advocated violence in pursuit of Marxist-Leninist class warfare by targeting and sabotaging Italian factories. The Israeli-Palestinian conflict simmered, each side claiming ownership to land occupied by Israel, and airplane hijackings had become so common that Israel placed air marshals on all El-Al flights. In the United States, demonstrations against the "conflict" in Vietnam became more and more hostile.

Amazingly, the casual approach worked well for ten days. But everything changed on the eleventh. Nirvana plunged into darkness.

Olympic Park consisted of three areas separated by two major roadways. Olympic Stadium, Olympic Hall, the aquatics facility, and several other sports stadiums and warm-up areas dominated the southern segment. A smaller section immediately to the north was shared by the Olympic Village on the east and numerous training facilities and the volleyball hall on the west. The press complex—tiny by comparison—occupied the northwest sector just beyond the major north-south thoroughfare.

Shortly after four o'clock on the morning of September 5, eight young Palestinian terrorists approached the wall at Gate 25a in the southwest corner of the Olympic Village. Dressed in athletic sweats with Arab country names emblazoned on them and carrying sports bags, they looked like Olympic athletes as they scaled the wall like countless others had done during the week. In fact, a group of mischievous Americans arrived at the gate about the same time and, innocently, helped who they thought were fellow athletes clamber over the wall. Once on the other side, though, the two groups separated in location and deed. The Americans went to their rooms. The fedayeen donned ski masks and pulled machine guns and grenades from their bags before quickly and quietly covering the eighty meters to their targets.

The Israeli contingent at the Olympics numbered twenty-eight athletes and officials. The majority shared five apartments in the three-story building at 31 Connollystrasse. The entire group had spent the evening in Munich watching a live performance of *Fiddler on the Roof* starring a renowned Israeli actor.

The eight commandos arrived first at Unit 1, which housed seven members of the Israeli staff. A scratching sound from outside the apartment alerted one of the men, a wrestling referee, who arrived at the door in time to see masked men and gun barrels before the terrorists burst in. Shouting *"HAVA TISTALKU!"* ("Take cover, boys!"), he valiantly barred the entrance with his hulking frame long enough for one coach to escape. As the invaders rounded up hostages, a wrestling coach attacked with a fruit knife, a move that drew a bullet to the face but did not kill him.

Inexplicably skipping Unit 2, which lodged five Israeli athletes, the incursion continued in Unit 3, where six Israeli athletes stayed. A weight lifter lunged for a terrorist's gun and later died of blood loss from the resulting fire while the bound hostages and ruthless militants looked on. The wounded wrestling coach charged again, this time disrupting a terrorist from firing at an escaping athlete. The bullet to his chest at close range killed him; the athlete survived.

In less than an hour, the terrorists had overcome and bound nine Israeli coaches, athletes, and officials. When the police arrived about an hour after the attack began, a terrorist dropped two pages of demands from a balcony on the second story of the complex. The document identified the group as members of Black September, Yasser Arafat's faction of the Palestine Liberation Organization and the most extreme. The auxiliary unit of the resistance movement was named not after the Olympic tragedy but to remember an event two years earlier in which the King of Jordan ordered tanks and armored cars onto the streets of Amman to bombard known and assumed Palestinian guerilla positions.

Primarily, they demanded the release of more than two hundred prisoners, most of whom were being detained in

Israel and including leaders of Baader-Meinhof. They also sought three planes to move the hostages to another country. If their 9:00 A.M. deadline was not met, the extremists would begin executing two hostages every thirty minutes. The Germans found themselves in a cruelly ironic situation. Jews were again being imperiled in their country. The fact that the antagonist came from beyond their borders mattered little to the officials harboring residual guilt from the Nazi regime. Their need and desire to consult often with officials in Jerusalem, especially early on, complicated matters.

The terrorists' demands were not well received by Israeli prime minister Golda Meir, who unequivocally refused to comply or negotiate. "If we should give in, then no Israeli anywhere in the world can feel that his life is safe." She advised the German government not to negotiate with the terrorists, knowing that giving in would only prompt them to ask for more. Israel also requested that its counterterrorism group take command of the crisis, but German officials denied the petition. The only concession Meir was willing to make was letting the terrorists leave the country, but only if the hostages remained.

Even with the crisis at high risk, few people knew about it for some time. Two hundred yards away, West Germany played Japan in volleyball. Ten other sports continued on as usual, including—incredibly—a few in which Israel had athletes. Not until ABC went live during the siege did word of the tragedy spread, and even then officials provided only fragmentary information to the press. Peter Jennings managed to gain access to the Village—the only reporter to do so—and Jim McKay anchored the coverage that broadcast live around the world. No one issued a warning to other Olympic Village residents, who were left to glean sketchy details from television news sources. Finally, IOC president Avery Brundage gave in to mounting criticism and suspended the Games at about 3:45 P.M. True to form, the insensitive octogenarian appeared unmoved by the human suffering unfolding before the horrified eyes of the world. The continuation of his beloved Games ranked higher than any mortal suffering. Afraid that the conflict would tarnish the Olympic image, Brundage—thinly veiled behind the IOC—intensely pressured German officials to somehow move the battle out of the Village.

The first deadline passed with no resolution except the setting of another deadline three hours later. First the police chief and then the chief negotiator separately confronted the extremists' leader in person, but most communication took place between the balcony and grounds below. The Germans convinced the terrorists that Israelis may be coming around to the idea of freeing their prisoners. Officials offered huge sums of money in exchange for the hostages but were refused. At one point, the courageous negotiators volunteered to exchange themselves for the hostages, but the terrorists declined the offer. Police considered at least three different tactics to liberate the hostages by force—sharpshooters on a nearby roof; through the basement; and under the guise of delivering food—but all were derailed for one reason or another.

Passersby did their part in antagonizing the militants and showing solidarity with the hostages as the mood went from the pre-attack frivolity and focus, to fear, to—once the crisis seemed to be contained—fury. Athletes sporadically yelled at the radicals to put down their guns. A German Olympic hostess told the terrorists to leave the country without the hostages. Young Jews boldly sang "Hatikvah," Israel's national anthem, and the U.S. civil rights hymn "We Shall Overcome" nearby.

Negotiators managed to extend the deadline several times throughout the day, but as afternoon gave way to evening, the situation became more and more tense. The terrorists, concluding that Israel and Germany would not submit to their demands, offered an alternative—fly them and the hostages to a sympathetic Arab country in one plane, not the three originally requested. The German government feigned agreement but had no intention of acquiescing. Just past 10:00 P.M., the terrorists and captives bussed to two helicopters for the twenty-minute ride to the nearby Fürstenfeldbruck airfield, where a Boeing 727 awaited. Hoping to kill or capture the terrorists on the tarmac, the police hastily assembled a group of snipers positioned around the airfield buildings and undercover police on board the jet dressed as its crew.

The attack was poorly planned on a number of levels. Faulty intelligence indicated only five terrorists instead of eight, and only five snipers were dispatched to the airfield, an unreasonably low number for even five targets in a nighttime ambush. The snipers, at least one of whom didn't consider himself as such, turned down night-vision goggles because they had not been trained to use them. Their rifle barrels were shorter than recommended for the distances from which they'd be firing, their positions were unknown to each other—one was inexplicably placed in another's line of fire—and they had no form of communication among them. An amateur could have guessed that the chances of a coordinated and successful rescue effort were minimal.

Making matters worse, if that were possible, the undercover officers voted to abandon the operation shortly before the helicopters arrived. They probably accurately assessed their position trapped on a ten-thousand-gallon gas can as untenable and simply weren't willing to expose themselves with little protection but a faulty plan.

Disaster predictably struck. Two terrorists guarded the helicopter pilots on the tarmac while another two inspected the plane. Sensing a trap, they ran back toward the choppers, at which point the ill-trained, isolated snipers opened fire in an uncoordinated effort. Two of the fedayeen died instantly, but a chaotic and gruesome battle ensued for about an hour. It ended when a terrorist tossed a hand grenade into one chopper, blowing up it and its helpless passengers, and another terrorist shot the Israelis on the other chopper at close range. In the end, eleven Israelis, five terrorists, and one West German police officer died. The other three terrorists ultimately surrendered.

Incredibly and rather immediately, rumors spread through reputable news organizations that the terrorists had been captured and the hostages freed despite no confirmation from German police. Some newspapers went so far as to go to press with the unsubstantiated account. Corks popped in celebration throughout Israel, and the world rejoiced at the remarkable news.

But the news was false. A few hours later, German authorities finally addressed the two thousand press members with the truth. After forty-five minutes of agonizing details about the conflict, they finally admitted that all of the hostages had perished. ABC had not broadcast the erroneous reports, and shortly after the press conference, Jim McKay updated American viewers by saying, "We've just gotten the final word. When I was a kid, my father used to say our greatest hopes and worst fears are seldom realized. Our worst fears have been realized tonight. They have now said that there were 11 hostages. Two were killed in their rooms this morning—excuse me, yesterday morning. Nine were killed at the airport tonight. They're all gone."

Eighty thousand people attended the memorial service in the Olympic Stadium later that September 6 morning, three days before Rosh Hashanah, the Jewish New Year and one of the holiest days in the Hebrew calendar. The crusty Brundage, in his final major act before his scheduled retirement after the Games, spoke to the crowd in characteristic heartlessness. He droned on about various attacks on the Olympic movement. His only reference to the hours-old massacre equated it with the "naked political blackmail" that resulted in Rhodesia's banishment from the Games because of their government's racial injustices, a decision Brundage resented. In his view, the issue at hand was how the bloodbath and the political boycott against Rhodesia had tarnished his glorious Olympic Games, not the suffering of the Israeli Olympic family.

Given the scope of the tragedy, many called for a halt to the Games, but the ever-predictable Brundage announced that the "Games must go on." Despite Brundage's history of bigotry, most agreed and strong applause greeted his announcement. The brief postponement of events ended at about four in the afternoon. An incredulous Israeli delegation protested by leaving the country. Athletes from Holland and Norway also refused to participate further, and many others agonized over their decision to continue. *Los Angeles Times* sports columnist Jim Murray complained, "Incredibly, they're going on with it. It's like having a dance at Dachau."

❗❗❗

About four hours after the terrorists breached the Village, Mark awoke in his apartment unaware of the melee. Content and at ease, though groggy after a hard week of swimming, a long night of celebrating, and a short morning of sleep, he prepared for the special press conference at which he would address the media for the first time during the Games. All week he had refused interviews, answering every inquiry with a short "No comment" to avoid the same mistakes he made in Mexico City. He was looking forward to talking freely and reveling in his status as the new golden boy of swimming.

During the preceding week, Mark only spoke to two reporters, Jerry Kirshenbaum of *Sports Illustrated* and Ray Kennedy from *Time* magazine. He liked Kirshenbaum and knew his comments wouldn't be printed in the weekly magazine until after his Olympic swims were over. He granted an interview with Kennedy as a favor to Kirshenbaum because of the same time lapse as long as Kirshenbaum joined them.

It was a godsend that Kennedy's article wouldn't hit the streets until after Mark was finished in the water. At a nice restaurant, Kennedy leisurely interviewed the swimmer while Kirshenbaum smiled at Mark's deft responses. The unprecedented string of levelheaded, tactful quotes was broken, though, in an imprudent moment at the end of the interview. Kennedy asked Mark if, as a Jewish athlete, he felt any irony about participating in the Munich Olympics. "Actually, I've always liked this country," Mark responded before tactlessly tapping his finger on a lampshade and adding, "even though this lampshade is probably made out of one of my aunts." Kirshenbaum sighed, knowing the ill-fated attempt at humor would be a setback to Mark's reputation. "I knew Mark meant that he recognized the irony, but his brazen sense of humor backfired," he later recalled.

Unaware of the hostage situation, Mark, Chavoor, and Daland walked jubilantly that morning toward the press center anticipating a hero's welcome. Mark wondered what questions would be posed to him: "What was it like being Jewish, competing in Germany?" "Did you think you could win seven gold medals?" "Will you still be going to dental school?" "What was your toughest race?"

When Mark, Daland, and Chavoor entered the press center, Kirshenbaum knew immediately that the trio didn't know what had transpired hours before. "They were smiling and joking with each other—acting in an inappropriate manner for the circumstances," said Kirshenbaum. He immediately rushed over to the trio and asked, "My God, you don't know, do you?" Startled at his demeanor and the number of media present, Mark asked, "Know what?" As Kirshenbaum briefed them, he realized that neither the USOC nor the Munich Organizing Committee had advised Mark of the situation or, given its gravity, canceled the press conference.

Mark, who had expected a couple dozen reporters to show up, suddenly realized the hundreds milling around were waiting for breaking news about the atrocity. Mark was no longer the story. The plight of the Israelis was far more significant. Chavoor, visibly upset, began arguing with a nearby Olympic official about getting Mark a bodyguard. Hearing that he needed a bodyguard made Mark uneasy. "My seven gold medals suddenly didn't seem so important. I began to wonder if I was a target and was angry that I was allowed to walk over to the press center without any protection," Mark recalled.

Tension seemed to compress the air around him. His mind began to wonder. He traced his movements from the night before. Did the terrorists see him being dropped off at the Olympic Village? Did he walk past them? Was he a target? If the terrorists were interested in relatively unknown Jewish athletes, wouldn't he be a better prize? Kirshenbaum later came to the chilling realization of the close proximity in distance of where they had left Mark about two hours before the attack in relation to where the terrorists jumped the fence. "One can only wonder whether they were milling around when we dropped Mark off that night," said Kirshenbaum.

As Mark was guided into the large, theater-like conference room, he winced as he overheard someone asking whether Mark might be a target. Although he had considered that very possibility a few moments earlier, hearing someone else say it out loud made it seem much more possible. He then recoiled at overhearing another person ask his companion if he thought a terrorist could be in the room. The whole scene was extremely unsettling.

As he waited, Mark panicked a bit when he it dawned on him that the assembled press would be asking him about the attack, not his Olympic achievements. He knew little about what happened and felt ill-prepared to answer the pointed questions reporters would surely hurl at him. He could hear Daland and Chavoor arguing with Olympic officials about whether Mark should even comment on the hostage situation, but nobody was stepping up to offer Mark advice. He turned to Kirshenbaum and asked him what to do. The reporter thought for a minute before telling Mark to expect the first question to be about what happened in the Village. He encouraged Mark to say what he felt but counseled that the worst thing he could say was, "No comment," as he had done all week.

Mark looked up to see four German security guards, rifles prominently displayed, taking positions in the press room. This did little to assuage Mark's distress as he was being tugged toward the speaker's platform. With every step he scanned the faces in the crowd and wondered if any belonged to terrorists.

Kirshenbaum's easy prediction about the nature of the first question came true. Ill-prepared, poorly focused, and still nervously searching the crowd for signs of danger, Mark lamely responded, "I think that it is very tragic. I don't have any other comment." Kirshenbaum cringed, but it got worse. Mark's mind blurred. He couldn't follow all of the questions, and his answers were disjointed. Kirshenbaum remembers a chaotic scene in which Mark looking very scared. A reporter returned to the hostage situation, asking, "You are a Jew. Jews are being killed. What does that mean to you?" Desperately searching for the right words, Mark blurted out, "I didn't come here as a Jew. I came to the Olympics as an American athlete, to represent my country, my teammates, and myself." Mark looked to the side and saw USOC officials nod with approval. He knew the answer was a bomb, but there was no coordination of the press conference and reporters kept shouting over each other, hoping their question would be the one caught by Mark.

Mercifully, the press conference ended, but Mark second-guessed his answers. "Why didn't I tell them that I know what it's like to be a Jew and that I had felt the sting of anti-Semitism? Why didn't I say something heartfelt about the poor people who had been murdered? Why didn't those SOBs at the USOC prepare me for this awful press conference?" he wondered. Nonetheless, he honored a previously scheduled interview with

Jim McKay on ABC television after producers promised that McKay would ask no questions about the hostages. McKay kept to the script, and the interview was largely uneventful.

Mark walked to a waiting van with Chavoor, Kirshenbaum, and Anita Verschoth, another *SI* reporter. Sherm kept muttering about getting protection for Mark, making Mark edgier and edgier. Abruptly, a man in a U.S. military uniform appeared. He looked Arabic, and Sherm brusquely demanded to see his identification papers. Once he assured Sherm of his loyalties, the soldier informed the group that he had been assigned to guard Mark for the day.

When the van reached the Olympic Village, the scene had totally changed. The grounds teemed with military and police. Soldiers with machine guns guarded the entrances and exits. Officers sealed off the entire village to anyone who didn't live there. Kirshenbaum and Verschoth hoped their affiliation with Mark might gain them access. No other reporters except Peter Jennings were inside the Village, and the opportunity for exclusive reports was attractive. A guard at the main gate asked for credentials, looked to see that the photographs matched the faces, and ordered Kirshenbaum and Verschoth out of the van. Mark protested, telling the guard, "It's okay—they are with me," but to no avail. The guard looked menacingly at the two and sternly repeated, "Get out!" Mark was the most recognizable athlete in the Village, but this meant nothing to the guard. Joviality had done an about-face.

When Mark reached his apartment, he looked around and counted eight guards in plain view. Remarkably, many of the athletes were still unaware of what had transpired. The German organizers made no attempt to tell the athletes what happened or advise them about what they should be doing, although the government soon requested that Mark leave the country immediately for his own good. He had planned to leave the next day anyway, and, in light of the situation, moving his travel up a day was a welcome relief. He packed his bags and waited in a small room with Chavoor and the military guard, watching the news on a small television. One report had Mark in Frankfurt. Another said he was out of the country. He wondered if the government had slipped that information to the press as a diversionary tactic. He didn't have a clue, but it made him feel better.

When Chavoor and Mark entered their London hotel room that evening, the standoff at the airport had not yet concluded. It wasn't until Sherm picked up a newspaper the next morning that they learned of the fate of the nine hostages in the badly bungled rescue attempt. Trying to lighten the mood, he said to Mark, "Boy, you're dangerous to be around." Mark closed his eyes, dropped his head, and tried to make sense of overwhelming triumph in his first eight days and then the previous twenty-four hours of what seemed like a continuous sucker punch. He found it hard to speak. The only response he could muster was "Not really," indicating the events still fogged his mind. He loved Israel and felt a special bond with the country and its people, and he felt guilty for even thinking about his gold medals. He'd competed twice in the Maccabiah Games and enjoyed the kinship he felt with the other Jewish athletes, a rare treat in his polarizing career. He wondered when, if ever, he would recover from the radical highs and lows of his Munich experience.

Fortunately, a busy and chaotic schedule would temporarily distract Mark from the tragedy.

CHAPTER 15

‼‼‼

IGN OF THE TIME$

STILL STUNNED by what they had just read, Mark and Chavoor were a bit rattled when the phone in their London hotel room rang. The German weekly news magazine *Stern* ("Star" in English) wanted to book a photo shoot with Mark before he left for the United States. Chavoor transformed from swim coach and mentor into agent and manager with his next words, roles for which he had little preparation other than having earned the trust of his swimmer/client. When Mark heard Chavoor start the negotiations at $10,000, his head started swimming. After a few minutes of haggling, Chavoor cupped his hand over the phone and asked Mark if he would accept $7,500. Nodding in dazed astonishment, Mark thought, "Wow! I've never seen that much money in my life. That's almost two years of tuition for dental school."

Chavoor and *Stern* arranged the shoot for later that day. Mark felt guilty posing in his red, white, and blue swimsuit with seven gold medals draped around his neck so soon after the bloodbath in Munich. But, he reasoned, he couldn't do anything for the victims, and the German government had virtually commanded him to leave their country before the situation's resolution, making him unable to attend the memorial service. Besides, passing up the whopping sum of seventy-five hundred bucks seemed irresponsible to the newly retired amateur.

The image emerged as perhaps the most iconic and enduring of Mark's storied life. *Stern* sold the photo to a company that printed it as a poster, and two million copies later it became the most popular poster in the world until Farrah Fawcett's likeness in a red swimsuit retailed eight million copies a few years later. *Stern* exposed Chavoor's inexperience in cutting the initial deal by offering a flat fee, and months later it took threats from Mark's attorneys to reach a fair, royalty-based agreement. Mark got fifteen cents for each poster sold.

The long, polar-route flight from London to Los Angeles gave both Mark and Chavoor time to contemplate the whirlwind of their lives. Mark tried to make sense of the horrific tragedy that occurred so close to him in terms of physical proximity and the frightening similarities between him and the victimized Jewish athletes. The shock and confusion dulled his senses on the Pan American jet until a random thought nudged him back into his current reality. The president of Daimler-Benz had offered Mark a Mercedes-Benz 450 SL as "a gift from the German people," which he was to have picked up in Stuttgart the day before. Instead, the Germans hastily swept him out of the country, and he wondered if he'd ever get the car. He didn't.

Then Mark remembered the two bags he hadn't let out of his sight since leaving the hotel. One held the photo-shoot cash, which made Mark feel daringly rich to carry. The other bulged with letters and telegrams he received in Munich. One invited him to be on *The Dick Cavett Show*, ABC's late-night opponent to Johnny Carson. Another wanted him to participate on *The Dating Game*. Ray Stark, a Hollywood film producer whose *Funny Girl* launched Barbra Streisand's career in 1968, sent a telegram that read: "HI. YOU ARE DOING A GREAT JOB FOR AMERICA. I'M CASTING A NEW MOVIE AND WOULD LIKE TO CONSIDER YOU FOR A PART. PLEASE CONTACT ME. RAY STARK." Most of the correspondence, however, came from agents begging to represent him, each claiming to know exactly how to capitalize on the swimmer's fame to create a fortune. Mark recalled Kirk Douglas's message to his parents—"Your lives will never be the same."—and began to realize it might hold some veracity. Chavoor looked from the bags to Mark and said, "You're going to be sitting around in luxury for the rest of your life." Mark just laughed—half nervous, half excited—but Chavoor continued, "Look, you nut. Just remember that I told you so."

By the time the plane landed in Los Angeles, Mark's thoughts focused on the future, but the bleak circumstances of the recent past remained on everyone else's minds. Secret Service agents steered Mark and Chavoor in a private car to the waiting Pacific Southwest Airlines plane for the final leg of their journey to Sacramento. Those agents would follow Mark everywhere for the next three weeks. As Mark and Chavoor boarded the plane, the duo quickly realized the flight would not be normal. Somehow, about a dozen members of the media learned of Mark's itinerary and purchased tickets in hopes of garnering an exclusive interview. The intense commotion surrounding Mark forced Chavoor to shout at the reporters to get back to their seats, assuring each an opportunity to spend time with Mark during the flight. Sherm then ushered the media two at a time to conduct their interviews. Creighton Sanders, a sportscaster from Sacramento, piqued the swimmer's imagination when he speculated on Mark's soon-to-be millionaire status. In an interview with the *Sacramento Bee*, Chavoor peered even further down the golden brick road and speculated that Mark's medals would translate into five million dollars in endorsements. Mark rolled his eyes at the astronomical sum, but Chavoor's prediction turned out to be amazingly accurate for a guy in his first and only week as an agent.

Back in Sacramento, representatives from numerous management agencies bombarded the Spitz residence. Almost daily, Mark returned home to find an agent talking with his parents, bragging about his current clientele and the bucketfuls of money he could bring Mark from endorsements and entertainment contracts. One day the pop singer Vikki Carr showed up with her husband and Hollywood agent Dann Moss. Meeting the singer impressed Mark, but Moss's lack of experience in the sports world prompted him to decline their offer.

Uncertain about how to proceed at such a critical juncture in his life, Mark called Mark McCormack, an attorney who represented sports figures such as Jack Nicklaus and Arnold Palmer. An aide in his New York office said that McCormack, on safari in Africa, couldn't return his call for at least a week and mentioned McCormack's fee of twenty-five percent. Stunned at the aggressive rate, Mark shared his feelings but nonetheless gave his number to the aide. A couple of days later McCormack called, saying he would be in San Francisco the following week and suggesting they meet at his hotel. Mark balked at the two-hour drive into the city, what with everyone else trekking to their house, and countered with a meeting at the Spitz home or at least a halfway point. McCormack seemed put off by the proposal, and the conversation sputtered to an end.

At first, the agents' interest flattered Mark, but he soon grew weary of their persistence and the strain of the decision looming over him. So when his mother mentioned that Norman Brokaw from the William Morris Agency rang, reminding Mark that Kirk Douglas spoke highly of the company, he sighed and thought, "Here we go again." But on the phone Brokaw didn't sound full of himself as others had, and he volunteered to fly from Los Angeles to Sacramento to meet with Mark and his parents. So far, so good. Mark's interest increased somewhat when research revealed that WMA, the largest theatrical agency in the world, also contained a small sports division. Brokaw further impressed Lenore during the trip in a spiffy suit with his initials monogrammed on the cuffs. His pitch, delivered in a likeable and straightforward style, sounded less like a spiel and more like the outline of a respectable partnership. When he unflinchingly responded to Arnold's blunt question that he personally would handle Mark's accounts, the Spitzes knew they had finally found their man.

V V V
○ ○ ○

Multimillion-dollar contracts, lucrative endorsements, and targeted sponsorships were unheard of in 1972, especially for swimmers. In those days, the term "amateur athlete" still had an authentic innocence about it, having yet to morph into an oxymoron. Had the new millennium's practice of compensating champions for their athletic exploits and lavishing those lucky enough to be marketable with millions for affixing their name or image to a product, Mark might have dominated the 1976 Olympics as well. But faced with the choice of swimming mind-numbing laps four more years or signing fat contracts, the twenty-two-year-old understandably picked the latter.

Almost instantly, it was clear that Mark could fashion an excellent living from endorsements under Brokaw's attentive and strategic direction. Mark earned $30,000 for a two-hour photo shoot. Schick paid him $50,000 to shave off his famous mustache for a television commercial, which evolved into a long-term contract worth six figures annually. Mark signed agreements with the California Milk Advisory Board and Adidas Swimwear. He promoted swim goggles and Spartan Pools, a swimming pool manufacturer, and he later added pharmaceutical companies to his portfolio. But when a brewing company presented a deal worth $250,000, Brokaw turned it down. "It's the wrong type of company for a hero," he told his initially incredulous client.

John Chancellor, anchor of *NBC Nightly News*, noted that "since [Mark Spitz's] return, he has attracted numerous offers. . . . According to Brokaw, the offers will lead to contracts worth five million dollars, which, when you divide by seven gold medals, comes out to $675,000 per medal. According to NBC's calculations, it is the largest paycheck for a single performance in history, considering that, at times, Spitz only swam for fifty seconds."

Chancellor exaggerated somewhat. Mark never swam for only fifty seconds. His seven winning performances ranged from 50.91 to 2:00.70, but that doesn't count his six preliminary races. All totaled, he swam about seventeen minutes and twenty-four seconds in Olympic competition in Munich, making his projected earnings about $287,356 per second. But that doesn't count his warm-ups and cool-downs in Schwimmhalle, nor the previous dozen years of his life in which he swam between two and four hours on the vast majority of days. When put into that context, his annual "salary" for twelve years of swimming and three of endorsement appearances came to "only" a third of a million dollars. To put $5 million dollars in perspective, according to Thomas Bussa, a partner in a "Big Four" CPA firm in Los Angeles, $5 million in 1972 would be worth over $26 million in 2008.

¡¡¡

Other swimmers had parlayed athletic success into income endorsing products. Joe Ruddy, who won gold medals in swimming and water polo in the 1904 Olympics, extolled the virtues of certain brands of toothpaste and vitamins. Johnny Weissmuller pitched, among other things, BVD swimsuits and beer, as did 1932 Olympic backstroke champion Eleanor Holm. Esther Williams, the 1939 national champion in the 100 freestyle and one of many athletes for whom World War II supplanted their chance for Olympic glory, cashed in on Corn Flakes and Canada Dry. Some even signed with cigarette manufacturers before the effects of tobacco came to light. Helen Wainwright, who won a silver medal at the 1920 Paris Olympics, claimed that Lucky Strikes didn't affect her wind or throat. Peter Fick, who broke Weissmuller's world record in the 100-meter freestyle in 1934, and 1932 Olympic silver medalist Harold Dutch Smith endorsed Camels.

No, Mark wasn't the first swimmer to earn money by pumping products, but he certainly raised the bar for himself and future sports stars. His early contracts netted a healthy seven figures at a time when minimum wage was $1.60 and a gallon of gas cost fifty-five cents. "Mark benefited from a confluence of events," explained Evan Morgenstein, president of the athlete representation company Premier Management Group. "Sure, he won seven gold medals, but the Munich massacre drew significant attention to him as well. That tragedy was the first terrorist act that affected the world in a global way, and as a Jewish athlete, Mark was swept up in the coverage of the event. Also, at the time, there were only three television stations, and the Internet was decades away, so there was a tremendous focus on Mark that will probably never be matched again by any athlete. All of this made Mark extremely marketable."

Bruce Wigo, CEO of the International Swimming Hall of Fame, agrees. "Even today, you can ask someone on the street if they have heard of Mark Spitz, and most people will know who he is. Today's greatest swimmer is Michael Phelps, but if you ask that same person who he is, you often get a blank stare."

Previous swimmers had laid the foundation for Mark to flourish in the entertainment industry. After the 1928 Olympics, Weissmuller became Tarzan. After the 1928 and 1932 Olympics, Buster Crabbe became Flash Gordon. Esther Williams starred in twenty-seven movies for MGM Films and Universal Studios in the 1940s and '50s.

With Mark's newfound fame, Brokaw and Mark's press agent, Jay Bernstein had no difficulty placing him on television. Although Mark failed to convince Ray Stark of his acting abilities, and thus did not appear in the box-office hit *The Way We Were* with Robert Redford and Streisand, he did appear on *The Bob Hope Special* in 1972, *The Sonny and Cher Comedy Hour* and

The Tonight Show Starring Johnny Carson in 1973, and *The Merv Griffin Show* in 1974. He roasted Ronald Reagan in 1973 and Jack Benny in 1974 on *The Dean Martin Show*. He guest-starred as a deranged husband who accidentally killed his wife on the weekly drama *Emergency!* in 1974, and he competed on the game show *Celebrity Sweepstakes* in 1975.

An especially enjoyable assignment involved cohosting the daily talk show *The Mike Douglas Show* for a week in March 1974 with signer Jaye P. Morgan and a last-minute performance by a young comic. "This guy was really good," Mark recalled. "The next day we received a lot of inquiries about him." Freddie Prinze hit the big-time within months, starring in the series *Chico and the Man* and comedy clubs before tragically taking his own life less than three years later.

But Mark's most important television appearance might have been *The New Bill Cosby Show* shortly after returning home from Germany.

$$\text{\bf !!!}$$

One early fall day in 1972, Bob Wicker, a heavy equipment salesman in the Bay Area, sat in Herman Weiner's office. The Jewish owner of Los Angeles-based Weiner Steel Corporation proudly displayed on his desk photos of his daughter, Suzy, a twenty-year-old part-time model and UCLA student. Wicker immediately recognized the star of television commercials for McDonald's, 7-Up, Chrysler, and Honda, and then a light bulb went off in his head.

"I know this couple in Northern California whose son just returned from the Olympics," Wicker started. "Maybe you've heard of him. Mark Spitz?"

"Of course I've heard of him," Weiner exclaimed. "Everybody knows who Mark Spitz is." When Wicker suggested that he take the photo composition to his friends' house to show Mark, though, Weiner hesitated. His beautiful daughter resisted the numerous matchmaking attempts by friends, much less strangers. But Wicker persisted, and Weiner consented.

Mark arrived home shortly thereafter to find Wicker in the living room talking with his parents about the Weiner family. He showed Mark the photographs and suggested he call on Suzy. The woman's long, flowing hair and pretty face appealed to Mark, but he, too, doubted the success of such a setup. Nonetheless, partly out of curiosity, partly out of respect, he called the Weiner residence. Herman answered the phone. Mark nervously identified himself and asked to speak with Suzy. She was at school, so Mark said he'd try back in a few days. Herman wavered on whether to give his daughter the message, anticipating her irritation, or anger, at the meddling arrangement. But the coed asked if anyone had called when she got home, and Herman came clean. "I was pretty excited, because Mark was a household name at the time," Suzy remembered. "When my father mentioned that he knew I didn't like to have dates fixed up for me, I told him 'That kind of fixing up I don't mind.'"

As fate would have it, Mark was due in Hollywood later that week to film an episode of *The New Bill Cosby Show*. When Brokaw heard about Mark's reticence about calling Suzy, he encouraged Mark to give it another shot. Herman answered the phone again, but as he offered to summon Suzy, she had already grabbed another handset and said, "I've got it, Dad."

Comments from her friends about Mark's conceited and arrogant reputation tempered the thrill that she was talking to America's hero, but they hit it off from the beginning. Mark liked that Suzy didn't seem overly impressed with him, and Suzy liked Mark's polite and down-to-earth demeanor. Mark promised to call again after he returned from Bloomington to attend Indiana's homecoming football game, an October 14 match-up between the Hoosiers and the Wisconsin Badgers.

Given that he lived in the Bay Area and she in Southern California, Mark mulled ground transportation options in L.A. When he called to arrange their first date, he asked if she had a car and if she'd mind driving. "Why don't we wait until you get your own car?" she recommended, stunning Mark with her resistance. "She let me know right away that she wasn't about to be my chauffeur," he recalled. "Luckily, I remembered Schick was delivering a new 1973 Lincoln Mark IV to Brokaw's office the next week, so I quickly told her that I could pick her up."

Mark made reservations for dinner at the Beverly Wilshire Hotel in Beverly Hills, but he neglected to communicate the plan to Suzy. She'd already eaten, but she kindly offered to join Mark at the world-class restaurant so he could dine. Their conversation flowed easily, and Mark considered it a favorable omen that she, like him, did not smoke or drink alcohol. His trademark confidence abandoned him on her doorstep, though. Unable to muster the courage to kiss her when the enjoyable evening ended, he was immensely relieved when she agreed to see him the next night.

They were both smitten and neither tested the waters with others again. It took only three dates to confirm their ardent desire to spend the rest of their lives together. Mark asked Herman for permission to marry Suzy after two short months, and both Weiners readily assented. "I had decided very early that the press accounts of his arrogance were unfair," Suzy said later. "If he was that way, I would never have agreed to a second date. To me, Mark was shy and loveable, not arrogant, but dating him wasn't exactly normal. When we went out, people stared at him, and he constantly got letters and telephone calls from other girls."

On May 6, 1973, the stunning pair exchanged wedding vows in a Reform Jewish ceremony at the famed Beverly Hills Hotel, Suzy in a traditional white floor-length gown and Mark in an elegant black tuxedo. The *Hollywood Reporter* called their wedding invitation the hottest ticket in town. Over 300 guests gathered in the gaily decorated Crystal Room. Mark's cousin Sherman served as best man.

After the wedding, Mark and Suzy moved into Mark's condominium in Marina Del Rey, a culturally distinct section of Los Angeles, surrounded by boats and fashionable restaurants. A sightseeing boat would inform its passengers by loudspeaker of the building's famous resident.

Another round of awards had begun to pile up. The Associated Press honored Mark and gymnast Olga Korbut as its 1972 male and female athletes of the year. The news organization had selected only one other swimmer as the world's best athlete, amateur or professional, in the forty-one-year history of the award—Don Schollander in 1964. LifeSavers Candy also chose Mark as the nation's top athlete that year, presenting him a second Triumph sports car, like the one he had purchased while in college, which he promptly gave to his sister Heidi.

One award he didn't garner was the Sullivan Award. The committee, allegedly reluctant to set a precedent of bestowing the award to the same person two years in a row, instead picked Olympic marathon champion Frank Shorter, peeving Mark. "Awards don't mean all that much to me, but it irked me that I had smashed the Olympic record for medals in one Olympic Games and they refused to give me the award," he complained afterward.

Five years later, he entered the International Swimming Hall of Fame, the first of several into which he would be inducted. In 1979, the International Jewish Sports Hall of Fame welcomed him, and he helped comprise the first class of athletes inducted into the U.S. Olympic Hall of Fame in 1983.

¡¡¡

In sharp contrast to his endorsement business, Mark's acting career never took off. Of course, it would have taken a Herculean effort for Mark to measure up to expectations out of the pool, given his overwhelming success in it. Suzy joined him on-screen as his dead wife on *Emergency!* and as a guest on *The Mike Douglas Show*, but Mark didn't have the staying power of Crabbe, Weissmuller, or Williams, his visible discomfort in front of the camera a primary hindrance. "I wasn't prepared for acting," Mark conceded. "It isn't that easy. Everybody said I looked wooden in front of the camera, and they were right. People don't believe that I'm pretty shy, and I'd become famous by swimming face down in a pool for more than ten years. That's not a good combination for performing in front of bright lights and a camera."

Bruce Wigo's comparison of Mark's era with that of Crabbe, Weissmuller, and Williams makes the divergent results understandable. According to Wigo, "When Buster, Johnny, and Esther were competitive swimmers, workouts were minimal, rarely more than 1,500 yards, and swim meets were thought of as opportunities to promote swimming as a fun sport and to entertain the public. There were very few events in those days, so serious races were often part of 'water carnivals' and aquatic shows that would often include clown diving, synchronized swimming and life-saving exhibitions performed by the swimmers themselves, so they were comfortable entertaining live audiences. Weissmuller actually performed a comedy diving routine with Harold 'Stubby' Kruger on off days at the 1924 Olympic Games and it was this act, as much as his swimming, that made him the most popular athlete in Paris. Weissmuller and Kruger, who became a famous Hollywood stuntman and character actor, reprised their act for the famous Billy Rose Aquacade shows of the 1930s and 1940s."

"But people started losing interest in swim shows in the 1950s, and at that time many pools were being shut down across the country as an alternative to allowing integration, so fewer pools were available for shows," said Wigo. "That combination took away a big opportunity for swimmers to perform. Plus, by the late '50s and early '60s, training methods had changed dramatically and swimming got more serious; times and records became more important than having fun and entertaining audiences. The fifteen-hundred-yard workouts were replaced by workouts five to ten times longer, so performing was no longer an option. Since then, no swimmer has made much of a dent on television. Summer Sanders has had some success, but the only current superstar swimmer who seems to have an inclination toward Hollywood is Amanda Beard."

Although Mark's acting career failed to flourish, he stayed busy as a swimming commentator for television. Brokaw negotiated a deal with ABC for Mark to provide color commentary at major swim meets such as AAU Nationals and the Santa Clara Invitational, as well as the Duke Kahanamoku Surf Classic. A couple of years later, CBS offered a better deal, guaranteeing Mark a minimum of ten broadcasts, so he changed networks. They paid in full but came through with only four assignments in two years, including the 1975 Pan Am Games and the 1975 FINA World Championships, so Mark returned to ABC for the 1976 Olympics in Montreal.

In 1978, Mark and Jim Lampley covered the FINA World Championships in Berlin, Germany, for ABC. At a preproduction meeting, directors instructed the pair to comment only on what appeared on the television monitor in front of them. The winners would likely be in lanes three, four, and five, and that's where the cameras would be aimed and what viewers at home would see. Mark explained that swimmers from the outside lanes occasionally challenged for the lead, but the directors admitted they hadn't positioned the cameras to cover lanes one or eight and reiterated, "So don't say anything about events or swimmers that are not on the monitor."

Naturally, a swimmer in an outside lane figured prominently in one of the finals. Appalled at the shoddy decision anyway, Mark simply couldn't keep viewers in the dark about the actual race in the 200 breaststroke. "Too bad we can't talk about anything that isn't on the monitor," he explained on-air. "American Nick Nevid in lane eight is way out in front and is swimming under world-record pace." In his earphones he could hear the producer swearing and screaming at an unnamed employee to "get a damn camera on lane eight." The crew reshuffled locations quickly and caught Nevid's last lap as he held on for the victory, but not the record.

Mark continued to work for ABC periodically. He was scheduled to commentate on the 1980 Olympic Games in Moscow before President Jimmy Carter announced the United States' boycott to protest Russia's invasion of Afghanistan. "Carter said that the invasion violated the principles of the Olympics, but that was crazy," said Mark. "Using athletes as weapons in politics never serves any purpose. The political cause is never advanced, and the athletes are the ones who are hurt." Mark concluded his sports commentating career at the 1984 Olympics in Los Angeles.

CHAPTER 16

BACK IN THE WATER

THE ELEVATOR in a downtown Los Angeles hotel descended to the first floor, and Mark emerged distractedly. As he'd done hundreds of times since 1972, the thirty-nine-year-old had attended a business meeting. Since his competitive swimming days, Mark had applied the same discipline, confidence, and aggressiveness that elevated him to rare heights as an athlete to his business endeavors. The parties had just brainstormed, discussing proposals, ideas, and scenarios. Although neither conclusive nor extraordinary, the appointment had been well worth his time. But on this day in 1989, Mark wasn't crunching the data presented moments before, as was his custom. He wasn't tuning in to what his gut said about the information he just received, as he'd trained himself to do. He wasn't thinking about the meeting at all.

Instead, his mind lingered on what may have been a throwaway comment by a young executive at the business meeting who had mentioned that he was a former collegiate swimmer and that he and some teammates had joined a local Masters swim club after years out of the pool. Possibly eager to impress his sport's most iconic figure, or to flatter him—or perhaps both— the man marveled that they all were churning out times as fast as they had in college years earlier. Continuing in that line of thought, he suggested that Mark consider a comeback. Mark instinctually shrugged and smiled as if to thank the young man for the compliment while summarily dismissing the notion.

Seventeen years removed from reaching the pinnacle of athletic feats and then somewhat abruptly retiring, the thought of making a comeback never seriously entered his thinking. Certainly the subject arose before. Fifteen years earlier, midway between the Munich Games and those in Montreal, friends, acquaintances, and strangers broached the subject, eager to predict the future by holding on to the past. But he'd moved on, convinced no other challenges lay in the water worth chasing and unwilling to risk or alter the perfect ending to his career.

It wasn't as if Mark feared a loss of speed. A chance workout five years earlier proved otherwise. As part of ABC's telecast for the 1984 Olympic Games in Los Angeles, for which they hired Mark as a commentator, the network planned a special segment analyzing Mark's freestyle stroke and comparing it to that of Rowdy Gaines. Gaines had set world records in the 100 free and 200 free, won thirteen national titles, and took second at the Trials in the 100 free. The feel-good story of the '84 swim team, Gaines theoretically had missed his chance at Olympic glory when the United States boycotted the Moscow Games in 1980 during his supposed peak.

Mark and a film crew spent a few hours in Mission Viejo, California, at the pool where the Olympic team trained, capturing images of both swimmers in action with an underwater camera. They finished as Richard Quick, the assistant coach for the men's and women's teams, prepared his sprinters—including Gaines—to swim eight 50-yard freestyles in descending time against the clock. In other words, each 50 would be faster than the previous one, with the athletes swimming one at a time. Quick looked over at Mark and saw a comparatively out-of-shape man a dozen years past his prime. Half joking, he asked if Mark wanted to join them. To Quick's mild surprise, Mark accepted the invitation and took the position following Gaines. Gaines swam the first lap somewhat conservatively, and Mark swam just a bit faster. Gaines picked it up slightly on the second lap; still, Mark swam just hard enough to beat Gaines' time. This pattern continued, and by the fifth lap both posted very fast times. Mark barely managed to outsprint the twenty-five-year-old on the sixth lap and, recognizing he would be unable to keep it up, wisely and gracefully bowed out of the last two.

Reflecting on the scene, Quick couldn't believe what he saw. "I remember looking down at Mark and thinking, 'Wow, what a fabulous talent.' He was definitely out of shape, but he had a tremendous stroke and was a tough competitor. To keep up with Rowdy, the premier freestyle swimmer in the world at the time, was amazing." Gaines went on to collect three gold medals at the Games in the 100-meter freestyle, 400-meter freestyle relay, and 400-meter medley relay.

Now, though, five years later, the idea of racing again loitered several minutes longer than it ever had. That fact in itself was curious. He'd never been measurably tempted with previous overtures, but for some reason this was different. Maybe it was the evidence from the young executive that getting back to top speed was possible, albeit speeds much slower than his best. Maybe the business world had gotten a little boring. Maybe the memory of sprinting against Gaines weaseled its way into his consciousness alongside the intoxicating feelings of being the best in the world and enjoying the subsequent adoration.

For whatever reason, the crazy idea created a tiny ripple in his brainwaves, intriguing him just enough to telephone his old buddy, Mark Wallace. In addition to being a close friend, the former Indiana University team manager also remained one of Mark's biggest fans and a swimming enthusiast. Wallace wrote periodically for Agence France-Presse (a wire service) and worked most national championship meets, during which he'd signal from the deck to Marge Counsilman in the stands after 100 fly races the place Mark's time in Munich would have fared.

He knew his immediate reaction was emotionally filled excitement based on nostalgia, but he also knew enough about the current swimming scene to recognize the real possibilities. It took only minimal research to discover Mark's 54.27 would have won Nationals in twelve of the twenty long-course races between 1973 and 1989, placing several more times in the top three and always finaling. It also would have got him third at the 1984 Trials and sixth in 1988. "A bit astonished, I called Mark back and told him how he stacked up," Wallace remembered. "I could tell Mark was excited with the news, and I think at that point he began seriously considering a return to the pool."

Many world-class athletes dream of a comeback after retirement, wondering how they'd fare against the stars that supplanted them in the public's heart. The glory of supremacy, the feeling of invincibility, and the boost both have on an ego sometimes trigger a glazing effect on the mind, enabling the athlete to remember the triumphs, fame, and laurels while conveniently forgetting the arduous work, sacrifice, and pain. Mark actually had the opposite problem to an extent. Sure, his ego and undying confidence fed the concept. But as much as the challenge piqued his interest, he remembered all too well the laps and hours and miles that went into achieving those times. His well-known distaste for training in his heyday tempered his thoughts, knowing that the process would be even tougher at his age. "Some people crave working out, but I was just the opposite," Mark explained. "I knew that a comeback would require extensive workouts if I was going to have a chance, and I wasn't sure I was willing to commit to it."

That summer at a function, Mark bumped into Bud Greenspan, the award-winning director, writer, and producer who had earned acclaim with his Olympic documentaries, and bounced the idea off him. Mark's musings absolutely enchanted Greenspan, especially after hearing that Mark's 100 fly time from Munich was still competitive. He took Mark firmly by the arm, looked him in the eye, and probed, "Does anybody know about this? We have to talk." Clearly, Greenspan saw a gold-medal film in the making, but contrary to popular belief, Greenspan did not offer Mark a million dollars to follow through with the plan.

Greenspan's exuberance rubbed off on Mark, who began talking openly about a comeback. Soon, word of it reached Ross Wales, who had competed against Mark in the 1968 Mexico City Olympics and in dozens of other national and international competitions. A young partner in the prestigious Cincinnati law firm Taft, Stettinius & Hollister, Wales had worked his way up the ladder in the nation's aquatic organizations before serving the sport internationally. After four years as secretary to FINA's Technical Swimming Committee, he had recently been elected as the organization's Honorary Secretary. Among his duties in that role were editing and publishing the FINA Handbook, making him well-versed in the intricacies of the sport's rules.

Wales quickly called Mark to confirm that he was serious about the comeback and reminded him that he had a technical hurdle to clear before getting too invested in the plan. "Mark had certainly broken the rules on amateurism as they existed in 1972, when he earned millions in endorsements after the Munich Olympics," Wales explained. "By the time Mark started his comeback effort, the rules regarding professionalism in the Olympics had been changed to allow athletes to earn endorsement money as long as they put the funds into a trust fund reserved for training expenses. That wasn't an option in 1972, and even if it was, Mark had no intention of a comeback when he retired."

It wasn't clear how the rules applied to Mark, but he definitely was at risk of being ineligible for Olympic competition if he didn't take preemptive action. Wales suggested that Mark write a letter requesting the FINA Bureau to clear him for competition, which Wales would hand-carry to the next meeting. Wales knew the Bureau, made up of officials from every continent in the world, could be very unpredictable. The savvy sports politician reasoned that the group would be more likely to approve Mark's request in 1989, when the prospects of success were low, than shortly before the 1992 Olympics, if it looked like Mark could qualify for the Games. As Wales surmised, the Bureau cleared Mark with minimal discussion, most considering his new adventure a long shot at best.

Mark had consulted Wallace. He'd excited Greenspan. He'd persuaded FINA. But he still hadn't convinced himself it was a good idea. His old world record only showed how he stacked up against current athletes back when he was in his prime. The real questions were, could he swim that fast again—or at least close enough to make the Olympic team—and was he willing to work hard enough to have a real shot at it? His size 28 Speedo swimsuits from 1972 were long gone, but it didn't matter. He probably couldn't have pulled them past his thighs anyway. After captivating the world at a solid but trim one hundred and seventy pounds, he now carried two hundred and ten on his frame and found it difficult to squeeze into a size 32. As he examined his body in the mirror, relatively round by comparison, he knew the journey would be grueling.

Mark took a three-week vacation to Hawaii and bodysurfed for three to four hours a day. "I didn't want to start with pool workouts, because they are so boring," Mark said, rationalizing a strategy that sounds more like fun than work. "I love to bodysurf, so I knew I could stay in the ocean for hours a day." When he returned to the mainland, he began swimming by himself in a recreational pool at UCLA three or four times a week, but with no coach to push him, he struggled to log more than two thousand yards a day. After a few weeks, though, several things encouraged him. His body shrank by twenty pounds, his stroke smoothed, and his speed made brief appearances. He wasn't actually swimming at meaningful speeds for meaningful lengths of time, but he was getting close enough for his muscles to remember how it felt.

Mark admitted to Greenspan that the notion was gaining steam. Delighted, Greenspan wrote an article for *PARADE* magazine in September about the possibility, interviewing Sherm Chavoor and Mark's friend Skip Kenney, the men's head swim coach at Stanford and a USA assistant in '84. Both offered the same opinion: for anybody else, a comeback after seventeen years would be ridiculous, but if anybody could do it, Mark could. After the article appeared in newspaper inserts across the country, Bryant Gumbel of NBC's *Today Show* asked Mark to appear live on the next day's telecast. Mark agreed, and a limousine shuttled him to the Burbank studio at 4:15 A.M. From their New York set, Gumbel and Indiana University alumna Jane Pauley interviewed Mark in the prime slot before millions of viewers, prompting hundreds to write Mark letters encouraging him to pursue the inspirational undertaking.

Recognizing that the point of no return loomed very near, hiring a coach became Mark's next priority. He first considered Kenney but quickly realized that would require a move to Northern California. He then approached Ron Ballatore. The head swimming coach for UCLA had significant Olympic experience, serving as coach for Peru at the 1968 Olympics, Ecuador in 1972, and Israel in 1976. In addition to his strong credentials, Ballatore also made sense because the UCLA pool was only minutes from Mark's Brentwood home. In their first meeting, Ballatore asked Mark about his workouts since the 1972 Olympics, and his jaw dropped upon hearing that swimming's most famous athlete had virtually abandoned the activity. Playing in the ocean on Hawaiian vacations and cooling off in his backyard pool had been about his only connection to the sport. After a serious inquisition to convince himself that Mark understood and was committed to the exhausting regimen required for such a comeback, the duo joined forces.

Ballatore quickly increased Mark's daily yardage to more than ten thousand a day from Mark's paltry two thousand and added dry-land exercises to his routine. After several months, when Mark began to cruise through his workouts, Ballatore upped the daily yardage to thirteen thousand. Things were going well until Mark ruptured a disc in his back during dry-land training in January 1990, forcing him out of training for two months and causing unbearable pain. Treatment from an acupuncturist didn't improve his comfort, but the cortisone shots administered by an orthopedist at Cedars-Sinai Medical Center in Los Angeles did. They also had the unfortunate side effect of making Mark yearn for food. Flat on his back for six weeks, the calorie-craving comeback candidate reverted to his previous weight, and then some. By the middle of February, he was pushing two hundred and twenty pounds. In early March, he finally felt good enough to get back in the pool and worked hard to make up for lost time. Incredibly, by the end of April, he slimmed back down to a svelte one hundred and seventy-eight pounds, only eight more than he weighed in Munich.

❗❗❗

A Japanese film executive caught wind of Mark's ambition and began producing a documentary covering the comeback. Curious about how Mark's butterfly stroke compared with other swimmers—past and present—he asked USA Swimming's executive director, Ray Essick, for permission to test Mark in the flume at the Olympic Training Center in Colorado Springs. The flume, a sort of swimming treadmill, measures stroke strength and efficiency by simulating a current up to three meters per second, against which an athlete swims; capturing three-dimensional images of the stroke; and analyzing the results. Essick agreed, and Audrius Barzdukas, Director of Sports Science Services for USA Swimming, administered the test that would calculate Mark's efficiency in terms of energy usage and stroke pattern as well as his strength by determining how much Mark's stroke propelled him forward.

Barzdukas set the flume's current to world-class pace, the strongest level set for any swimmer, and Mark struggled initially. His fastest split ever in a 100 fly race converted to about two meters per second, and he was more used to slicing through the water rather than the water rushing toward him. The flow pushed him back a couple of feet before he found a rhythm and regained his position in the tank for the rest of the forty-second test. After digitizing and analyzing the images, the flume's computer printed out a graph with two lines, the top measuring Mark's potential with perfect mechanics and the bottom representing the actual effectiveness of his stroke. The difference between the two indicated how much Mark could improve with better technique.

Barzdukas knew he was witnessing what had been one of the most impressive athletes of all time, and he marveled at the camera views of Mark's stroke. Still, he was unprepared for the efficiency rating that rolled out of the printer. Stunned and more than certain the computer malfunctioned, he ran the graph again. The second readout confirmed the first. Thousands of swimmers had been tested in the flume, including almost every top USA male and female swimmer and Olympians from around the world, but Mark's results set yet another standard. Incredibly, the two lines matched almost exactly. Mark just executed the most efficient stroke ever tested. "Even at the age of forty, Mark was getting everything out his stroke," confirmed Barzdukas. "He didn't fight his own body. He had the most natural and fluid stroke I had ever seen or tested. One of the biggest challenges swimmers face in the flume is maintaining stroke efficiency through the entire test, because fatigue makes technique erode. Mark was incredible, because he maintained his stroke technique throughout the test. Mark's stroke was the same to swimming as Bobby Jones' swing was to golf." Doc

Counsilman had been right more than twenty years ago. There was no way to improve Mark's technique.

▽▽▽
○ ○ ○

Wanting to increase his exposure, which in turn would increase pressure to continue training hard, Mark pitched to ABC television the idea of broadcasting match races against current world-class swimmers. The network showed significant interest in airing the races live on its acclaimed show, *Wide World of Sports*, but only if Mark secured the funding to cover ABC's expenses of producing and airing the segment. Mark had recently agreed to use and endorse Clairol's Option Instant product line of hair dyes to conceal his emerging gray hairs, so he approached the company with the idea of sponsoring the races. The executives jumped at the perfect opportunity to showcase the aging swimmer's use of their product in what ought to be a highly publicized and watched event.

The first swimmer asked to participate was German Michael Gross, the six-time Olympic medalist in the freestyle and butterfly events in 1984 and 1988. His exceedingly long wingspan earned him the nickname "The Albatross" and gave him widespread recognition, and his domination during most of the '80s prompted American swimming sensation-turned-commentator John Naber to suggest in a *Sports Illustrated* article that Gross was better than Mark. The potential existed to create the type of quick rivalry that could boost ratings, but Gross declined the invitation.

Eventually, Americans Tom Jager and Matt Biondi each agreed to square off against Mark. Both men had impressive international credentials. In the 1988 Olympics in Seoul, Jager won a silver medal in the 50-meter freestyle and a gold as a member of the 400-meter freestyle relay. Biondi, the first swimmer in sixteen years to threaten Mark's record of seven gold medals in one Olympic Games, was even more remarkable. He matched the number in Seoul but not the hue, collecting gold in the 50 free, 100 free, and all three relays in addition to a silver in the 100 fly and a bronze in the 200 free. Also, both Jager and Biondi were actively training for the 1992 Olympic Trials and Games, giving Mark a true gauge of his progress and prospect of making yet another Olympic team. In addition to buying advertising spots, Clairol agreed to award $20,000 to the Spitz-Jager winner and $35,000 to the Spitz-Biondi winner.

As part of the deal, Mark chose the race's stroke and length. He selected the 50-meter butterfly against both opponents, figuring the combination of swimming his best stroke at the shorter-than-normal distance gave him the best chance to win. When the media asked ABC producer Kim Belton why she approved a non-Olympic event, she replied, "I think people want to see Spitz race, no matter what the length is." Belton also revealed ABC's plans to conduct live interviews during the segment with George Foreman, in the midst of his own comeback, adding, "We're going to milk this as much as we can."

The first of two nationally televised races was set for April 13, 1991, against twenty-six-year-old Jager in Mission Viejo. Although Mark's forty-one-year-old back still had not completely healed, causing some occasional pain, he and Ballatore decided not to reveal that fact for fear that disclosing it would diminish interest in the comeback. ABC, meanwhile, splurged for the affair, using a total of six cameras for the two swimmers, including two hand-held and one underwater.

At race time, Mark and Jager entered the pool area to a surreal scene. People packed the aquatic center, standing three and four deep in hopes of catching a glimpse of the quadragenarian swimmer. Jager, a seasoned competitor, was surprised when he realized his level of anxiety. "The media for that event was more aggressive than any other swim meet I attended, including the Olympic Games," he admitted. "The crowd was electric, and I found myself getting very nervous. Before the race, I told Mark that I was going all out. Mark smiled and said he was, too."

Jager reacted exceptionally to the gun for a tremendous start, but Mark was slow off the blocks. Jager's dive was also better, and when he surfaced for his first stroke, he led Mark by almost half a body length. Mark lost very little ground to Jager once his near-perfect strokes powered him through the water, but he couldn't close in on his younger adversary. Jager finished just more than a body length ahead in 24.92 to Mark's 26.70.

According to John Leonard, executive director for the American Swimming Coaches Association, starts and dives are all about trajectory. "Swimmers in Mark's era used a flat-angle start in which the swimmer tries to stretch out flat over the water, minimizing the time underwater," Leonard explained. "By the time Mark had his matches with Tom and Matt, swimmers were using dives with steeper angles of entry. This deeper dive, sometimes called a single-hole entry dive, allows the swimmer to glide longer under the water and to reach the surface with greater velocity. The newer technique is really quite faster."

Ballatore agreed. "Starts had changed dramatically from those used in 1972, and Jager hammered Mark. Plus, at the age of forty, Mark didn't have the same spring in his legs that he had in 1972." Even Jager himself admitted the dive was the difference. "Starts had changed quite a bit since 1972, and I was able to get a good advantage immediately. I think that if we had swum from a push start in the water, the race would have been a lot closer," he conceded.

Essick was less charitable. "Mark didn't do his research. This was obvious when he used an outdated start in the match race against Tom," he groused.

Despite Mark's loss, the ratings pleased ABC. The race drew more viewers than the vaunted Masters Golf Tournament at Augusta National, which aired opposite of *Wide World of Sports* that week. Two weeks later, on April 27, Mark took on Biondi. This time, Mark reacted to the starter's gun more quickly than the twenty-five-year-old, but his flat dive again hampered his positioning. By the time Biondi surfaced, he held a slight lead. Unlike Jager, though, Biondi continued to put distance between him and Mark, posting a 24.51 to win by exactly two seconds.

Mark's comeback was the talk of the Masters Swimming community. "Even though he lost to the younger Jager and Biondi, Mark's times were incredible. Had Mark been swimming in an official Masters meet, his 26.51 time would have beaten the existing Masters world record in his age group by over a half second," stated United States Masters Swimming president Rob Copeland. "Interestingly, in 1991, the third fastest swim in the world for men over 40 was by Jerry Heidenreich, Mark's long-time rival, who clocked a 27.32."

$$\underset{\circ}{!}\underset{\circ}{!}\underset{\circ}{!}$$

In the end, Mark failed to qualify for the 1992 Olympic Trials. Needing a 55.59 in the 100 fly, his best time was a 58.03. Ballatore thought the international attention hampered Mark's preparation. In addition to the Japanese documentary, Mark's comeback attempt generated considerable interest overseas. Several countries and race officials offered Mark handsome sums of money to swim at their meets. They didn't particularly care if Mark swam fast. They just wanted the superstar's presence to create excitement and draw attention, fans, and money. Eager to earn the "show up" money, Mark traveled often to such events.

"Mark's comeback generated a lot of media interest, and he and I were invited to travel to many countries," Ballatore said. "I think that had a negative effect on his comeback. At times it seemed like the trips were more important than training." Mark's Indiana buddy, Mark Wallace, concurred. "I was talking with Charlie Hickcox about Mark's comeback, and we both agreed that Mark could have been successful if he didn't travel so much and didn't make so many personal appearances. Mark obviously enjoyed the attention, and it disrupted his efforts in the pool."

Wallace was also critical of the distance of the event. "Mark wasn't a raw speed burner like Jager and Biondi. These two guys were the fastest 50-meter swimmers in the world at that time. The 50-meter race put a premium on fast-twitch muscle fibers, which Mark had less of than his two younger opponents," Wallace said.

The comeback elicited diverse reactions from the public. Many considered it inspirational, as evidenced by the dozens of letters Mark received. Jim Booth, owner of the Jim Booth Swim School in Northern California, stated, "I found Mark's comeback to be invigorating. I'm about his age and watching him compete prompted me to get seriously involved in the sport." Others were not so kind, viewing it as little more than another failed public relations venture. ESPN posted a Britney Spears-inspired article to its Web site on September 11, 2007, entitled "Comebacks? More like train wrecks." It listed Mark's comeback as one of the most ill-conceived of all time, along with those of roundballer Michael Jordan, pitcher Jim Palmer, boxer Riddick Bowe, and hockey player Guy Lafleur. The author offered some tongue-in-cheek solace to Mark, stating that his comeback outshined Spears' because "Spitz probably comforted himself on his piles and piles of Olympic Medals."

For the most part, though, Mark found the experience to be positive. "I enjoyed the competition and, naturally, the attention my comeback generated," he admitted afterward. "I'd matured quite a bit, so I wasn't the brash, cocky kid some people remembered in 1968. I changed the attitudes of a lot of people about me. If I'd known they would react so enthusiastically, I'd have done it years ago."

CHAPTER 17

PRESIDENTS, KINGS, AND QUEENS

FEW PEOPLE personally converse with a U.S. president, and fewer still gain recognition or an audience with worldwide leaders. But Mark's success in the pool, exposure, intelligence, and dignity resulted in associations with five presidents, a queen, a king, an emir, and a prime minister.

The one president Mark never met was Richard Nixon. Nixon's first term in the Oval Office was winding down in 1972 amid the beginnings of the Watergate scandal when Mark set the ridiculously high standard against which future Olympians, especially Olympic swimmers, would be judged. Inviting the nation's most celebrated athlete from Munich and reportedly the second most recognizable person in the United States—the president himself being first on that list—may have helped Nixon's cause at that troubled time in his life. The thirty-seventh president enjoyed hosting champion athletes and teams at the White House. Apparently, the practice extended well beyond major sports or household names, as he even entertained the Vanderbilt University national championship bowling team at Pennsylvania Avenue the year before.

The White House never called. Sherm Chavoor tried to arrange an official visit, but at least two factors worked against him. First, Nixon's anti-Semitism ran deep, a view unknown to the general public at that time but which came to light when later-released White House tapes captured the President repeatedly lashing out at Jews.

"All right," President Nixon instructed his chief of staff, H.R. "Bob" Haldeman in 1971, "I want a look at any sensitive areas around where Jews are involved, Bob. See, the Jews are all through the government, and we have got to get in those areas. We've got to get a man in charge who is not Jewish to control the Jewish . . . do you understand?" Haldeman said he did, and Nixon continued. "Second, most Jews are disloyal. . . . But Bob, generally speaking, you can't trust the bastards. They turn on you. Am I wrong or right?"

Haldeman affirmed, "Their whole orientation is against you. In this administration, anyway. And they are smart. They have the ability to do what they want to do, which is to hurt us."

Clearly, receiving a request to honor the most famous Jewish athlete at the nation's capital would rankle Nixon, who agonized about the dilemma of extending his invitations to champions to the most decorated Olympian ever. Charles Colson, Nixon's chief counsel, vilified Mark, saying he'd seen the swimmer in a television interview and "it seemed as if he was on drugs." Despite adding that he knew Mark was clean, Colson achieved the intended effect of maligning Nixon's perception of the Olympic champion.

The second obstacle in Mark visiting the White House turned out to be an inaccurate assumption of Nixon's, who rationalized the snub by assuming that as a Jew, Mark probably aligned with Democrats and would vote for George McGovern. Ironically, when the 1972 election in November afforded Mark his first opportunity to cast a ballot in a national election, he supported the incumbent.

After the Watergate fiasco forced Nixon to resign his seat to Vice President Gerald Ford in 1974, Mark's agent, Norm Brokaw, picked up the mantle and carried it with more success. The night after Ford's second presidential debate with Jimmy Carter in the fall of 1976 at San Francisco's Palace of Fine Arts Theatre, Ford stayed at the Beverly Hills Hotel in Southern California. Brokaw arranged for Mark and his wife Suzy to attend at a small reception in the hotel's twenty-five-hundred-square-foot Presidential Suite.

The couple mingled with Los Angeles Dodger great Steve Garvey for a few moments before President Ford materialized. Looking over the crowd, he turned to one of his guards and asked, "Am I off duty?" The agent responded, "Yes, Mr. President." Ford smiled and said, "Then I want a drink." From out of nowhere, an aide appeared with a bottle of beer. Brew in hand, President Ford joined Mark and Garvey. Predictably, they discussed sports, and Mark pointed out that both he and the President were "Big Ten people." Ford played for Michigan from 1931 to 1934, helping the Wolverines win the national championship his sophomore and junior seasons, and he boasted of Michigan's football prowess. Mark responded in kind about Indiana's swim team, six-time national champs. Feeling on shaky ground against such accomplishments in the pool, President Ford rather forcefully replied, "Yes, but in football we used to always kick Indiana's ass." Mark, quickly recognizing the inappropriateness of one-upping the United States Commander in Chief, responded demurely, "Mr. President, you still are," which drew a welcomed chuckle from Ford.

The nation's most athletic president in history then pulled Mark aside. Having recently installed an outdoor swimming pool on the White House grounds, Ford asked Mark for a good workout about four hundred yards long. Mark recommended two laps to loosen up, a series of one-lap sprints to elevate his heart rate, and an easy hundred yards to cool down. Ford summoned his personal physician, who nodded with approval at the President's personalized training regimen from the world's best swimmer.

The conversation ended with Ford inviting Mark to swim with him the next time he was in town. Mark chuckled and said,

"You mean I can walk into the White House and take a swim?" The President smiled and reassured him that he would arrange it. Unfortunately, the two never rendezvoused. Jimmy Carter defeated Ford exactly a month later to take control of the White House and its aquatics facilities.

❗❗❗

Mark maintained the longest and most personal presidential relationship with fellow Golden State resident Ronald Reagan. After the Munich Olympics, Reagan, in his second term as governor of California, invited Mark to the state's capital in Sacramento, beginning a friendship that lasted into the 1990s. The two strengthened their acquaintance at Republican Party fund-raisers during Reagan's drive for the presidency in 1980, at which Mark contributed his popular presence.

One time that year, when Mark worked as a color commentator for an international swim meet in Mission Viejo, Reagan and his horde of Secret Service agents visited the venue during a campaign stop. During one of Mark's infrequent breaks, an agent entered the restroom, identified himself, and politely asked everyone to clear the room for Reagan. As Mark exited with the others, the governor spied him and said, "He doesn't have to leave. I know him. That's Mark Spitz." The two chatted for a few minutes, Reagan asking about Suzy and Mark asking about the campaign. Reagan later won the election and invited Mark and Suzy to attend the Inauguration, but the Spitzes opted for their preplanned trip to Europe.

In July of 1990, about a year after Reagan's administration ended, Mark answered questions lobbed by Larry King from Turner Broadcasting at the Goodwill Games in Seattle. The major international sporting event, the brainchild of broadcasting mogul Ted Turner, was in its second staging after debuting in

Moscow in 1986. After the interview ended, Mark and King struck up a conversation with Arnold Schwarzenegger, who was also in the studio. King, pointing to a nearby curtained-off area guarded by the Secret Service, mentioned that President Reagan had arrived. Sensing an opportunity to catch up with one friend and impress a couple more, Mark casually announced his intent to talk with him. Skeptical, both King and Schwarzenegger chided Mark with comments such as, "Right, like you know the President," and "Sure, Mark, good luck." Undaunted, Mark walked over to an agent, introduced himself, explained his relationship with Reagan, and asked to say hello. Dutifully, the agent nodded and vanished behind the curtain. About thirty seconds later, he reappeared and said, "Sure, go on in. He's waiting for you." Before entering, Mark turned and waved to King and Schwarzenegger with a righteously indignant smile. The stunned duo, with jaws dropped, sheepishly waved back.

Once inside, Mark talked with the President for fifteen minutes. As always, Reagan asked Mark about Suzy. He then mentioned his satisfaction with the Goodwill Games and his pride in and appreciation of Ted Turner for pulling them off a second time, explaining how important they were to U.S.-Russia relations. Reagan asked Mark if he would have competed in the event if it was around in his day. Mark assured him that he would have in a heartbeat, adding that he broke world records in Russia, where some of his toughest competitors had lived.

After Reagan left office in early 1989, he and his wife Nancy moved to the Bel Air community in Los Angeles, not far from the Spitz residence. Reagan frequently took long walks in his neighborhood and, on at least one occasion, strolled near Mark's house. On that day, Mark drove home, a Secret Service agent politely detained him, explaining that President Reagan was walking up ahead and the delay would only last a couple of minutes. Mark again described their relationship and asked for permission to catch up with his old friend. After a moment, the agent granted the wish. When Mark pulled into his driveway, Reagan was only a few yards away. Despite having recently announced in 1994 that he suffered from Alzheimer's, Reagan immediately asked about Suzy. The two spoke happily for a few minutes before Reagan continued on. It was their last communication before Reagan succumbed to the disease in 2004 at the age of ninety-four.

❗❗❗

Although he wasn't as close to George Bush, Sr., Mark continued to help with Republican fund-raisers, and his support yielded an invitation to the 1989 Inauguration. This time their schedules permitted Mark and Suzy to attend the exclusive ceremony, to which they brought their eight-year-old son, Matthew. Matthew couldn't see the President beyond the large crowd, so Mark lifted him up on his shoulders. As few people could do, Mark and his son diverted CBS cameras away from the President to catch the scene of father and son watching the proceedings. Mark may not have believed it, but his mother-in-law back at home had caught the CBS-broadcast shoulder ride on tape.

During that trip, Mark, Suzy and Matthew toured the White House, with stops in the famous Red Room, Green Room and Blue Room. Matthew, who had covered the same ground the year before when Reagan had invited the family to visit, expressed his childlike exasperation at the redundancy of the tour. When he recognized the rooms he exclaimed, "Again? I've already seen these rooms!"

In the receiving line at one of the parties that evening, First Lady Barbara Bush remembered a previous encounter with the swimmer and said, "Mark, it's so nice to see you again." She turned to her husband. "Poppy, Mark is going to give the grandchildren swimming lessons, and if you're good, I might arrange a lesson for you to get one as well." President Bush chuckled and said, "I'd like that."

❗❗❗

Although Reagan quickly became his favorite president, Mark thoroughly enjoyed his exchanges with Bill Clinton. The first occurred in Atlanta just prior to the 1996 Olympic Games. Mark served as one of the last of the 12,467 torchbearers who carried the Olympic flame around the United States. Soon after finishing his leg in Atlanta hours before the Opening Ceremonies, Mark was due to join President Clinton and fellow Olympic stars in a ceremony for the 1996 U.S. Olympians in the Olympic Village. With no time to return to his hotel, he wandered over to President Clinton's temporary offices in the Olympic complex with his torch, creating a possible security dilemma.

Spotting Leon Panetta, Clinton's chief of staff at the time, Mark walked over and introduced himself. "Hi, Mark. What can I do for you?" Panetta responded. Mark explained the situation: insufficient time to return to his hotel, his requested presence with President Clinton at the upcoming athletes' ceremony, and his possession of a possible weapon. Mark asked if Panetta could have the Secret Service inspect the torch so he could take it with him to the ceremony. Catching Mark a bit off guard, Panetta suggested, "Why don't you ask the President yourself?" For some reason, Mark felt compelled to tell Panetta that while he would love to meet the President personally, "he should know that I am a Republican." Panetta assured, "That doesn't matter. I'll be right back."

A few moments later, he ushered Mark into the President's private office space. As Mark entered the room, he eyed Hillary Clinton and her daughter Chelsea talking with another woman. When Hillary looked up to see who was entering the room, she exclaimed, "Hi, Mark Spitz. You made such a commotion during the torch relay that we were stopped in traffic for a half hour." Mark grinned and asked how she knew who he was. An amused First Lady responded, "Because you look like Mark Spitz, you're carrying a torch, and you have a torch relay outfit on." Everyone laughed.

At that moment, President Clinton came through the door and said with a huge smile, "Mark Spitz! Mark Spitz, how are you?"

"I'm fine, Mr. President."

"Mark, you can call me Bill," the President proposed.

"Yes, Mr. President," Mark ignored lightheartedly.

Clinton playfully pushed him on the left shoulder, repeating like a star-struck boy, "Mark Spitz . . . Mark Spitz," as if he couldn't believe he was actually in the same room as the superstar. Hillary chastised, "Hey Bill, you can't hit Mark like that." But the President responded, "Sure I can. He's an athlete, and he's used to it, right, Mark?" The athlete smiled and said, "Well, Mr. President, I'm a Republican, and I can't take it." Clinton laughed and punched Mark on the shoulder again.

The two fraternized for twenty minutes. Clinton, only four years older than Mark, said how much he enjoyed following Mark's swimming career, asked about the 1972 Olympic Games, and inquired about Mark's current endeavors. When he inspected the relay torch, Clinton gushed, "How cool!"

"Mr. President, I'm sure you have the wherewithal to get one for yourself," Mark reminded him. Clinton laughed and said, "Please call me Bill."

"Yes, Mr. President."

When aides finally tore Clinton away from the conversation, which carried on so long he was late for his next appointment, the President invited Mark to the White House in the fall when Clinton would host the nation's newest Olympic champions. As Mark left, Panetta caught up to him and said, "The President told me that he invited you to the White House. You can stay overnight if you like, but I need to know how to get in touch with you." Mark smirked playfully and said, "He's the president. I'm sure his staff can figure out how to find me." Panetta seemed taken aback but softened when Mark handed him a business card, and asked what Mark would like to eat at the White House. "If I get to come to the White House," Mark answered, "I'll be in awe and won't care if we have McDonald's hamburgers." Panetta guaranteed him, "We can do better than that."

Mark indeed received an invitation to attend the fall ceremony, albeit with no offer to stay overnight in the executive mansion. Arriving slightly late because of a coincidental business meeting that day in Washington, D.C., he entered the room as President Clinton began to address the Olympic champions:

"You know, I grew up in a small town in Arkansas, but what a great country this is. I was elected governor of Arkansas and was fortunate to be elected President of the United States. As president, I get to meet many wonderful people, and just last summer in Atlanta, I got to talk with Mark Spitz for thirty minutes. Can you believe that? Mark Spitz!"

After the speech, Mark and a dozen or so Olympians formed a half-circle greeting line, with Mark at the end of the line on the left. President Clinton's aides directed him to start on the right side, but when he spied Mark he walked directly to him.

"Hi, Mark! How are you?"

"Fine, Mr. President."

"Oh please, Mark, call me Bill."

"Okay, Mr. President."

"Mark, have you tried these desserts my chefs prepared? They're great."

"No, Mr. President, I'm waiting for my tester to try them first."

"Your tester? Who is your tester?"

"It's you, Mr. President."

With that last comment, President Clinton burst into laughter and, characteristically, hit Mark on the shoulder. He walked away chortling, shaking his head, and muttering, "That Spitz, he's quite a character."

※ ※ ※

While Mark's interaction with five United States presidents dominated his contact with rulers, it by no means monopolized them. He also managed to bump into or be approached by presiding royalty and heads of governments from time to time.

For the 1976 Montreal Olympics, ABC hired Mark to provide color commentary for its broadcast of the swimming competition. One day near Olympic Pool, Mark waited with others behind a cordon while the Queen of England walked by. Flabbergasting Mark, Her Highness walked over to him and volunteered to later would grace the "swimming facility" to cheer on David Wilkie, Great Britain's best hope for a swimming medal. Mark respectfully related to the Queen his memory of Wilkie from the 1972 Olympic Games, where the Scot won a silver medal in the 200 breaststroke. The Queen smiled, quite pleased that Mark knew of her subject.

Days later, as Mark and Keith Jackson discussed the upcoming 200 breaststroke and its finalists, the Queen took her seat a few rows beneath their booth. She looked up at Mark but refrained from acknowledging his presence. When Wilkie won the gold medal, though, the proud monarch turned around, waved to Mark, and said, "Our boy did pretty well." Mark smiled, waved, and nodded. An astonished Jackson turned to his partner and said, "You've got to be kidding me! You know the Queen of England?"

In 2000, the British Broadcasting Corporation honored Steve Redgrave as its Sports Personality of the Year. Redgrave had just returned from the Sydney Olympic Games, where he won his fifth-straight gold medal in rowing dating back to 1984. A Commander of the Order of the British Empire, Redgrave repeatedly attributed his motivation in sports to Mark's performance in 1972, so the BBC quietly commissioned Mark as the surprise presenter. As Mark stood behind a backdrop, waiting to be introduced, Prime Minister Tony Blair walked over, introduced himself, and told Mark he'd been anxious to meet him. A bit stunned, Mark said the honor was all his and conveyed his esteem for Redgrave's accomplishments.

In 2005, Mark and several other sports stars, including soccer great Pelé and gymnastics idol Nadia Comaneci, participated in the grand opening in Doha, Qatar, of Aspire Zone, an international destination for sports, entertainment, recreation, and education. Hamad bin Khalifa, the Emir of Qatar, granted several of the sports legends a one-on-one meeting. During Mark's, the Emir noticed the American admiring his watch, so he allowed Mark to inspect it. The next day, Comaneci told Mark she had received from the Emir a very lavish watch encrusted with diamonds. Later that day at the Hamad Aquatic Center, a man approached Mark with a wrapped box and asked Mark to sign a form acknowledging he had received the gift. He also cautioned him not to let the box out of his sight. When he was finally alone in his room later that day, he opened it to find an exact replica of the Emir's watch.

While loitering in Harrods, the world's most famous department store, during his layover in London on the way home, Mark noticed they carried the same brand of watches. He showed his to the salesman and asked its value. Upon inspection, the salesman directed him to the next room and the salesperson who handled their most expensive watches. Mark repeated his question to the second salesman, who examined the unique timepiece with interest. He estimated the value of Harrods' closest match to be $37,000 but explained that appraising its precise value was impossible given that Mark's had to have been specially ordered. When Mark revealed the watch's origin, the salesman deemed it priceless.

Mark and forty-two other of the greatest living sports legends from around the world comprise the Laureus World Sports Academy, a group that strives to use the power of sport to promote unity and enrich the lives of young people worldwide. The ultra-exclusive alliance also annually selects the Laureus World Sports Awards winners. At the 2006 banquet in Barcelona, Mark and his friend Roger Schuster sat next to Juan Carlos, the King of Spain. Later that evening, when Mark spotted His Royalty in the lobby talking on a cell phone, Mark joked to Schuster, "Look, there's the King of Spain telling somebody, 'You won't believe who I met this evening—Mark Spitz!'" The King heard him, lowered his cell phone, and admitted, "You know, that is actually what I just said."

A year later, the King invited Mark and Schuster, already in Spain, to a reception that U.S. actor Cuba Gooding, Jr., also attended. Nervous, Gooding asked if they were Americans and how one should address a King, joking that the only Kings he knew were Martin Luther and Rodney. Mark said he'd met the King before and recommended Gooding address him as "Your Excellency." Later, when Mark asked Gooding how it went, Gooding laughed that the first thing the King said was, "Show me the money!" a reference to Gooding's famous line in the 1996 blockbuster hit *Jerry Maguire*.

More amazing, perhaps, than the Queen of England recognizing Mark, the Emir of Qatar gifting a priceless watch, or the King of Spain knowing Gooding's most famous line is the fact that Gooding did not know who Mark was.

CHAPTER 18

!!!

SIMILAR GOALS, DIFFERENT JOURNEYS

CHANCES ARE, whoever first suggested that records are made to be broken was not a philosophical athlete whose previously unmatched accomplishment just became second best. The thrill of setting records is undeniable. Some use the possibility as motivation; for others, it's simply a consequence and side benefit of their approach. But it's safe to say that once they have set themselves apart from their peers in some way, they'd prefer it to stay that way, no matter how gracious they sound when the mark is in jeopardy.

Certain record-breaking performances defied logic to such an extent that they seemed immortal, such as Babe Ruth's seven hundred and fourteen home runs, until Hank Aaron topped it thirty-nine years later; Bob Beamon's twenty-nine-foot, two-and-a-half-inch-long jump at altitude at the 1968 Olympics, until Mike Powell flew two inches further in 1991; and Lou Gehrig's endurance record of 2,130 consecutive major-league baseball games, until Cal Ripken, Jr., blew past him fifty-six years later.

Records stir up a number of emotions in fans, as evidenced by the great deal of blather generated about them in conversations at the water cooler, on e-mail and blogs, over airways during sports talk shows, and in print media and books. The old-timers usually root against the up-and-comer on the verge of erasing a legend's mark, believing the changes to rules, technology, or circumstances prevent fair or accurate comparisons. Younger fans often side with the challenger, not having the emotional attachment to the aged or deceased star that comes from witnessing the original feat firsthand. But for most fans, it's not that clear cut. Their mixed emotions range from feeling empty or sad when a sacrosanct record is about to fall to excited about watching history being made, and their intensity increases in direct proportion to the age of the record.

Regardless of their allegiances or sentiments, sports fans yearn for a connection between the two athletes when the challenger threatens to supplant the record holder in the annals of sport. Those resisting change want to see youth pay homage to those that came before. Those hoping to see history want the aging star to gracefully step aside and accept the accomplishments of the challenger. Both can bolster their fan base if they can at least be respectful and knowledgeable of the other.

A direct interaction isn't always possible. The more amazing the exploit, the less chance it's surpassed during the record holder's lifetime. The Babe, for example, passed away in 1948, twenty-six years before Hank Aaron slugged his seven hundred and fifteenth home run. Most baseball partisans delighted in experiencing Aaron's pursuit of the record, but not all of them. Some clung to Babe's sacred record for nostalgia's sake; some did so out of racial prejudice. Aaron received hate mail and death threats from bigots not wanting to see a black man surpass Ruth on the chart. Ruth's widow played a major role in the public's acceptance of Aaron as the home run king when she cheered his efforts and publicly denounced the racists who belittled Aaron, guaranteeing that her husband would have also condemned the racists.

Gehrig's reliability record arguably topped the immortality list, and Ripken tirelessly effused about the example and achievements of the original "Iron Man" as he neared the milestone.

Someone suggested that Ripken sit out the game after he tied Gehrig out of respect, but Ripken felt the act would have a different effect. "I believed sitting down after I had tied Lou Gehrig's mark would dishonor both of us by implying that the record was a purpose and not a by-product of my simple desire to go out and play every day, which would have been Gehrig's desire, too," he explained after the fact. "Lou Gehrig would not have wanted me to sit out a game as a show of honor. No athlete would. Take that to the bank." Ripken became the new "Iron Man" to highly positive fanfare.

The sensational running back duo of Emmitt Smith and Walter Payton developed a special bond, often discussing the inevitability of Smith eclipsing Payton's NFL all-time rushing record of 16,726 yards. After Payton died in 1999, Smith stayed close to the Payton family, and he broke down in tears when talking about Payton after breaking the mark in 2002. Fans applauded his attitude as much as his athleticism.

Tiger Woods has done the same with Jack Nicklaus, whose record eighteen major PGA tournament championships was thought safe until Tiger began prowling the links. More than simply connecting, Woods and Nicklaus were described as "de-facto presidents of each other's fan clubs" by *USA Today* columnist Ian O'Connor in 2006. If Woods wins number nineteen, Nicklaus hopes to be one of the first to congratulate him in what would be a special moment in sports.

By contrast, legend has it that certain members of the 1972 Miami Dolphins—who finished their season a perfect 17–0—break out champagne each year when the last undefeated NFL team loses a game, certainly not in the spirit of applauding outstanding achievement. Further, as the New England Patriots steamed toward an undefeated season in 2007, Coach Don Shula of the undefeated Dolphins criticized the Patriots after New England got caught filming their opponents' coaches signaling in plays to the huddle, a clear violation of league rules.

Shula's suggestion that an asterisk be placed next to their name in the record book if the Patriots finished the season unblemished came across as childish. Had Shula made a positive comment, he would have been admired. His spiteful remark, while not contemptible, cast an unnecessary shadow over his status.

❗❗❗

When the Olympic Torch ignites the cauldron near the Beijing National Stadium to officially commence the 2008 Olympic Games, Mark's "unbreakable" record will be thirty-six years old, its longevity placing him in illustrious company. Current challenger Michael Phelps will take his second swing at a standard that has survived two legitimate attacks. Matt Biondi medalled seven times—but "only" five wins—at the 1988 Seoul Olympics, and Phelps' first try dominated headlines leading up to and during the 2004 Olympic Games in Athens.

The possibility of Phelps rising to rarified heights first surfaced at the 2003 FINA World Aquatic Championships in Barcelona, Spain, where he broke five world records. Two more bookended the meet for a total of seven in a forty-nine-day span. (Mark's two best runs were seven in seventeen days in 1971 and twelve in thirty-four days to end his career.) Speedo, Phelps' sponsor since 2001, recognized the potential significance of the upcoming Olympics and inked the phenom to a six-year deal, reportedly the richest sponsorship contract in the company's history. Most intriguing to fans, the agreement included a clause to pay Phelps a one-million-dollar bonus if he matched or bettered Mark in 2004 or 2008.

Just as with Mark three decades earlier, Phelps first had to succeed at the Trials, which in 2004 were held in Long Beach in mid-July. Phelps qualified for and entered eight events, but he and his coach, Bob Bowman, remained tight-lipped about which events he would ultimately swim, his exceptional versatility keeping the doors open.

The press inundated Phelps shortly after his arrival in Long Beach, asking about his events and his contract and his iconic predecessor. This was the moment fans and media had waited for: Phelps' first public words regarding the man who set the standard for swimmers. But unlike Woods, Aaron, Ripken, and Smith, Phelps said little about the sport's hero and endeared himself to on-lookers and listeners even less with his seemingly total indifference and somewhat irreverent regard to Mark.

When asked by reporters about the Speedo bonus, Phelps was flippant, saying, "In addition to the whole Spitz thing, there's the million dollars out there now. That's just going to make me work harder." Bill Plaschke, a writer for the *L.A. Times,* chided Phelps' blasé attitude about the Spitz legend. When Phelps responded to a question about whether he could win seven gold medals by rationalizing, "Spitz did it," Plaschke wrote an article the next day entitled "It's Mr. Spitz to You."

Phelps opened the Trials by knocking almost seven-tenths of a second off his year-old world record in the 400 IM final, and already high expectations skyrocketed. The entire venue buzzed with bated breath. The chase, whether active or passive on Phelps' part, became the featured attraction of the Trials and then the Games.

Swimming fans longed to smooth their conflicting feelings and support both. Phelps' current undertaking as it related to Mark's previous feat thrust their sport into the forefront of the sporting public's collective mind, and they appreciated the publicity and attention. A warm, meaningful connection or exchange between the duo would have eased the fans' discord, but none came.

A few days later, after he'd won the 200 free in a meet record, a somewhat forced meeting took place. Organizers had slated Mark to present the medal to the winner of the 200 butterfly. As expected, Phelps won, beating his closest competitor by more than three seconds, an astounding margin. Afterward, Phelps was ushered around the pool to acknowledge the cheers of the fans and walked directly in front of Mark, who was sitting in the front row of a box suite at the start-finish line. Phelps appeared oblivious to Mark's presence and paraded by without a wave, nod, or glance. Mark sat stoical, apparently unruffled by what people in surrounding box suites openly and cynically criticized as a blatant slight by the nineteen-year-old.

Moments later, Mark prepared the medal ceremony. It had been thirty-two years since his last trip to a medal stand. Virtually all competitors and many spectators had not yet been conceived when Mark beat the world seven times in record fashion, and Mark had fairly low expectations of the crowd's reaction: polite applause, but eager for the "real" moment. The air, though, palpated with excitement. When the announcer finally directed the fans' attention to the podium and introduced Mark as the presenter, ten thousand people sprang to their feet and erupted in thunderous applause and roaring cheers. Bob Bowman described a scene in which reporters climbed over each other to see. Mark draped the medal around Phelps and climbed on the podium to raise Phelps' arm. The two had a very brief and vanilla exchange, but that was it. No affection, no good feelings, nothing for fans to ponder intellectually or embrace emotionally.

Phelps went on to qualify for the Olympics in six individual events, winning the 200 free, 200 fly, 200 IM, and 400 IM; finishing second in the 200 back and 100 fly; and earning spots on the 4x100 freestyle, 4x200 freestyle, and 4x100 medley relays. With his decision not to swim the backstroke event, eight gold medals were within reach. He came tantalizingly close to matching Mark in Athens with an extraordinary showing: six gold, including four of his five individual events and two relays (the 4x200 free and 4x100 medley), and two bronze, in the 200 freestyle and 4x100 free relay. Eight medals, but Mark's record remained. Phelps would have to wait four more years for another try.

Oddly, neither USA Swimming nor Olympic broadcaster NBC television made an effort to publicly link Mark and Phelps before the Trials, at the Trials, between the Trials and the Games, or after the Games. Opportunities existed. Among others, Spitz and Phelps held press conferences in Long Beach at the Trials three hours apart, but the two never met. They never spoke by phone, they didn't pose for photos, and they didn't bump into each other and chat informally at the aquatics center. Except for that brief moment at the medal ceremony, it was as if they lived in parallel universes.

Later there were brief exchanges at USA Swimming's "Golden Goggle" awards in 2005 and 2007, the latter at which Mark awarded the Male Swimmer of the Year to Phelps. The audience winced when Phelps failed to mention Mark in his acceptance speech, and as the two made their way back to their tables, Phelps proceeded first into the backstage walkway and continued on without turning to acknowledge Mark in a private moment.

Almost everyone around Mark seemed upset about Phelps' lack of appreciation or respect—except for Mark himself, who later defended Phelps by admitting he would have acted the same way. "The mental toughness to achieve greatness is rare, and I think Michael has it," Mark explained. "Michael and I are on different journeys. I completed mine, and he is in the midst of his. He needs to focus on his journey, not mine. The last thing he needs to do is personalize or humanize Mark Spitz, and I don't want to disrupt his concentration by foisting myself on him. When his journey is over, I'm sure we will meet and exchange views on what happened to us."

Mark's record almost certainly will be broken, if not by Phelps in 2008 then by another brilliant swimmer in the near or distant future. But pundits will continue to link the two—just as they do Ruth and Aaron, Ripken and Gehrig, Nicklaus and Woods, Payton and Smith—even if nothing else does.

It happened to Mark, less with Schollander—a more tidy comparison—than with Johnny Weissmuller. Equating that pair's accomplishments was nearly impossible, and a debate ensued. For the same reasons—different eras presented varied stroke technique, training regimens, competition, and meet and event opportunities, among other factors—a comparison between Mark and Phelps is unfair.

The suit Mark wore in 1972 seemed state-of-the-art compared to its predecessors. Speedo, a company founded in 1928 on Bondi Beach near Sydney, Australia, introduced the risqué, form-fitting, cotton Racerback the next year and has led the swimsuit industry ever since.

Mark's tiny iconic Speedo brief featured a fabric and style that benefited from early hydrodynamic research and experimentation, but the subsequent advances in swimsuit technology have been phenomenally more revolutionary. In fact, "the nylon suit worn by Mark in 1972 is now a standard, high-drag swimsuit that male swimmers use to increase drag during training," explained Stu Isaac, vice president of marketing for Speedo USA. In other words, now swimmers wear them to make their workouts harder.

Speedo has poured huge sums of money into their innovations at their top-secret Aqualab, with staggeringly improved results. The old nylon suits gave way to Lycra, a man-made fabric ingredient with elastic properties that improved fit, freedom of movement, and durability. "Woven suits" and polyurethane/polyester blends followed, significantly reducing drag.

Design and fabric continued to break new ground, often because of each other. Speedo developed the first fast fabric in 1992 with the S2000. More than half the medalists in the 1992 Barcelona Games wore Speedos. Four years later, they introduced the Aquablade, with an advanced texture slicker than human skin and designed to channel water away from the body. After years of shaving fabric from suits under the assumption that less is more, the speedy Aquablade reversed that trend by covering part to all of the legs. Speedo clothed seventy-six percent of the medalists in Atlanta in 1996. In 2000, the pioneering company unveiled Fastskin. The full-body suit featured fabric designed like sharkskin and included a muscle-compression component that reduced muscle vibration, a major source of power loss and fatigue for swimmers. Speedo's monopoly on Olympic medalists rose to eighty-three percent when the Games ventured Down Under to the company's native land.

Not content to rest on its laurels, Speedo continued to lead the industry with the Fastskin sequel, FSII, with faster fabric texture, and the FS-Pro, a full-body suit with superior muscle compression, increased water repellency, and lower drag. In February of 2008, Speedo introduced the LZR Racer made of LZR Pulse, a high-density, water-repellant fabric that further reduces drag, improves compression, and actually speeds muscle recovery after the swim.

About the only thing Speedo hasn't done is keep track of how much faster each new suit is from all of its forerunners. "Each generation of suit is only compared to the previous generation," said Isaac. "There have been no studies comparing Mark's nylon suit with the LZR Racer. It is fair to say, though, that if Mark wore the LZR Racer in 1972, his world records would have been faster."

In addition to improved suit technology, pools are faster today than in 1972. "Although the Munich pool was the most advanced design of its time, it lacked the sophistication of modern pools," explained Trevor Tiffany, former Canadian national swim coach and president of Myrtha Pools, USA. "The lane lines did not have the wave-quelling features that are standard nowadays, and the gutter systems then were of inferior design. Basically, pools today are much faster because they are designed to keep the pool surface as calm as possible, eliminating waves and splash back. The perimeter gutters are deep and do not allow the waves to rebound back into the pool."

In addition, there have been significant changes in technique and training methods, which make it unfair to compare today's swimmers with those of Mark's era. According to Mark Schubert, USA Swimming's National Team coach and general manager,

> Starts, turns and stroke technique have changed drastically. When Mark competed, swimmers tried to dive as flat as possible. The thought was that a shallow dive would allow the swimmer to start his stroke more quickly. Today, the idea is to dive deeper to take advantage of underwater speed. Instead of extending out as far as possible, swimmers try to dive so that their entire bodies go through a single hole. The angle of the dive is steeper and generates much more velocity going into the water. While they are underwater, the swimmers utilize strong dolphin kicks to speed them to the surface. By the time they get to the surface they are moving faster than if they did the old conventional type of start. Likewise, the old turns were twisting motions with wasted energy. Swimmers came out on their stomachs, would use a flutter kick and would quickly surface. Today swimmers go into the turn with their bodies more aligned and they drop their heads and dive into the turn. Instead of twisting, they push off on their backs and turn quickly to their sides. They use powerful dolphin kicks until they reach the surface.

Schubert, who was previously the head swim coach at the University of Southern California, has also seen a dramatic change in training methods. "In Mark's era, swimmers plodded through high yardage workouts, usually 10,000 to 12,000 yards a day. Today, workouts for top swimmers usually average about 7,000 yards, but there is more intensity in the workout. Swimmers swim more laps at race pace," explained Schubert.

Of course, suits, pools, technique, and training only take into account differences in speed between eras, making it inadequate for a conclusive assessment. Domination over opponents is another parameter, but again not one without complication. One possible yardstick is comparing the number of world records, but changes to the financial side of the sport muddy those waters. Mark swam in two Olympic Games and could have competed in at least one more had today's rules regarding amateurism and professionalism been in effect. His choosing to make a living slammed the door on an extended career. With the "amateur only" rule eliminated many years ago, top swimmers are compensated handsomely for their commercial endorsements and can afford to stay in the competitive arena longer. Phelps will swim in his third Olympic Games in 2008 at twenty-three years old, making a fourth in 2012 plausible.

Most experts agree it will be harder for Phelps to win seven gold medals than it was for Mark, because more countries qualify better swimmers for the Olympics now than then. In 1972, swimmers from ten countries won medals, but by 2004 that number increased to twenty-one. In addition, Phelps will have to swim in more races. In 1972, only one event—the 100 free—included a semifinal. In 2008, three other events will also have semifinals: the 200 free, 100 fly and 200 fly, some or all of which Phelps is likely to swim. Mark swam thirteen races in Munich; Phelps swam fifteen in Athens.

At least one factor, though, weighs in Phelps' favor. In 1972, each country entered up to three swimmers in each individual event; now only two are allowed. Given the United States' consistent supremacy in the pool, with the third-fastest American often possessing the ability to win Olympic gold, that change decreases the American team's medal collection but improves individual Americans' chances. In the 1968 U.S. Olympic Swim Trials, Ken Walsh placed third in the 100 freestyle but went on to beat Mark in the Mexico City Olympics. Under today's structure, Walsh would have watched the race from the stands.

Some observers consider Phelps' seven gold medals at the 2007 FINA World Championships in Melbourne, Australia, the equivalent of Mark's feat. In fact, he likely would have earned eight golds if Ian Crocker hadn't disqualified the U.S. team in the preliminaries of the medley relay. An Australian newscaster commented after his seventh win, "Well, now he's done it, tied Mark Spitz's record of seven gold medals."

But few in the know agree. "The World Championships is a fantastic event," said Olympic legend Rowdy Gaines, "but it isn't the Olympics. The World Championships have fewer spectators, fewer members of the press, and there is significantly less pressure on the athletes." So the real test is still before Phelps; he needs to repeat the feat in the Olympics.

Even if Phelps breaks or ties Mark's record, it is doubtful he or any other Olympic athlete will reach the levels of fame Mark enjoyed. This says much less about current athletes' marketability than it does mass communication in Mark's era. Times were simpler in 1972, with far fewer choices in entertainment and media. People used to rely on a newspaper, a magazine or two, and three television stations—ABC, CBS, and NBC—for their information. Personal computers and cell phones were in their infancy, and the Internet was a distant dream. Now, hundreds of channels and the Web are available 24/7, creating a glut of information.

People choose when and where they get their highly specific news, but the focused messages of Mark's day is gone.

This widely complicated and diverse news and information delivery system provides athletes with numerous avenues to get in the public eye. Conversely, the average sports fan cannot keep up with the multitude of reports, so the performances of nonprofessional athletes are often beyond their headlights. As Premier Management Group's president, Evan Morgenstein, said tongue-in-cheek, "It's harder to get exposure for athletes in today's marketplace. If one of my athletes gets a world record and sets himself on fire, people won't notice because they're watching *Extreme Makeover* on television."

Mark's name and image were known in nearly every household across the country. Winning seven gold medals and emerging as an international sex symbol was only part of it. Mark was also thrust on the world stage because of the massacre in Munich, which etched his face on the minds of hundreds of millions of people worldwide who might have ignored his performance in the pool. The media frenzy over the massacre created a stage from which he gained more visibility than any previous Olympian.

In the '70s, Mark could hardly appear in public without people excitedly exclaiming, "Hey, you're Mark Spitz!" Mark's fame presented an amusing incident for his cousin, Sherman Spitz. Shortly after the Munich Olympics, Sherman met a fellow UCLA student who informed him that her last name was Spitz. Not knowing Sherman's identity, she immediately volunteered that Mark Spitz, the famous swimmer, was her cousin. With a chuckle, Sherman responded, "Really? If you're Mark Spitz's cousin, then that makes you my sister." Embarrassed, the young coed quickly turned and walked away. As the years passed, though, public recognition of him dwindled significantly. The chiseled sex-symbol looks of his youth had morphed into mature, handsome, distinguished features.

In 2000, Mark attended the Olympic Games in Sydney, Australia, courtesy of Air New Zealand. As he watched the track and field competition one day, he overheard two attractive women in front of him talking, one in English with a British accent and the other in French, each obviously understanding the other. Fascinated, Mark leaned forward to express his amazement at their dual-language discussion. It turned out they were sisters, one living in England and the other in France.

Mark continued the conversation, asking if they were enjoying the Olympics. They nodded, but one conceded they'd been disappointed with their experience at the swimming venue the day before. This puzzled Mark, who recounted watching Ian Thorpe break a world record. "Yes, that was nice, but we were hoping to see Mark Spitz," one explained. "Oh, he was there, I saw him," Mark assured them, barely able to suppress his laughter as he described where he sat. The discussion turned to other subjects, but the sisters never realized whom they were talking to.

About a half hour later, several Air New Zealand employees arrived and sat next to Mark, almost all of them asking Mark to sign their programs. Curious bystanders slowly began to recognize Mark, whisper to their neighbors, and make their way to him. Soon a long line formed, which the sisters couldn't help but notice. When they finally discovered Mark's identity, they simultaneously shrieked and covered their lips with their hands, chiding Mark with excitement for keeping them in the dark.

‼‼‼

Over the years, Mark has engaged in various business ventures, developing condominiums and working as a stockbroker among them. He still commands a five-figure sum for appearances and is often booked as a motivational speaker.

Mark didn't leave his competitive nature in Munich. In 1973, Schick bought a thirty-six-foot racing sailboat and leased it to Mark for $1 a year. Naming the boat *Sumark 7* in an obvious reference to Suzy, himself, and his famous record haul, he competed with success in the Southern Ocean Racing Conference. He also sailed *Sumark 7* three times in the annual Transpac race from Los Angeles to Honolulu, placing third in his class in 1981.

A significant component of Mark's journey has been his long and successful marriage with Suzy and raising their two sons, Matthew, born in 1981, and Justin, born in 1991. Neither son took to swimming competitively, and understandably so. Who would want to enter a novice meet under the name Spitz? Expectations would be way too high. Mark even refrains from the typical father/son races in the family swimming pool. He knows he has an ultra-competitive mentality and doesn't want to create a negative situation for his sons. Both sons were attracted to "land sports." Matthew became a top-level golfer with a "plus 2" handicap and hopes to turn pro. Justin likes basketball and hopes to play that sport in college.

❗❗❗

Mark's journey has indeed been extraordinary. It is hard to imagine any Olympic athlete reaching the level of fame that Mark achieved. According to former USA Swimming president Dale Neuburger, "Mark's seven gold medals in Munich, combined with the Munich massacre occurring the morning after he won his seventh medal, gave Mark media coverage that will probably never be duplicated. It is unlikely that any Olympic athlete will be as recognizable as Mark was in 1972." Indeed, the media was much simpler then, with only three television stations, and far fewer newspapers and periodicals. The present-day explosion in the number of media outlets and the incredible amount of options on the Internet make an intense international focus on one athlete unlikely. There are simply too many distractions now.

One thing is certain, though. Mark is a complex person revered by millions who have never met him. The sport of swimming, and the experiences associated with his involvement in the sport, have made him a unique person. While some still find him confusing, most people who thought him to be arrogant and abrasive three decades ago are now pleased at how he has matured. Mark continues to evolve and his journey is far from over.

‼‼‼

WHERE ARE THEY NOW?

RON BALLATORE

Ron was the head men's swimming coach at UCLA for sixteen years before the program was disbanded in 1994. He was a coach on five Olympic teams (USA, 1984 and 1988; Peru, 1968; Ecuador, 1972; Israel, 1976). In his career, Ron coached twenty-eight Olympians, who won twelve medals in the Olympic Games, ten of which were gold. Ron is retired and lives in Florida with his wife, Ann Claire. They have five children.

GREG BUCKINGHAM

Unfortunately, Greg died of a heart attack in 1990.

MIKE BURTON

Mike is living in Billings, Montana, where he works at Billings Hospital. He coached age group swimming for over thirty years. He is married to Anne, who is his second wife. According to Mike, their family is sort of like the Brady Bunch. Anne brought four children from a previous marriage to the family and Mike added two of his own.

SHERM CHAVOOR

Sherm sold Arden Hills in the late 1980s and retired from coaching in 1990. Over his coaching career, his swimmers set one hundred world and American swim records. His swimmers also won thirty-one Olympic medals, twenty of them gold. He wrote a great book entitled *The 50-Meter Jungle* detailing his most famous swimmers, including Mark, Debbie Meyer, and Mike Burton. The book is out of print, but worth the price if you can find it. Sherm remained close to Mark until he died of cancer in 1992, at his home in Gold River, California.

GARY CONELLY

Gary retired from swimming in 1974. He married the former Kathy Healey in 1975. Gary and Kathy had two children, Emily, a ballet dancer, and Cody, a graphic artist. Both were involved with youth sports, but neither displayed any interest in swimming. In 1989, Gary was appointed to be head swim coach of the University of Kentucky Wildcats and he continues in that position today. He coached forty-two swimmers to All-American status. Two of his swimmers, Rachel Komisarz and Nikia Deveaux swam in the 2004 Olympic Games, Rachel for the United States and Nikia for the Bahamas. He was inducted into the Indiana Swimming Hall of Fame in 1973. Gary is a history buff and especially enjoys reading about the Middle Ages, Roman history, and major U.S. wars. He and his wife Kathy enjoy sailing and traveling, and are "rabid" Scottie dog owners.

JAMES "DOC" COUNSILMAN

Doc retired in 1991 after thirty-three years of coaching. During his career, he won twenty consecutive Big Ten Championships and six consecutive NCAA Championships. In addition to Mark Spitz, Doc coached swim greats Jim Montgomery, Gary Hall, John Kinsella, Charles Hickcox, Don McKenzie, Chet Jastremski, George Breen, Mike Stamm, Alan Somers, Ted Stickles, Larry Schulhof, John Murphy, and Fred Tyler. In 1979, Doc successfully swam the English Channel at the age of fifty-nine.

Doc passed away on January 4, 2004, after years of Parkinson's disease. He is survived by his wife Marge.

PETER DALAND

Peter retired from coaching in 1992 after thirty-five years of collegiate coaching. He is regarded as on of the greatest college and international swim coaches ever. He guided USC to nine NCAA team championships, with eleven runner-up finishes. Peter and his wife Ingrid live in Ventura County, California. Peter wrote a treatise called *History of Olympic Swimming, Vo. I*, which covers Olympic swimming from the 1890s to 1964. In 1977, Peter was inducted into the International Swimming Hall of Fame.

ROWDY GAINES

In the 1984 Olympic Games, Rowdy won three gold medals. In 1991, the swimming world was shocked to learn that Rowdy had contracted Guillain-Barré syndrome, an affliction of the autoimmune virus that attacks the nervous system. Completely paralyzed for two weeks, Rowdy fought back and overcame the disease one year later. Rowdy is a regular announcer for televised swimming events, and called his fourth Olympic telecast for NBC at the 2004 Athens Olympic Games. He will be a part of the NBC team for the 2008 Olympic Games in Beijing. Rowdy and his wife of twenty years, the former Judy Zachea, have four daughters, Emily, Madison, Savanna, and Isabel. When asked what he and his wife do in their spare time, Rowdy responded, "Are you crazy, I have four daughters."

DON GAMBRIL

While coaching at Long Beach State, Don's 49er team placed as high as fifth place in the NCAA Championships and they were 48–3 in dual-meet competition. In 1971, he was lured away to Harvard University where he coached for two years before landing up at the University of Alabama. Prior to hiring Don, the Crimson Tide had only earned one point in NCAA Championship history. In Don's first year, he placed nineteen swimmers in the championships and in 1977 his men's squad placed second in the NCAAs. He was an assistant Olympic coach in 1968, 1972, 1976, and 1980 and head Olympic coach in 1984. In his career, his swimmers broke twenty world records and won fourteen gold medals in the Olympic Games. Don is semiretired; he still teaches classes at Alabama, which provides him a little extra money to fund his hunting and fishing expeditions. He is a big game hunter, having hunted in North America, Africa, and Mongolia. He pilgrimages to Alaska every year to fish and hunt. He and Teddy, his wife of fifty-five years, reside in Tuscaloosa, Alabama. They have three children and eight grandchildren.

STEVE GENTER

Steve moved to Switzerland in the '70s and has lived there ever since. He is divorced from his first wife, but they have five children, all of whom know how to swim, but none took the sport as seriously as their father. He works for McKenzie & Company, which Steve describes as a low-key company in the computer industry.

GEORGE HAINES

George passed away in May of 2006, four years after suffering a severe stroke. He was the foremost producer of Olympic champions in the history of competitive swimming, having coached fifty-three Olympic swimmers who won forty-four gold medals, fourteen silver medals and ten bronze medals. In 1974, George was inducted into the International Swimming Hall of Fame. In 2000, he was voted Swimming Coach of the Century by USA Swimming, and the Santa Clara International Swim Center was renamed in his honor as the George F. Haines International Swim Center.

GARY HALL

In 1976, Gary qualified for his third Olympic Games, competing in the 100-meter butterfly. In 1981, he was inducted into the International Swimming Hall of Fame. Gary was a popular ophthalmologist in Phoenix, Arizona, for twenty-five years. In 2006, he and his wife Mary moved to Islamorada, Florida, where Gary directs the swimming programs for "The Race Club." He continues doing research in ophthalmology and has developed a line of children's sunglasses called "Frubi Shades." He serves as vice president of the United States Olympians. He also gives motivational talks. When his son Gary Hall, Jr., qualified for the 2004 Olympic Games in Athens, the duo became the first father and son combination to each compete in three Olympic Games. Gary and Mary had five other children, all of whom were good swimmers.

FRANK HECKL

Frank is an orthopedic surgeon in Albuquerque, New Mexico, specializing in sports medicine and arthroscopy. He served as a physician volunteer at the Summer Olympic Games in 1984. He has also served as a team physician for the USA National Swim Team. Frank has been married for twenty-five years to Vicky Perrigo, who is also a board-certified physician. They had three children, Alison, Emily, and Tyler. All were involved in age-group swimming, but the girls were more attracted to volleyball, each earning a college scholarship, Alison at St. John's University in New York and Emily at Winthrop University in South Carolina. Tyler was tragically killed in a car accident at the age of nineteen. The Heckls are actively involved in their church and are ardent followers of USC football.

JERRY HEIDENREICH

Jerry retired from swimming after the Munich Olympics. He returned to Dallas, Texas, where he started the SWAM swim club (Swim with American Masters) and later formed an age-group club with his brother-in-law called The Atac. Jerry was inducted into the International Swimming Hall of Fame in 1992. He was married three times and divorced three times. His son Austin was his only child. At the age of fifty-one, Jerry had a stroke. According to his long-time friend, James Dolan, Jerry was troubled by alcoholism and drug abuse. He became very depressed about his physical condition after the stroke and encountered some financial difficulties. At the age of fifty-two, he committed suicide by an overdose of prescription drugs.

RONNIE JACKS

After competing for Canada at the 1972 Olympic Games in Munich, Ron retired from swimming and worked on a master's degree in wildlife management. After five months in Africa, he decided that he missed swimming too much and he returned to Vancouver to open up a swim club. He has been coaching in Vancouver and Victoria ever since. He is presently the head coach of Pacific Coast Swimming, a club associated with the University of Victoria. He is also the Canadian National open water coach for the Beijing Olympics. He has been married to the former Patricia Anne McGavin for thirty-eight years. They have two sons, Jesse and Greer, and both were swimmers. Jesse was a two-time Canadian National champion in the 200 butterfly (same stroke as his father). Ron is still interested in wild animals and animal photography. He also loves skin diving and surfing.

TOM JAGER

Tom is the women's swim coach at the University of Idaho. He's been married to Becky for twenty-two years. They have two boys, Wyatt and Cy, who are successful age-group swimmers. In the 1992 Olympics in Barcelona, Tom won a gold medal in the 400-meter freestyle relay and a bronze in the 50-meter freestyle. When he retired from swimming he was the world-record holder in the 50-meter freestyle. In 2001, he was inducted into the International Swimming Hall of Fame.

JOHN KINSELLA

After college, John swam the English Channel in record-breaking time. He went to Harvard Business School and is an investment officer with RBC Dain Rauscher. In 1986, John was inducted into the International Swimming Hall of Fame.

JERRY KIRSHENBAUM

Jerry retired from *Sports Illustrated* in 1998. He lives in New York City with his wife Susan, who is a soap opera writer. They enjoy traveling and going to the theater. Their son David is a composer. Jerry recently returned to Munich where he dined at the Käfer-Schänke restaurant. His waiter had just started working at the restaurant when Jerry dined with Mark the night Mark won his seventh gold medal. The waiter remembered that historic evening and told Jerry that the whole restaurant staff was buzzing about hosting Mark that night.

KURT KRUMPHOLZ

Kurt retired from swimming after the 1976 Olympic Swim Trials. The world record he set in the prelims of the 400-meter freestyle at the 1972 Trials held through the 1972 Olympic Games. It was broken in September of 1973 by Rick DeMont. Kurt was the vice president of Speedo USA for over twenty years, then joined BetterTimes, a swim accessory company. In 2007, he formed his own company Pool Tools, Inc. He is also a principal of Impact Pools, a distributor of Myrtha pools in California. In 1983, he married Debra Peacock and they have three children. Katie played water polo at UCLA and son J.W. plays water polo for the USC Trojans. J.W. is also a member of the USA National Men's Water Polo Team and was a member of the 2005 World Championship team. Kurt's second daughter Kari is a student at Foothill High School, in Santa Ana, California, where she is on the swim and water polo teams.

JIM MONTRELLA

Jim lives with his wife Bev in Mission Viejo, California. He currently works for USA Swimming as a Master Coach Consultant. After a brief stint at Indian River Junior College in Florida, Jim was the head coach of the women's swim team at Ohio State University, a position he held for eighteen years. During that time, his squad won five Big Ten titles. After that, he was Mark Schubert's assistant at USC.

RICHARD QUICK

Richard was the head coach of the United States Olympic Team in the 1988, 1996, and 2000 Olympic Games and was an assistant at the 1984, 1992, and 2004 Olympics. While at Stanford, Richard coached ninety-six All-Americans. His swimmers won a combined sixty-three NCAA individual and twenty-nine NCAA relay titles. He has won numerous Coach of the Year honors. Richard is now the head swim coach at Auburn University. He has been married to the former June Brooks for eighteen years. His son Michael swam at Auburn and his daughter Kathy swam until she developed a disc problem. He is stepfather to June's two children, Tiffany and Benjamin.

CARL ROBIE

Carl's gold medal victory in the 200 meter butterfly in Mexico City was the last time anybody beat Mark Spitz in Olympic competition. After the 1968 Olympics, Carl retired from competitive swimming and returned to Dickinson Law School (now Penn State Dickinson School of Law). He graduated in 1971 and currently maintains a law practice in Sarasota, Florida. He practices in real estate and civil litigation. In 1968, he married the former Christine Von Anderson, who is also his paralegal. This year they will celebrate their 40th wedding anniversary. The Robie swimming tradition continued with their children, C.J. and Amanda, who enjoyed successful swimming careers at the Bolles School in Jacksonville, Florida, and continued for C.J. at the University of Texas at Austin and for Amanda at Louisiana State University. Carl has received many awards over the years for his contributions to various swim teams. Carl and Christine are active in their church and enjoy chocolate, gold, and cross-country skiing.

DOUG RUSSELL

Doug lives in Austin, Texas. He recently remarried his high school sweetheart. He is an area manager for a company called HD Supply. He is often asked to speak about his Olympic experiences and refuses to accept money for doing so. He coached Little League baseball for fifteen years and his youngest son was drafted out of high school by the Atlanta Braves.

ROSS WALES

After the 1972 Olympic Swim Trials, Ross retired from competitive swimming. In 1974, he married Juliana ("J.J.") Fraser. Ross graduated from the University of Virgina School of Law in 1974, and is a partner in the prestigious Cincinnati law firm, Taft, Stettinius & Hollister, where he heads the firm's international practice group. Ross held numerous offices in the aquatic sports for over twenty-five years, including president of United States Swimming, various positions with the United States Olympic Committee, and president of United States Aquatic Sports. From 1984 through 2002, Ross held important positions with FINA, rising to the office of vice president in 1992. Ross and J.J. have two sons, Dod and Craig, who became successful swimmers at Stanford and Princeton. In 1999, Dod was the NCAA champion in the 100-yard butterfly, setting an American record. Dod followed in Ross's footsteps, placing third in the 100-meter butterfly at the 2000 U.S. Olympic Swim Trials. Unlike his father, Dod didn't get to go to the Olympic Games, because in 1980, FINA limited each country to two swimmers per event. Craig was the captain of the Princeton Swim Team in 2001 and was a consistent finalist at the Eastern Swim Championships.

KEN WALSH

Ken retired from competitive swimming after the 1968 Olympic Games, but he briefly considered a comeback in 1972. He moved to Hawaii in 1972 and lives on the North Shore of Oahu with his wife Marilyn. They maintain a second residence in Big Sky, Montana. Ken is a self-described surf nut. Ken and Marilyn have two children, Michael and Debby. Debby had some success in high school swimming, but was a member of the crew team in college. Michael also swam a bit, but like his father became a surfer. Ken is a hand-held cameraman for NBC Sports. He works the PGA golf tour and every four years gets to be the hand-held cameraman for the U.S. Olympic Trials and Olympic Games.

MICHAEL WENDEN

The 1968 Olympic champion from Australia retired from competitive swimming in 1974. He has been married to Narelle since 1971. Michael and Narelle have five children, Karen, Gabrielle, Alister, Joshua, and Rebecca. Michael originally went into banking. He and Narelle decided to venture off for a year or so to operate a sports club in Palm Beach, Australia, and some thirty years later, they are still at it. The Wendens enjoy raising Arabian horses on the side. Michael has been actively involved in the Olympic Movement. In 1992, he was a member of the Brisbane bid committee for the Olympic Games. He has been a member of the Australian Olympic Committee since 1989 and has been a staff member for the Australian Olympic Committee every year since 1992.

MARK SPITZ'S WORLD RECORDS

DATE	EVENT	TIME	PLACE
9/4/1972	4 x 100 medley	03:48.16	Munich, Germany
9/3/1972	100 freestyle	00:51.22	Munich, Germany
8/31/1972	4 x 200 freestyle	07:35.78	Munich, Germany
8/31/1972	100 butterfly	00:54.27	Munich, Germany
8/29/1972	200 freestyle	01:52.78	Munich, Germany
8/28/1972	4 x 100 freestyle	03:26.42	Munich, Germany
8/28/1972	200 butterfly	02:00.70	Munich, Germany
8/5/1972	100 freestyle	00:51.47	Chicago, Illinois
8/4/1972	100 butterfly	00:54.56	Chicago, Illinois
8/4/1972	100 butterfly	00:54.72	Chicago, Illinois
8/2/1972	200 butterfly	02:01.53	Chicago, Illinois
8/2/1972	200 butterfly	02:01.87	Chicago, Illinois
9/10/1971	4 x 200 freestyle	07:43.30	Minsk, Belarus
9/10/1971	200 freestyle	01:53.50	Minsk, Belarus
9/4/1971	200 freestyle	01:54.20	Leipzig, Germany
9/3/1971	4 x 100 medley	03:50.40	Leipzig, Germany

DATE	EVENT	TIME	PLACE
8/27/1971	200 butterfly	02:03.90	Houston, Texas
8/25/1971	100 butterfly	00:55.00	Houston, Texas
8/23/1970	100 freestyle	00:51.94	Los Angeles, California
8/22/1970	200 butterfly	02:05.40	Los Angeles, California
7/12/1969	200 freestyle	01:54.30	Santa Clara, California
10/17/1968	4 x 100 freestyle	03:31.70	Mexico City, Mexico
8/30/1968	100 butterfly	00:55.60	Long Beach, California
6/23/1968	400 freestyle	04:07.70	Hayward, California
10/8/1967	200 butterfly	02:05.70	Berlin, Germany
10/7/1967	100 butterfly	00:55.70	Berlin, Germany
8/12/1967	4 x 200 freestyle	07:52.10	Oak Park, Illinois
8/12/1967	200 butterfly	02:06.40	Oak Park, Illinois
7/31/1967	100 butterfly	00:56.30	Winnipeg, Canada
7/26/1967	200 butterfly	02:06.40	Winnipeg, Canada
7/7/1967	400 freestyle	04:08.80	Santa Clara, California
6/25/1967	400 freestyle	04:10.60	San Leandro, California

INDEX